Partnership Games

Partnership Games

The Musings of a Recently Retired Psychiatrist

Sanford L. Billet, M.D.

AUTH VILLAGE PUBLICATIONS • Camp Springs, Maryland

Author's Note

In this book I present my thoughts, feelings and recollections, not facts. I refer to people, real and imagined, but the book is about me and my efforts to learn some truths about myself.

First Edition

Sanford L. Billet, M.D.
Auth Village Publications
5018 Braymer Avenue
Camp Springs, MD 20746, USA

ISBN 0-9659365-0-3

Library of Congress Catalog Card Number 97-94034
Biography

Manufactured and Printed in the USA

Acknowledgments

This book became a reality through the enthusiasm, generosity, and talented teamwork of the management and staff of Technical Typesetting Incorporated of Baltimore, Maryland. My daughter Deborah provided me with essential support and many hours of hard work from the beginning of this project to its completion. I thank them and the many others who have encouraged me to record my musings.

L'chaim

Contents

Campaigning for Your Vote

Tired a lot, achy, shaky, unsteady, scaly, bloodied and decrepit but happy to be here; so far I've had a very easy life. Thank God I'm not religious or superstitious, knock on wood and no evil eye; I have been very lucky. It amuses me when people who are inclined to be the way they think they are supposed to be become self-righteous rather than realizing how lucky they are. My good fortune has been multifaceted, but the icing on the cake is that this is a very political year and I intend to watch it unfold.

The South Carolina primary takes place today. I awakened to a luminescence and looked out at a winter wonderland: the trees and bushes adorned with gobs of fluffy snow. So lovely, and to make it even better there was no snow on the driveway. Two weeks ago, while shoveling the snow, I slipped and badly bruised myself. The pain is gone, but aches and tenderness persist. The good news is that I did not break anything and the bad news is that the fall did not cure me of any of my obscure chronic conditions.

Last night I put some black beans in water to soak. The beans were simmering before the newspaper arrived, and the snow had dissolved from the tree branches before the beans were done or the paper finished. No one ever asked me to cook. I have no prejudice against cooking and get a big kick out of making things that taste good. Much of what I cook is an attempt to recreate dishes my mother made. I'm a sentimental bloke.

The beans were tender but bitter by 10 A.M. I added some candied ginger and liked the results. I'll serve them to my daughter tomorrow. Everything will be homemade.

Fish cake sandwich on a homemade roll
Potato salad   Sweet and sour cabbage
Meat loaf with black beans and rice
Mixed fruit tart

Mother never cooked black beans, but she would recognize everything else on the menu.

At 12:30 I left for my regular Saturday afternoon duplicate bridge game. When I closed my office three months ago I took my high-backed office chair to the bridge club. It helps me to sit more comfortably through the three hour bridge game, but it has not improved my game. There was no political talk at the club. A few old jokes were told; I'll spare you.

This evening I watched the news and political shows, followed by a terrific 1985 Martin Scorsese movie, *After Hours*. Teri Garr played a ditsy dame and did her usual marvelous job.

A decisive victory for Dole in South Carolina has put him ahead in the delegate race.

Last year included several major changes, not surprises, in my life. Ria died in February. She ran out of breath. We had parted thirteen years earlier after thirty-two years of marriage. I had expected she would die the previous year; a shock, especially for our children, but not a surprise. Pat moved to Florida in early November. She told me she was going to move more than a year before—that was a surprise—and expressed her hope I would join her. We met several months after Ria and I separated and I was exclusively hers for more than ten years. In late November I closed my medical practice and discontinued my professional liability insurance. I gave lots of notice. I retired "to protect the public." When asked if I might change my mind I would say that I had an imaginary picture on my refrigerator door of an infamous old Democratic politico who stayed on too long and made a damned fool of himself.

It is Sunday. The big print headline is DOLE WINS DECISIVELY IN SOUTH CAROLINA PRIMARY. It is a fulgent, gusty morning. A slip of paper flying through the backyard appeared birdlike. The first robin of spring must be out there. A squirrel was hanging like a bat from a tree limb to reach the bird feeder. One or another squirrel has been eating from that stretched out, upside down position all winter.

I am frequently asked how I like retirement; it is too early to tell. The winter has been confining. My activities are hardly different. The biggest change I have noticed is that I read the morning newspaper more slowly and more thoroughly. Sunday, however, is not different because of retirement, but because most Sundays I would spend with Pat. The Sunday newspaper, "Meet the Press," "This Week with David Brinkley," rest and relaxation, early dinner; all with Pat. Now I do about the same but by myself. Often I will skip dinner. I read a little more and I write a bit.

Monday evenings I usually cook dinner for my daughter. Deborah chipped a tooth last week and we decided to have dinner today and maybe tomorrow also if she feels up to it after her dental appointment. The fish cake sandwich was very large. We had it with potato salad and cabbage. We decided to save the beans, rice and meat loaf for another time, perhaps tomorrow. The mixed fruit tart was delectable.

Deb and I customarily talk for an hour or two after dinner. We retire to my bedroom where she sits in a comfortable cushioned chair and I go recumbent on my bed. Now that retirement I like a lot. These dinners and talks are important to me.

It is an exciting time for Deborah. She was on the verge of quitting her job and did quit soon after her mother died. Now, almost a year later, she is starting to work as an independent contractor. It is an adventure that I hope she will enjoy. She is aware of my view that when you have a job with a company you have a boss but when you work for yourself everyone and anyone is potentially your boss; sort of like being a physician in private practice. After dinner and a chat Deb left for home. I was asleep before the 10 o'clock news.

Monday morning and Dole's big primary victory in Puerto Rico is on page seven. It is a cold but beautiful morning. There is much activity in the yard; lots of birds and squirrels, but still no robin. At 9:30 a special news report that the fourth Hamas suicide terrorist attack in nine days occurred this morning in Israel. Orthodoxy alarms me; it is so often divisive, oppressive, even deadly. Those who know in their heart how things are supposed to be are going to try to force me to follow their rules. Religious and ethnic wars are in progress. Are we close to a repeat inquisition or holocaust?

The important questions, fears and events do not deter me from following my usual Monday routine. After reading the newspaper, a daily event, I showered and shaved, occasional activities for me in retirement. At 9:30 I sliced two loaves of mixed grain bread to take to the bridge club and started off to the Monday morning pot luck game that starts promptly at 10:30.

Gloria has been my regular Monday morning bridge partner for about two years; that ended today. Before the lunch break, during the play, I was aware of her censorious, and of course unjustified, grimacing. Following another hand she criticized my bidding. I told her she did not know what she was talking about and that it was time for us to end our bridge partnership. Bridge partnerships often break up; it is primarily a matter of ego with a touch of grandiosity. The joke is that the bridge expert in court was asked who is the world's greatest bridge player. He testifies that since he is under oath he has to admit it is he.

My training tells me that behavior is overdetermined; more than one motive is likely. This morning's breakup was waiting to happen and had little to do with Gloria's facial expression or fault finding. It was motivated much more by my uncertain feelings about what I want with a woman. I have become wary about how I will proceed since it became clear to me that Pat would move to Florida.

The close attachment to one woman has provided me with feelings of safety and stability. When Ria and I uncoupled I was fifty-six years old. It was very clear to me that I would seek and find a satisfactory new relationship with one woman. My cocksureness was apparent and some found it disquieting. It annoyed some who were dissatisfied with but afraid to break out of their marriage. That was then; now I am uncertain and ambivalent about establishing a marriagelike relationship. Why isn't it enough to have children, grandchildren, other family and friends? So I have unloaded both of my regular woman bridge partners.

It is arrogant of me to think they might be available for courting, but more than that it is a problem for me that I consider it.

Gloria and I had a pretty good final game. I did not wait for the results, but I think we were first or second.

Home again after the game, rested, watched the news (increasing body count), read the mail (medical junk) and thought about dinner. Deb called about 5 o'clock and was ready to eat. Her dental appointment was not painful. We had salad, potato blintzes with sour cream and yesterday's black beans, rice and meat loaf. Dessert was chocolate pie. Often I put a secret ingredient in things I cook and then forget what it is. Deb figured out that the secret ingredient in the chocolate pie was hot peppers. After dinner we called Teresa, Steven, David and Kelly, and then Saria, Adam, Allison and Michael. All was well. Adam and Steven are my identical twin sons. They are fourteen months younger than Deborah. They did a wonderful thing when they provided me with four grandchildren and Deb with two nieces and two nephews. Each has a terrific wife too. What good luck.

Tomorrow is another big political day. Junior Tuesday may settle the Republican primary process.

The human nervous system is fascinating and marvelous; when it goes awry the results can be bizarre. It is easy for me to know when I am falling asleep because I revert to normal functioning when the sleep process begins. My body returns to regular alignment, all unwanted and involuntary movement ceases, hypertonic muscles relax and I feel grateful. My tired, tender body welcomes the sandman. If I turn onto my side while watching the 10 o'clock news, I will miss it. It happened again last night. Four or five hours of sleep usually suffice. On awakening the surcease persists for a bit and I treasure the comfort. It doesn't last long. That is when I appreciate living alone. I moan and groan and whine and wail; loudly. Solitary living unencumbers all kinds of useful and satisfying noisemaking.

It is Junior Tuesday; another big political day. Today for the first time in my memory I voted in the afternoon. The last few years of my practice, when I worked less than twenty hours a week, I continued to schedule a full day on Tuesdays. Several times I have cast the first vote at Skyline Elementary School in Maryland's fourth Congressional District. Today I voted at 2 o'clock. I counted eight precinct workers and one voter, voted in the Democratic primary and returned home. How is that for excitement? All the passion, excitement, uncertainty and interest is connected with the Republican race.

Tuesdays and Wednesdays remain unstructured for me. Every day I am aware that I am off duty. A part-time psychiatric practice required full-time availability and responsibility from me. On Tuesdays and Wednesdays there was no room for activities other than work. On the other days of the week scheduled activities were interruptible when duty called. That arrangement suited me and I miss it. For about forty-five years my focus was my work with and for patients. A sixty hour work week was usual in the early days but for the past thirty years I scheduled less then forty hours with patients and much less than that for the last five years. Although I managed this light workload easily I have had doubts for several years about my ability to manage a crisis. I have diminished stamina and resilience. Questions about meeting my own standard for practice were very important in my decision to retire soon after my sixty-ninth birthday. I retired because I thought I should, not because I wanted to experience retirement.

The Junior Tuesday news is in. It is a clean sweep for Dole. Perhaps all the excitement and uncertainty will subside.

It is Wednesday, the day between Junior Tuesday and the New York Primary. Very large headlines proclaim Dole's decisive victory. His 276 delegates are far short of the 996 needed, but he has the big MO on his side and the pundits say it is just about over. As the day proceeds Alexander and Lugar withdraw, Texas governor Bush endorses Dole, Kemp supports Forbes and Buchanan proclaims his crusade will continue.

Wednesday is one of my unscheduled days. Since my retirement I have spent Tuesdays and Wednesdays cooking, reading, writing and sightseeing. December was just right for sightseeing, but then the weather and the government shutdown made it more attractive to stay at home. Cooking and baking have taken a lot of my time. Last week I took some of my kitchen creations from my freezer to my friends Alice and Herb. Alice had just returned home following a hip replacement.

They received chicken soup, dal, black bean soup, beef and barley soup, brisket in onion gravy, curried beef, lamb stew, jelly torte and a loaf of bread. All of that was cooked after I retired. Working in the kitchen is not difficult for me, although I sometimes pay for it later with muscle spasms, back discomfort and fatigue. It is difficult to fathom why some ordinary activities relieve me while others are uncomfortable or unachievable. I feel entirely normal and comfortable when I am yawning or falling asleep. Eating quickly, especially while standing, gives me great relief. It is not much, but it is better than nothing. I can sit still only momentarily. A high-backed chair with strong back, neck and head support provides me with some comfort, and unwanted movements and spasms are reduced. A portable support seat makes it much easier for me to go to the theater or a bridge game. Sad to say, my symptoms are worsened by reading and by writing. I can perform these activities in bursts.

The evening report gives Dole 290 delegates and there is an eerie unanimity that Dole is a shoo-in.

Thursday, New York Primary day, and the tone of the Republican contest has changed substantially. A sure thing is hardly interesting and not at all exciting. Perhaps I can kindle some melodrama. Will Forbes nab the crown as D'Amato tries to place it on Dole's head? Will Buchanan splinter the Republican Party sufficiently to render this primary process ineffectual? Naah.

There is a bridge game at the Andrews Air Force Base Officers' Club every Thursday morning and I routinely play in it. It's about a mile from my house, within easy walking distance for me, but not today when I ache so much and the weather is uncertain. My twisted neck and torso don't prevent me from taking walks. Three miles is my maximum; more than that and I feel beaten up. I'm still modestly aerobically fit.

Around 1970 a patient, whom I'd encouraged to resume his previous athleticism, prodded me to get off my sedentary rump and begin aerobic activity. Gingerly I began and gradually, ever so slowly, I became fit. I jogged regularly, ran several ten mile races and became lean while eating large quantities of food.

Fitness is reassuring; it protects, but not entirely. The same guy who never dreamed of walking to his office at the USAF hospital, one mile from home, now occasionally jogged and walked to his office, eleven miles away, in downtown District of Columbia. It was fun. I was healthy although I suffered several recurring problems.

One morning, after I had eaten a full dinner for breakfast and while reading the newspaper, Ria asked me why I had my head turned. I was unaware that my head was turned. It was easily corrected. Soon thereafter I experienced a severe tremor of my left hand when I awakened in the morning; there was no difficulty with my right hand. The tremor was short lived but it recurred several times, always soon after I awakened. I knew I was in an early stage of a neurological disorder. It was 1979. I was concerned and I told Ria about it. I did not alter my activities and since it was very unlikely that I suffered a condition that would respond to quick or heroic treatment, I postponed having a neurological evaluation.

When I eventually went to see the neurologist across the hall from my office, I took a written personal history with me. It was obvious by then that I had a dystonia, a neuromuscular movement disorder, called spasmodic torticollis. I will try to get a copy of the history I took to Dr. Edelson who evaluated and advised me.

The resident robins are pretty smart; they have not arrived yet. They have avoided today's howling winds and three inches of snow. Yesterday's voter turnout in New York was light, partly because of bad weather, but the result was overwhelmingly in Dole's favor. He won 92 of New York's 93 delegates and is near the halfway mark. It is over.

The schools are opening late and there are many accidents today. No one has called to cancel the Friday morning bridge game at the Masonic Lodge, so I will be driving there soon. It is less than two miles from my home and I have walked there often. I call it "the food game" because so much food is served and I eat so much. Often I will bring bread, butter and strawberry jam to add to the feast. Anna's fruit pies are superior. She directs the Friday morning game.

Life can get complicated when you don't know the rules. The rule is, no Friday morning game when the schools are closed, and there was no game this morning. I figured it out when I saw the empty parking lot. I drove another few blocks and visited with Alice and Herb. We have been friends since Alice taught my boys in fifth grade. Alice and Ria were close friends and Alice, more than anyone, may have been aware of Ria's feelings and perspective. She had encouraged reconciliation when Ria and I decided to part. Our breakup startled and upset many who knew us.

Ria was sixteen, a high school student, and I was twenty-one and ready to start my second year of medical school when we met at the New Jersey seashore. We were strongly attracted to each other and we kept in touch after I returned to Ohio. We were together for the holidays and for summer break. We married two years after we met and we went to Cincinnati where I started my final year in medical school. I was eager to have her with me, to have her, and I knew of no acceptable way to accomplish that other than marriage. Ria was ready to leave her family and her parents seemed agreeable. My mother was covertly disapproving; I knew she felt I should complete my residency (another five years) before marrying. Mother understood that my decision was based on lust, with little thought about creating a family and fulfilling family responsibilities.

We lived on the $135 a month that Ria earned as a laboratory technician. She was pregnant when I graduated and Deborah was born in December 1951, a few weeks after Ria's twentieth birthday. Adam and Steven were born fourteen months later. So we went from no kids on Ria's twentieth birthday to three kids shortly after her twenty-first birthday. These pregnancies had been planned for a later date. As soon as we figured out what was causing them we modified our procedures.

Money was not a big problem. I joined the United States Air Force when I graduated and had very modest but adequate and regular pay. Things were still difficult. I was essentially unavailable during the first four years of our marriage; always studying and working. It is easy to see how Ria might view me as a taker, never a giver; she had no help. Early on I realized that her parents were not supportive or helpful, but that they could cause Ria to feel discomfort, sadness and guilt. I tried to treat her folks with affection and respect, but it was an act designed to protect us from them.

Early in 1955 a call from the office of the Surgeon General informed me that when I finished my training in July, I would be assigned to duty in Texas. Soon thereafter I received my orders to Clark Air Force Base in the Philippine Islands. There were so many unknowns. It felt precarious. The bureaucracy had not inspired confidence.

We drove to the West Coast with our three kids in the back seat. My cousin Ben and his wife were very helpful; they assisted our settling into an apartment in Los Angeles. Two weeks later I left and went to the Philippine Islands. In December Ria would drive the kids to San Francisco and then they would fly to Clark AFB. She had many administrative tasks to complete, plus the care of the children. She did it all and did it very well, but it was a very difficult time for all of us.

Clark Air Force Base had many of the features of a small southern United States city. It took awhile before we were settled. Then we had a nearly two year respite from the unsettling intensity we had imposed on ourselves. The meager military pay was irrelevant for we had the amenities associated with wealth. The military family might relax a bit in a large tropical house with two servants to take care of all the drudgery. We were one block from the Officers' Club with easy access to tennis, golf, swimming and arts and crafts. We had a car and a motor scooter. Neighbors and colleagues were mostly friendly and respectful.

It was not an entirely stress-free period; we brought our problems with us and, in addition, we suffered illnesses and threats. I was the only American psychiatrist in about a five thousand mile radius, most of it water, and I was subjected to the tensions that can occur when one serves two masters: my patients and the United States Air Force. I complained and resisted when my superior officer presented me with a problem and told me what I should find. At one point the commanding general threatened to reassign me to oblivion when he didn't like my findings.

Ria swam, painted, golfed, did ceramics and traveled to Japan and Hong Kong. We golfed together regularly and we played in a weekly duplicate bridge game at the club. We went to the movies together and shopped at the PX together; we experienced typhoons and earthquakes together.

I remember with pleasure some of the risible gaffes I committed when I went from my Air Force sponsored civilian training at Cincinnati General Hospital to Clark Air Force Hospital. I did not know the rules of military behavior and made some silly errors, but I was a quick learner and I appreciated the forbearance I was shown.

My most favorite memory of our time in the Philippines is of teaching our children to read. We used a phonics reader and we had great success, but the boys would not learn from me and Deborah would not learn from Ria. It was interesting and funny. Perhaps that pattern persisted. When we moved to Washington, D.C., in August 1957 our children could read anything written in English.

It is Saturday, March 9, 1996, and it is unseasonably cold; too cold for the snow to melt; a thin, lovely canopy persists on grassy areas. Today's news corrects yesterdays news; Dole won all 93 delegates in the New York Republican primary.

Wes called this morning to cancel our regular Saturday afternoon bridge game at the Washington Bridge Center. He is retired from the U.S. Navy, an MD and a DDS who has been subjected to multiple medical miracles. He is not feeling well today. Rather than scrounge around for a replacement partner I will stay home, write a bit and watch the college basketball playoffs. Having decided that, I invited Deb to come over for soup and bizarre pizza. I will invent the pizza soon; the crust is already in the freezer. How about baked apple and (commercial) almond cookies for dessert?

When I look out the kitchen window I see the backyards of several neighbors; my own backyard is only twenty feet deep. When we moved into this house in October 1957 there was little vegetation and no fences; the center of our block was as a common area. Now each property is fenced and there is much growth; lawns, trees, bushes, and in summer there are many flowers. Birds are attracted by the growth and by feeders.

Everyone who lived in this house, but I, grew up and left. That is a success story.

It was quite a stretch for us to buy this house; a small brick and block house on one third of an acre and costing $18,500. Houses that cost less seemed inadequate so we used all of our financial resources for a down payment. Six years later we would almost double the house size with an addition rather than move.

Just to my right, as I look out the kitchen window, is a black cherry tree. Its main trunk is over three feet in diameter but is only about three feet high; it was cut down at that height about twenty years ago. Steven, one of my Eagle Scout sons, assured me that he could get the falling tree to do no damage to our neighbor's fence. Later I wondered about having Steve's tree cutting badge revoked. Now from the main trunk of that tree there are four heavy major trunks and the tree rises about fifty feet; that is about twenty years of growth since the fated felling.

In 1958, the first spring in our new house, Adam and Steven excitedly ran to me on our barren yard. They had a small rooted sprig. I had no idea what it was. Solemnly we dug the ground, inserted the plant and agreed to care for it and watch it grow. I have gladly honored that pledge. This tree brings the robins to my yard. Each spring, after the leaves appear, thousands of drooping racemes of white flowers burst forth. These beautiful adornments produce a million deeply dark and delicious pea-sized cherries. Have you ever seen a robin salivate? The robins who own this place eagerly eat the fruit and broadcast the pits. Now, regular weeding prevents a black cherry tree forest from overwhelming the neighborhood.

Several years ago Adam told me that when he was growing up I was never here. I responded that when he was growing up I was always here. We were both telling the truth and perhaps we were both correct. When I was not at work I was at home, often in the yard. I encouraged the children to join me but I rarely insisted that they work with me. The kids often preferred activities away from home. My activities were worklike, not fun, although I enjoyed my home activities and I was often very pleased with the results.

Plants grow up but can't leave home. Before they die or are killed they often become overgrown, diseased and less attractive. Most of what is here is past its prime but still a joy. I built or planted much of it. Most of the azaleas were grown from cuttings and all of the dogwood trees are from seeds I dispersed. Not everything is old; young volunteers abound and there are about one hundred goldfish in the pond where they were born last spring. This past summer I started a bed of rhododendron cuttings and planted several hundred pink dogwood seeds and many seeds from a miniature leaf Japanese maple tree. There are five one year old dogwood trees in the front yard clumped around the stump of a double blossom Japanese ornamental cherry tree that was planted in 1964 and died eight or nine years ago. The birds are waiting to nest in those trees. Some of what I have built here has deteriorated. I recently repaired the pond; it is the third pond I've built here. The back stairs and front walk need repair but I will not tackle it and I do not plan to hire anyone to do the job.

The University of Maryland lost today in the basketball playoff.

Deb was here at 3 o'clock. We had beef and barley soup, bizarre pizza (made with tomato relish, onion relish, onions sautéed with ginger, meat loaf, cheddar cheese, mozzarella cheese and sweet and sour cabbage) and baked apple with cookies.

George Burns failed to live in three centuries; he died today.

It is 5 A.M., Sunday morning and I am well rested; missed the 10 o'clock news again. My nose awakened about 4:30 and once my nose is awake I might as well stop trying to doze and get out of bed. Everyone's nose is close to their brain but in my case it is very close. My nervous system has three modes: awake, asleep and doze. The nose is inactive, except in the awake state, and it often signals the onset of awakening. It is probably an instance of interaction between brain function and the immune system.

Today's atypical schedule stirs up so much, I will not be able to write about all of it. This evening, rather than lying in bed and watching PBS, I'm going to dinner at Jemma and Robin Smith's home. It is their son Andrew's fourteenth birthday; he was an infant when I first met him. Robin is the son of Pat's sister Connie.

This afternoon there will be a memorial service for Armand Gordon. I plan to go to it. Armand and I met thirty years ago; we served together on the alcoholism committee of the District of Columbia Medical Society. About ten years ago I started playing duplicate bridge with his wife Bernice. Our partnership lasted several years. We played once a week at a recreation center near my office. I would go directly to the office after the game and work for several hours.

When I was in high school, two fellows who knew how to play bridge tried to teach several of us so they could take nickels from us. It was not a fair arrangement, but it awakened my interest in an intriguing and creative partnership game.

Ria and I began to study bridge and to play a bit during our last two years in Cincinnati. Ria was very taken with the game and she was a quick learner; bridge provided her with much needed mental stimulation. Moreover this game required and rewarded competitiveness and Ria welcomed an acceptable way to compete. I was sometimes inappropriately competitive with her and she would try to minimize such exchanges and keep it light.

At Clark Air Force Base Ria and I played in a weekly duplicate bridge game. Duplicate is a very competitive form of the game. Ria was my only partner and I enjoyed our partnership. I don't know if she played with others. We came to our house in Maryland in anticipation of the opening of the Andrews Air Force Base Hospital. I was in the group that opened the new facility in August 1958. I never smoked in that hospital. When Ria and I first met I was an addicted smoker who was trying to quit. My medical school anatomy professor, an addicted cigarette smoker, told us that the first clear-cut scientific studies had been published showing that cigarette smoking was a major factor in the development of lung cancer and heart disease. He laughed and said he guessed he would die of lung cancer or a heart attack; he was smoking as he spoke. He died that year of a heart attack; I was impressed. Dad was right when he called cigarettes coffin nails.

The Andrews Officers' Club had a Tuesday evening duplicate game and we often played in it. Ria began to play in other games and she eventually started a game in our house where all the entry fees went to charity.

Ria smoked. She was very aware of my struggle to stop; she seemed to agree that our smoking was dangerous, undesirable and set a bad example for the children. We were in agreement, I thought, that the opening of the new hospital could be a watershed for us; we would stop smoking. When after a week or so of my abstinence, Ria asked me if I actually believed she had stopped smoking, I was surprised and thought it was sort of amusing. Later I was upset about her continuing to smoke; it became a great source of tension for both of us. She agreed—from her point of view she submitted—to my request that she not confront me with her smoking; but I was repeatedly confronted even though she did not smoke in my presence.

After several years I told Ria that I was unwilling to go places with her if she would smoke while we were out together. She could, of course, go where she chose to go, but not with me. She agreed, but did not follow the agreement. Eventually she told me that when I thought we had discussed some important matter and come to an agreement or mutual decision, she felt there was no agreement; she had simply submitted to what she viewed as the inevitability of things being done my way.

Perhaps Ria was right, but right or wrong I understood that she viewed me as unfair, oppressive and limiting. It was a very uncomfortable arrangement. I thought we had a fair deal with agreed upon sharing of power and duties; Ria felt powerless and stifled.

We had an enlightening exchange about money. Always I brought the money home and Ria handled the finances. She told me that she viewed all of our money as mine. I responded that I thought all we had was ours. Afterwards I thought a lot about that exchange and I realized that although I always put all the money in the pot, I might not if I did not approve of the way that money was used. Ria did what she knew I would accept and she felt under my rule. It is likely that she felt that not smoking would be another instance of submission.

My view of myself as fair and accommodating was not shared. Once I said I was sure we could come to an accommodation about something and Ria said, "Name one time when you have been accommodating." I was taken aback by that, but replied that after about a five year hiatus I had agreed to resume playing duplicate bridge because she had requested it. Ria said, "But you like playing bridge." I agreed, but felt it, nevertheless, was an important instance of accommodation and the fact that it worked out well did not nullify it. If one only gets credit when one suffers, one might tend to suffer a lot.

In 1961 I resigned from the Air Force and began working for the District of Columbia Health Department. I also started an evening private practice; it was one of those decisions we made together. My work schedule was very heavy and I did not play bridge for five years. It was 1966 when I left the Health Department and began full time private practice. Ria asked me to start playing bridge again; she wanted to play on the weekends in addition to her weekday games. I agreed to play with her on weekends.

Ria wanted to become a major bridge champion; she had the ability. I resisted; it would have included frequent travel and considerable expense. When our sons started college in 1970 I suggested that she go back to school. She did and she had what I thought was a very exciting and successful college experience. She made Phi Beta Kappa at the University of Maryland and then graduated from the Maryland College of Law. She was in law school while our sons were in medical school. When we separated in 1982, several years after she had passed the Maryland bar, I believe she expressed the idea that I had encouraged her to go back to school in preparation for getting rid of her. I remember fearing that we might break up much more than wanting it.

When our twenty-fifth wedding anniversary was near, I suggested that we hire a hall and throw a party. Ria said she preferred that we take a trip. I agreed and she arranged a theater package to London and Paris. We were together nearly continuously for two weeks. It was a fine, interesting vacation, but something was not right. Later I realized how troubling it had been for her to have me there and how she escaped me periodically to smoke.

It's late. I went to the afternoon memorial service and I spent an enjoyable evening at the Smiths'. I'm tired.

My nose was up at 4 A.M., my guts rumbled with last night's hot chili peppers, my thighs and belly itched and I scratched, got out of bed and went askew.

Yesterday's narrative did not focus sufficiently on my addiction and the distress I felt as an abstinent addict in a world that repeatedly exposed me to the stuff I craved. It is now over twenty years since I last lit up and smoked; the tension is very greatly reduced, but for many years the conflict was intense and included several brief cigarette smoking slips and a period of a few months when I was preoccupied with cigar smoking. My work taught me that addicts tend to have a slip when they feel they have their problem licked. I was chagrined to have that experience; even today I try to keep my guard up and assert that I am still quite vulnerable. I know that I am vulnerable even though I don't feel it. Maybe I'm due for another slip. Where is my amulet?

Bridge clubs and bridge tournaments are now nearly smoke-free. It was a long hard battle to achieve that and the battle continues. There has been much rancor, intolerance and maliciousness; friendships, marriages and partnerships have ended; lots of casualties in this battle, including many prolonged disabilities and deaths from the smoking.

When I returned to bridge the environment was smoke filled, irritating, fetid and grimy. I was already a soldier in the battle to extinguish my nemesis and I was early in the fight to change the rules of the game at bridge clubs and bridge tournaments. The rules are very important to the players and change requires much deliberation. Players are smarter than average and probably better educated and better informed than average. When a good player is faced with a problem, she will "work it out." The problem is still being "worked out."

A duplicate bridge session takes about three hours. During the game I would sometimes be aware that when Ria left the table it was to smoke. Our agreement was that she would not smoke when we went out together. After the game we both stank; all the players stank. The tension was intrusive.

Nothing is more destructive to a bridge partnership than competition within the partnership. All that competitive energy is best directed against the opponents. A successful partnership depends on the same stuff that makes for a successful partnership in life. What is on the list? "Work it out."

In 1982 Ria was doing some public defender work and other law work. I felt quite proud of her, but we were not comfortable with each other. She bought a small, sporty new car that I could hardly enter and I believe she knew that would be the case when she decided to buy it. I had stayed out of the selection process because she had complained, after the fact, about how I had influenced a previous purchase.

My neurological symptoms were mild, but we both knew something was developing. With all the tension in our relationship I knew I would not want to be under her care if I became disabled, nor would I want to care for her if she developed a serious illness, probably secondary to her smoking.

I stopped smoking in early August and many years I have experienced increased tension, a kind of anniversary reaction, around the first week of August. It was the first week of August when I came home, kissed Ria, smelled the tobacco on her breath and complained about it. She firmly said, "Accept it; just accept it." I said I would accept it and we both knew we would separate. We went to New Jersey to Ria's niece's wedding. We were civil; there was no discussion. I felt a great sense of relief. Ria moved into another bedroom and soon she was looking for a new place to live. I think Ria was frightened but determined. I felt a little sad but a lot relieved. We were in the house together until December. Ria moved into a new house in January. Ria drew up our separation agreement and it was changed very little by our mutual friend Murray Kivitz.

When we had been apart about ten years I met a bridge player who asked me if Ria and I were related. I responded, "Only by children." Ria and I saw each other regularly at local bridge games and the children would sometimes talk about their exchanges with her. I believe she continued to smoke until she developed severe lung problems; then she became a strong proponent for smoke-free playing facilities for bridge games.

Last night I enjoyed a delicious Indian dinner cooked by Jemma Smith and Cathy, her housekeeper. Jemma is a nurse and is from Goa. Robin, Pat's nephew, is an anesthesiologist and is from Bangalore, India. Their sons were born here. They are friendly, generous people and they are very fond of their Aunt Patty.

Pat and I met at a Christmas party in 1982. She is a nurse and she worked with the group of internists I worked with. I had spoken with her on the telephone, but we met at the party. She was wearing a sari and she looked lovely. She disagreed when I subsequently said that she initiated our friendship. She had introduced herself and later she lowered her eyes when I looked at her. Very erotic and forward, don't you think?

That December my son Adam married. Early in January my father died. I was alone in my house. Ria had moved out, things settled down and Pat and I courted. It was never light-hearted; our relationship became very important to me. I had a frolic with another admirable woman and enjoyed its ease and eroticism, but I was discomforted by what felt like a deception and I thought it would pain Pat.

Pat had an international perspective and many friends and relatives around the world. She was raised in southern India with Indian, Irish and English origins. As a young nurse she had been chosen to attend Rajenda Prasad, India's president, during his illness. She was trusted and admired. She married an American in our diplomatic service. They lived in Japan for two years with their young daughter before settling in the United States. Their marriage ended soon thereafter. When we met, Pat worked as an occupational nurse at the Pan American Health Organization. She lived with her mother and young teenage daughter. Her brothers and sisters were scattered: Canada, Australia, India, England and the United States. She is a gentle but determined woman; I enjoyed her sphere and admired her resolve. We enjoyed entertaining each other and found comfort and strength together. I find pleasure in being helpful to her.

My Monday routine has come to an end. The bridge game this morning, with a new partner, was not a winner, but I enjoyed it and the lunch was terrific. This evening Deb and I enjoyed our dinner and chat. She told me that the robins have returned. I have not seen them although I have been looking. Tomorrow is Super Tuesday; the media suggests that Dole's selection will go from a sure thing to an absolute certainty.

Super Tuesday; it is a bright, warm day. The last vestige of Friday's snow will melt today.

It will be a couple of days before I hear from the Neurology Center about getting a copy of the history I wrote before I first saw Dr. Edelson. It was probably 1984 when my symptoms accelerated. I was jogging to the office and I had reached the Mall when, in front of the Smithsonian castle, I stopped and could not continue. My coordinated movements had gone awry. I was able to slowly walk the remaining two miles and then I worked a full day. I went from feeling fit and vigorous to feeling uncomfortable and limited. It was not clear how severe my symptoms would become or how restricted I would be. Pat was quite concerned and very supportive.

A complete diagnostic evaluation revealed, as expected, no lesion or cause. Dr. Edelson was very generous and helpful; we agreed that the best course of action was to wait and see how my condition evolved. He told me that my mental capacity would not be affected by spasmodic torticollis. I was experiencing a great deal of torsion on my neck and back and the twisting and turning was worsened by various activities.

The biggest change was in my view of myself; I was no longer vigorous. It was the beginning of my decrepitude. There were fluctuations in my discomfort, but no new, big increase of symptoms, and I began to adjust to living with a chronic condition that was very unlikely to improve.

Pat stuck by me and was always encouraging. Another big health crisis struck when in September 1985 I was diagnosed with a malignant melanoma on my right arm. I underwent surgery that included a wide removal of tissue, skin graft and axillary node dissection. Following the surgery my right hand was paralyzed. I made a slow, painful recovery. Pat was with me as friend and nurse throughout that ordeal. I was frightened and I expected to die from that cancer. The surgery, done around my fifty-ninth birthday, was successful despite the complications and I subsequently recovered most of the strength in my hand. I stopped smelling frightened before the year ended and I am pleased to remember that I was happy and in good humor at the office Christmas party that Pat and I attended.

My children were concerned and attentive during that very difficult time. They wanted to help and they did help, but Pat was the care giver. She had my admiration, gratitude and affection.

Dole did it again.

Wednesday, March 13, 1996. David Broder declared in today's *Washington Post*: Fall Face-off Starts Now on Pennsylvania Avenue. The primary process is over, but Forbes and Buchanan have not gone away and the exit polls show little voter enthusiasm about the likely candidates. They need our votes and they will work hard to win our approval.

So much of what goes on in our relationships seems to revolve around the question, "How do you regard me?" followed by the request, "Prove it." It is connected with our uncertainty about ourselves; it is for me. I can be cherished by being consistently supportive and admiring, but I want to be cherished without trying very hard to please. I am not confidently pleased with myself unless I have at least a modicum of good feedback. I seek self-acceptance, but I wonder if I want it primarily to make myself invulnerable to the views of others. Blatant self-approval is so often laughable and arrogant or even bizarre; don't be too open about it if you have it.

Pat moved because she was persistently discontent. Her uneasiness was partly about how she perceived me and my regard for her. I tried to behave in a helpful manner with her and her family, but she questioned how I valued her. Her situation had evolved during our time together; her mother became elderly and her daughter had grown up and moved to Europe to study. Selena married and had two children. Pat craved more contact with her daughter and grandchildren.

Pat's decision to move to Florida surprised many of us. Her mother did not want to leave a comfortable situation with many friends and important family nearby. I suggested that Pat delay the move, but she felt it was now or never. When I realized her decision was firm and unwavering, I experienced a change in my feelings for her. She entered a new category that closely resembles the way I feel about my children. My interest in her welfare persisted and I tried to be helpful and assist her in making the change she wanted. I was helping her to leave me and soon I was ready for her to leave.

The stability and safety that I felt in our relationship faded away and I found myself in a new category: unattached and uncertain about how to proceed.

Most of my work as a physician, a psychotherapist, was based on forming an alliance with a person who would be the focus of our partnership. Their job was to make an attempt at an accurate self-presentation. My job was to encourage their attempt, consider what they presented and to react with the intention of helping them to clarify their important issues; perhaps helping to resolve troubling problems with resulting symptom relief, avoidance of future symptoms and improved quality of life. Often there is dramatic symptom relief early in this process, but, in spite of what medical insurers shortsightedly want, it is rarely wise to stop the work then for the vulnerability to recurrence is unchanged at that early stage.

In the treatment process I was intently focused on my partner. The process was devoted to the patient's productions and to attempts to nurture, assist and relieve that person. Now, if that ain't love, what is?

The word *love* and the word *really* are often used; they rarely clarify. I asked my patients to please avoid those words. Love is a cover-up word that helps one to avoid dealing with what one feels or what one wants. Really obfuscates. So a person might say, "It is true that you show intense interest in me and you focus all of your attention on me while I am with you but you don't really love me because…" or "If you really loved me you would…" or "Would you still really love me if…"; long lists can follow. In recent years I have often heard about commitment and about unconditional love. Examples of unconditional love are often weird. A woman still really loves her husband and wants him back after he has killed her parents, raped their children and broken her bones. Now that is commitment and true love; anything less doesn't cut the mustard.

Bill Clinton and Bob Dole would like us to really love them, but they will gladly settle for our vote.

I really loved my work.

Last year I sent a card to my eleven year old granddaughter, Allison. I covered it with REALLY written with many different crayons and using small letters so I could fit in many REALLYs. At the end I wrote: Love you a lot. One of these days when her father says, "I love you, Dad," I will say "Dear Son, I care deeply about you and would do anything and sacrifice all for your welfare and happiness."

So often a statement is part question and part request. "I love you." Tell me how you regard me and prove it.

It is a warm spring morning; perfect for a walk to the bridge game at Andrews. The next door neighbor, whose bird feeder provided me with theater all winter, tells me there were four robins in the yard this morning. I walk slowly and repeatedly press my fist against the small of my back. That manuever helps me to maintain my posture and reduces the torsion and disrupted coordination. The walk to the game and back was even better than the game and the lunch. It was my first walk since I slipped on the ice on February 16. I'm lucky that I can still enjoy walking.

Today's mail includes a letter from the Neurology Center. It contains a copy of the history I wrote in May 1984, just prior to my neurological evaluation. It reminds me that I had a tremor of my right hand intermittently for nearly a decade and that my terrible handwriting was getting worse. The involuntary head turning began in 1981. Around 1982 I first experienced pain and limited motion in my right shoulder. By 1983 I was experiencing pain in my neck and shoulder and my posture was deteriorating. It became very difficult for me to sit still. All of this became much worse in early 1984. Discomfort had turned into recurring pain and activities that had been easy and comfortable became difficult. I was dis eased.

In January 1985 I reported that my symptoms were much worse and new symptoms had appeared including facial movements and movements of my right shoulder and arm. I continued all my usual activities except jogging, but I was much less inclined to go to the theater or movies and I was reading less. On December 12, 1985, I wrote to Dr. Edelson about still more muscle involvement and about the malignant melanoma surgery. I am reminded now of how much pain I was experiencing and how frightened I was, but I was already improving and there was a clear decrease in my left hand tremor; a little good news is always welcome.

This evening I will watch the NCAA tournament. Forbes has withdrawn after spending thirty million dollars of his own money. Buchanan is still mouthing off. Congress has not passed a federal budget, but there is another continuing resolution to keep the government from shutting down again.

It is early Friday morning, I'm writing and I'm still feeling quite comfortable. "It" has not started yet.

Yesterday was unusual in that I got a telephone call from all three of my kids; on a Thursday. Steve called from his car phone as he drove to the hospital in Baltimore to see patients; just a friendly chat and he reminded me that his family is going on a skiing vacation next week. Last night Adam called from southern Virginia. We talked about his work, my writing and the premature death of two of his colleagues. He may drive up here to visit with friends this weekend and if he does he will sleep here and I'll make dinner for him. Deb called soon after; she had just gotten home from having dinner with an important man friend. She is feeling discouraged about getting her customer to help her gear up to do the job she's been hired to do.

All three kids have gotten the bitter and the sweet from their parents. Adam most overtly resembles me and it is not all sweet. He expresses a combined criticism and sentimentality about his childhood. He sometimes emanates a discontent in circumstances that almost anyone would envy. We are often honest rather than generous. He once told me that he wanted my respect and admiration. I responded that I wanted to respect and admire him. Why didn't I say "I respect and admire you"? I do respect and admire him, but not entirely. Like it or not, my feelings about him are all too similar to his feelings about himself.

Steven is genetically identical to Adam but presents himself as if much more lighthearted. He was my playboy son who finally settled down and married Teresa in 1988, six years after Adam married Saria. If he has a bone to pick with me, he doesn't reveal it. I am willing to drive up to fifty miles away on a day trip; it is likely that I picked that distance because the two places I go to see Steve and his family are fifty miles from my house.

Deborah has been telling me a little about herself for several years; it is part of her finding out about herself. She had a very difficult early life. When she was fourteen months old two small strangers stole into her home and kept her mother from her. Her father would show up periodically and distract her mother still more. Adam and Steven started walking when they were fifteen months old; Deb was running around the house when she was ten months old. We had a screen door between the living room and a front porch. Deb was eight months old when she decided to open that door to go out and then open it to come in. It was not easy, but she was determined, she persisted and she conquered. I was not aware of the extent to which she dominated her brothers until after they were adults. She did not forgive her brothers until after they left home. It did not matter that she had already left home; they had to leave before she would seek friendship with them. Deb married a very nice guy. I believe she wanted someone she could look straight across to rather than look up to. That was part of what made him suitable and that was a big part of what led to their divorce.

All of my children picked mates who had parents whom I found likable and admirable. That is lucky. My in-laws seemed very nice at first, but they were never helpful when they were needed and Ria was vulnerable to any discontent they expressed. Ria's father was a fraud. After he died I found myself feeling some sympathy and even affection for my mother-in-law, but she soon pulled a few tricks and I reverted to my negative view of her.

My mother never told me that she hated my father's mother, but I believe she hated and resented her. Mother's father died before my birth and her mother died when I was quite young. I remember Dad's mother. She was wheelchair bound after an amputation, her house smelled funny and it was unpleasant to visit there. Grandmother died when I was seven or eight. Dad's father was a pleasant and playful man who would visit us. He would "come on his horse"; walk with his cane. He enjoyed Mother's cooking. He died soon after Ria and I married. I believe my mother was always in competition with my father's family. She wanted all of his allegiance and rankled when he showed loyalty to his original family. I wonder if I have it right.

My brother Fred is five years my junior. He was a miracle baby; born prematurely and weighing less than three pounds. I think he was two months old before he came home. Mother recovered incompletely from the toxemia of pregnancy that precipitated Fred's early birth. I remember being introduced to my brother by my mother and running out to invite some neighborhood friends in to see him. He was tiny and delicate. My mother's tendency to be overprotective increased.

The neighborhood standard for strictness and probity was set by my mother. If the Billet boys were permitted to do something, anyone could get permission. There was an ongoing tension between the caution my mother felt and the desire to experience life that Fred and I felt. In my teens I felt unfairly ruled by my mother's anxiety. I developed a pattern of complying without quite complying. That is still my style.

I was not a very good brother. Fred was included in few of my activities and I was not affectionate with him, but I was a groundbreaker and I hope that made his life easier. Later on, Fred and Dad had an ongoing battle about showing respect. In the last few years Fred has been much less reticent with me and I'm very pleased about our friendliness.

Mother was probably recurrently angry and depressed. I did not realize the extent to which she was ruled by fear, anger and the avoidance of shame. I vaguely understood that we were poor and that Mother blamed Dad for selling his business and losing everything in the 1929 stock market crash. I also knew that I was not supposed to talk about Dad working for his brother in an illegal bookmaking business. Late in my teens, in a moment of anguish, my mother revealed how hurt, angry and ashamed (and unforgiving) she felt about contracting syphilis from my father when they married. They underwent prolonged arsenical treatment, in secret. Mother told me this as a warning. She was telling me to be watchful and circumspect.

I decided to become a doctor when I was three weeks old. Also at three weeks I knew I would be motivated to do good and not make too much money; everyone would be proud of me.

Dad was born in New Jersey and Mother was born in New York; their parents were immigrants from eastern Europe. They were hardworking people of orthodox Jewish background. I grew up in the voluntary Jewish ghetto in Newark that has been written about by so many. Several successful writers grew up in my neighborhood. It was as intellectual, upwardly mobile and sexy as has been written about. It was more like a small parish than it was like part of a big city.

My house was on the top of a hill. From the roof one had a view of Newark Airport, the Statue of Liberty and Manhattan. The airport was then the largest in the world; incoming planes would fly right over our house; I could almost reach up and touch them as they flew by. One day when I came home from school I saw a huge swastika hung across the alley between our house and the next house. I was frightened. It slowly moved and I realized it was the tail fin of the *Hindenburg*. The dirigible was circling Newark Airport before going to Lakehurst to moor. It burned just prior to landing. Later my mother said that it was a terrible tragedy, but that if it had to happen she was glad it happened before touchdown for surely the Jews would have been blamed if it had occurred after the landing.

All of my activities were within walking distance or easily reached by bus. Mother did not drive and we had no car until I was in high school. When I went to New York University I commuted by bus and train each day. When I was in my preteens I didn't understand that we would spend summer afternoons playing in the alley because there was no money to do things away from home. On some summer Sundays in my early teens our family and mother's sister Dotty's family would drive to Rahway park and have a picnic. The kids could swim for twenty-five cents. Later we would return to Aunt Dotty's house and Uncle Jack would make turkey club sandwiches slathered with Russian dressing. My mother still kept a kosher house so we couldn't have club sandwiches in my home; no bacon permitted. Aunt Dotty's son, Raymond, is the only cousin I have kept in touch with. I am the closest thing he has to a brother.

Elliott and Murray are my very close friends who live near each other in the Maryland suburbs. Both of them are from my boyhood in New Jersey. Murray and I were high school classmates. When I came to Maryland he was practicing law in the District of Columbia. We became close friends after he married Iris. Ria and Iris also became good friends. The Kivitz family has included me in their gatherings since Ria and I separated.

Jerry, Elliott's cousin, was my best friend in high school. I spent a lot of time at his house. The atmosphere was very relaxed and it was usually crowded with family and friends. Elliott went away to private school, but was usually at Jerry's house during holidays and summer vacation. Elliott, Fred and I were on vacation at the beach when we met Ria. My friendship with Jerry remained strong, but we got together infrequently. Elliott was doing research at the National Institutes of Health when my family came to Maryland. We have become very close friends. Elliott and his wife Jenny have been very thoughtful and helpful; a lot like family.

I and most of my friends and associates are affluent; we have come a long way from those days when I played in the alley. When I was in college I had a classmate who said, "My parents hocked the furniture to pay my tuition." I do not know if that was the truth or if it was meant to be symbolic, but it certainly captured the spirit of those times.

The political question this evening: Who will be Dole's running mate?

The early Saturday morning news had a long segment on the killing of sixteen kindergarten children in Scotland. A delusional man shot them and also killed their teacher and himself. The small community is in shock and mourning and things have been further complicated by a huge contingent of media people and equipment. The tragedy of foreshortened life and loss of loved ones agitates and interests us. It reminds me that life is just a flicker, but it is all we've got. Whether you are George Burns who lived one hundred years or those Scottish kids who died at five or six, it is a short stay. I try to give it meaning. Only rarely do I envy those who believe that life has intrinsic meaning. They are the same people who will go to heaven; God bless them.

My mother died before her sixty-fifth birthday; I was thirty-eight. All of my life I had been told how much I looked like her. I had been a tall, skinny, fair-skinned boy. Not long after Mother died I looked in the mirror and I saw my father; what an amazing transformation. It was the beginning of being full grown and near being old. Being old is close to being dead but for some, such as those Scottish children, death occurs well before old age. Thursday Adam told me about two of his colleagues who died in their prime of incurable cancer.

That malignant melanoma did not kill me. Dad lived to be eighty-eight; maybe I've got another twenty years. Why does that seem like such a long time when the past twenty went by so quickly?

My first experience of living away from home occurred when I went to Cincinnati to begin medical school. Except for vacations, I never lived in my parents' home again. I was almost twenty and I wanted my own place with my own rules, not Mother's rules. Dad would occasionally try to gently get Mother to relent, but he was characteristically passive when she delivered a ruling. I wanted him to actively oppose her on my behalf. I did not understand their arrangement and did not know its historical underpinnings.

During World War II bookmaking became a federal offense. Dad went into factory war work. He became more available and he seemed friendly and interested in me. Dad, Fred and I would go bowling together and I remember going with some regularity to wrestling matches and the fights. Dad knew a lot about the fights; those evenings were great fun for me.

Dad read a lot. He remained easygoing. He had an unusual memory; he seemed to remember everything. He learned to speak French while stationed in France and he remained fluent in French. When I studied biology in college, Dad knew all I had to learn; he remembered it from high school. I forgot most of it soon after the exam.

After my mother died Dad lived with his two older sisters in New Jersey, near my brother. After several years they moved to Miami Beach. Dad called Miami "the land of our people." He outlived both of his sisters and stayed in Florida. In 1976, eleven years after my mother's death, Dad hinted that he was having trouble taking care of himself. I discussed it with Ria and we agreed to invite Dad to live with us, but we planned to not greatly alter our activities. Dad arrived. We bought a dog and asked Dad to participate in its care.

My easygoing father had become somewhat anxious and unsteady. He did not want to be any trouble for us, but he was discontent with the amount of attention we showed him and he did not like the isolation of the Maryland suburbs. After more than a year with us he concluded that if he could take care of himself here, he could take care of himself in Miami. He returned to the residential hotel he had previously lived in and he remained there until his final illness. Dad had regained his confidence here and he was ready to be on his own again. I felt Ria had been welcoming and generous with my dad and I told her how much I appreciated her efforts.

Mother probably married because she was ready for the serious business of having and raising a family. She thought Dad was suitable for the job; he was tall, handsome, smart and he had money. She felt deceived when her husband infected her, putting a long delay on getting pregnant.

Marriage is serious business, not fun and sex. The pressure is on to accept the ordeal. We are taught that we are following the rules when we form a family and take care of it. It is written; is it a sacrilege to deny it? Family values and pressure to conform to traditional ways are prominent issues in this political year. Sleaze and character issues may be more important than most other matters in influencing the voters. It vexes me when the Republicans claim the high ground and it perplexes me when all those divorced Republicans claim to be the good family values guys.

The last blast of winter this Sunday morning includes high winds, rain and sleet. It is St. Patrick's Day. Yesterday I wore my Dukakis–Bentson button to bridge and when asked I said I was wearing it instead of wearing my green socks for St. Patrick's Day; I try to amuse myself. Why didn't we Democrats understand that our country was not yet ready to have a president named Dukakis; maybe soon, but not yet. Traditional thinking tells us there is us and there is them; Dukakis sounds too much like them.

People have told me a dream in which they are taking a trip and they have their luggage right there with them, but somehow it gets lost and they feel very upset. I have heard some variation of that dream a dozen times. We often fear what we want. The dreamer entered into a partnership with me with the hope of getting rid of a lot of unwanted baggage, but is fearful about how he will be and what he will do if rid of that baggage. Introspection and self-evaluation usually help us to reaffirm what we are about. A sense of freedom does not mean you will go hog wild, but we are often afraid that we will be disruptive or disrupted if we feel our freedom.

Two people decided to tell the shrink the exact same dream on the same day. After hearing the second telling, the shrink exclaimed, "That's the third time I've heard that dream today!"

What good luck I have had; my work was interesting, prestigious, remunerative and centered around forming constructive partnerships with wonderful people of great diversity. Many of those people were very intelligent. One of my strongest points as a therapist was my ability to work well with a person much smarter than I while we both acknowledged that difference.

Authority and responsibility went with my work. The old paternalistic model of medicine is largely gone, but even in the egalitarian model that I followed, society recognizes that the physician has immense power, authority and responsibility. Lucky me; I was never greatly tempted to misuse that trust.

Several years ago I attended a lecture sponsored by the George Washington University Department of Psychiatry. The title of the lecture was in code; the uncoded title was, "You Better Not Have Sex With Your Patients." The lecturer petitioned for someone in the audience to present a case where it seemed all right to have sex with a patient. When no one came forward he implored the audience, but no one volunteered; finally I volunteered. I did not get to finish my presentation. The lecturer dismissed me; my case did not suit his purpose. The patient I tried to present was ninety years old. The code of ethics for psychiatrists prohibits sex with a patient or former patient; it was not always so clear-cut. My personal code keeps me from having sex with anyone over whom I have authority or unfair advantage. The patient I tried to tell about was a wonderful, smart, creative woman who was very fond of her internist and cared almost as much for me. She had strong sexual feelings. Our work together helped her to resolve some difficult concerns about her family with great reduction of her anxiety and depression. I have rarely experienced even a soupçon of sexual feeling toward a patient (lucky me) and I felt no sexual feelings toward this lovely lady, but I think that if I had been eager to have sex with her she would have welcomed me and she would not have been injured in any way by our sexual union; even her children would have been pleased about it. The only problems would have been mine for my behavior would have been unethical and punishable by any usual standard, including mine.

We are barraged by instances of corrupt authority and abuse of power. I am dismayed that once again the Republicans claim the high ground in their electioneering as if untouched by perfidy.

The house is filled with the fragrance of fresh baked bread.

Pat called this morning. She planted a mango tree and a litchi tree. A neighbor gave her a dozen grapefruit. Every Saturday is like the fourth of July with a ten minute fireworks display after sunset. She is pleased with her new home and wants me to visit soon. My regular response is that I do not know what I'm going to do. I told her I'm scheduled for a cataract removal on April 23. Her mother's cataract surgery has been delayed. Pat has joined an exercise club. In the afternoon I called Betty, Teresa's mother, and sang "Happy St. Patrick's Day to You." I told her that Deb and I have almost finished the delicious almond cookies that she and Roy gave me for my birthday. Their robins have returned in full force and their home is north of here. Betty is sure that our grandson David is a budding genius. We have all felt confined by the winter and we welcome spring.

The more I learn about Senator Dole the more I like him. Don't get me wrong, I'll not vote for him. The candidates go through such contortions to get nominated and elected; the process makes them look bad and does not seem to clarify anything about their views or their character. Dole's history suggests that he is an admirable, compassionate and moderate man. Unlike Ronald Reagan, he seems not to have been greatly corrupted by power or money.

President Clinton and I share a problem; our facial expression is not always easy to identify. Many times I have been reprimanded for smirking when I was feeling chagrin; grinning while suffering. The president does not look serious enough. It creates a suggestion of insincerity when there is nothing other than his facial expression to support doubt about his authenticity. I have often been told to stop smirking. Dear Mr. President, please stop smirking.

This morning I trimmed my hair, showered and shaved, dressed, filled a basket with sliced bread and went to the bridge game. Safeway had good looking asparagus and grapefruit that I bought for dinner. The asparagus was on special, but the checkout scanner overcharged. I still have a depression era mentality so I noticed that error and had it corrected.

It has been about thirty years since I have had a barbershop haircut. Ria cut my hair until around 1965 and soon after I started cutting it myself. Everything we did in our family I claimed we did on haircut money: vacations, college tuition, everything done with haircut money. I think my sons made extra spending money while in college by cutting hair. Our family always had enough money because we never spent more than we had. Never being in debt is one version of being rich, so we were always rich. Now I am not only rich, but I have a little money.

Most of the people I know who have big money problems also have large incomes and extraordinarily large expenditures. It is all part of deciding what is important. When I was a kid we always had everything my mother thought it was important for us to have, but little more. Now I tend to impose a similar standard on myself. When Steve and Teresa asked for financial assistance to buy a place on the Chesapeake Bay I thought they were bonkers, but I agreed to help. Their purchase will probably work out well monetarily, but even if it doesn't they bought a very wonderful place that gives me and many others great pleasure. When they asked for the money I thought, if I spent money the way Steve spends it I would not have it to give. I am pleased that my kids have a more relaxed standard about indulging themselves and I hope that they never suffer a repeat of the 1930s depression.

Yes, I know candy bars do not cost a nickel any more and perhaps I will soon accept it. Suits cost what cars used to cost. Deb's car cost as much as my house, including the big addition. You've heard about the unfortunate fellow who recently graduated from college and was only earning $10,000 a year ... more than his father ever earned.

Let us have a balanced budget, but let us provide, as my mother did, everything that is important. Are we one family? I believe we are. It is not us and them, it is just us.

Last evening Deb and I had baked apple and fluden for dessert. Fluden is a kind of jelly torte that is cut into zwieback shaped slices. It is delicious. Ria got the recipe from Iris Kivitz, but it is very much like a cake my mother made that Mother called zwieback. It is not rusk, but is a very rich cake that is filled with jelly and coconut and then iced and sprinkled with additional coconut. Ria often made this treat for us; for me. After 1982 Deb made fluden for me on special occasions and she let me know how very difficult it was to make. I decided to make it myself and I found it was an awful chore. The rich dough tended to crack when folded and the filling would run out and eventually burn. I cursed a lot while rolling and shaping the dough and still more while trying to repair it before baking. I was not willing to suffer that much. It is a wonderful cake so I invented a no-curse, minimal-suffer method and now we have fluden with great regularity.

Suffering is often avoidable. A gift that causes the giver to suffer is often more highly valued. Around the holidays people will complain that their gift giving had not been difficult enough. When suffering is so highly valued it may seem desirable; there is extra credit for wearing a hair shirt. Unnecessary suffering is deplorable and sometimes deceitful. It can become a manipulative technique used to tip the balance in our struggles. The new fluden that I make with ease is even better than the original.

Back in the old days a patient complimented me on the beautiful shine on my shoes. I explained that I had used liquid polish. She was disbelieving and became angry. She felt that such a fine shine must be the result of hard work. It was as if I had misrepresented myself.

Important matters deserve close attention, diligence, hard work and even suffering. Needless suffering makes a mockery of the notion of worthwhile, intense effort that has a painful component.

Washing dishes for short periods helps to ease the discomfort I feel when sitting still at the dining table. I will wash a dish as soon as it is empty, before the next course. The dishes are not very clean; a little more soap and elbow grease would help do the job. My standard for cleanliness is not very high when I am doing the cleaning. If Ms. Macklin who cleans this house did such a poor job, I would not accept it. There is sometimes a discrepancy between the standard I hold for myself and the standard I apply to others. It is probably about role assignment and about arrogance and condescension.

Role assignment and role acceptance or refusal underlie so many of our adjustment problems and can lead to much discomfort. I have never had an easy time uncritically accepting authority. I tend to resist. I suffer from the chocolate ice cream dilemma; if you tell me that chocolate is the best flavor, it makes me less certain that it is my preference. If I liked chocolate best and you recommended vanilla, I would be more sure of my choice. Although the authority is often wise, benevolent and correct, questioning still suits me. Questioning has not led me to any great scientific or therapeutic breakthroughs, but it has done that for others. Orthodoxy resists change and punishes questioning that fails to reinforce the conventional wisdom.

My mother would have preferred that I become a surgeon or an internist, but I pretty much fulfilled the role she assigned me when I was three weeks old. Luckily my premature marriage gave her five extra years of glorious grandmotherhood. Unluckily she did not live to see one grandchild an internist and another a surgeon.

Spring is three hours old. The primary yesterday was so unexciting that I didn't bother to mention it. The bridge hands at the Andrews game were very interesting; I played well and stayed alert, but when I got home I was bone tired and fell asleep almost at once. The big news didn't reach me until this morning; Senator Dole went over the top and is the Republican nominee for president. Ross Perot is exposing himself again. Buchanan continues to arouse his ilk. The hoi polloi remain unenthusiastic.

There is snow in today's forecast; it's a raw gloomy morning. The side yard is littered with leaves and debris. The pond is full but the contraption that feeds water to it from the garage roof is toppled over. That work will have to wait; I am not yet ready to tackle it. Instead, I will make a potato pudding for the first Passover seder at the Kivitz's on April 3.

I bought a leg of lamb and many ripe bananas this morning so I'll have a busy afternoon in the kitchen.

Today the Virginia legislature passed a bill to make English the official language of that state. One legislator said the bill was "just a feel good bill." He didn't say who would feel good; certainly not those who vigorously testified against it; they feel the law would disadvantage and derogate them. Must we dominate or ridicule others to feel good? I hope humanity will overcome its small family values and develop big family values. The factionalists use language, nationalism, tribalism, race, religion and anything else they can find to assist in differentiating groups and dividing people.

Our small families remain too much like a hen house and our world view is still largely as that of small primitive tribes. There is not enough civility in our civilization. Nationalism and race are very prominent issues in this political year. So much of what the politicians say is shallow rhetoric that appeals to our prejudices and insecurities.

I hold to an unconventional definition of racist. A racist is a person who believes that current concepts of race make sense. There are five races, and then there is the Irish race and the Jewish race. All the diverse tribes in Africa are placed in one race and a similar combining of the heterogeneous peoples of Asia puts them into one race. A person of diverse origins is designated as belonging to one race in one location and to another race somewhere else. Intelligent and educated people believe in the moral and intellectual superiority of one of the races they create, usually their own, over the other races they have devised. The media reports that race is the most divisive issue in the Unites States today. No one in authority questions the reasonableness of the racial categories. There seems to be agreement that Colin Powell is a Black man. I wonder if he agrees. If he does, he meets my definition of racist.

The Democrats and the Republicans seem stuck with the conventional wisdom. It would cost too many votes to challenge the prevailing illogical beliefs. If you want to get elected you had better be very careful about what truths you tell.

The first full day of spring is blustery. The back yard is busy with boisterous birds and squirrels. I see several mockingbirds, but still no robins. It is a fine day for walking to the game at Andrews. I relished a refreshing and reassuring ramble, enjoyed the game and lunch and, declining a ride, walked home.

The mail included the income tax forms done by my accountant. It seems strange that I will not have to pay quarterly estimated taxes; retired, no income anticipated, no quarterly payments necessary.

The Speaker of the House—I like to think of him as Grinch Frankly Newrich—today proposed a bill to repeal the ban on assault weapons. He insists it is not about politics. Maybe he's right. Senator Dole can't welcome this dispute.

Tomorrow I will keep looking until I find a robin. They are out there.

I dozed through last night, never deeply asleep and often awake, but not sufficiently for my nose to awaken, turning frequently to avoid prolonged pressure and to reduce aches.

The route to the Masonic Lodge includes one major intersection that has been disrupted for months by the construction of an overpass. It will be a bit tricky and incautious but I'm going to walk through that crossing this morning carrying a backpack full of bread and butter. I prefer walking someplace rather than just strolling around. Walking is supposed to be good for one's health, but I walk to show myself I can do it. It does not increase my metabolism sufficiently to allow eating without weight gain, so in addition to my backpack I'll be carrying about twenty-five pounds of counterbalancing front side bread basket. Nobody is perfect.

My bridge playing companions tell me they want the bread I bring for them and they sometimes complain if I fail them. I repaired one disrupted relationship with the gift of a loaf of bread; it was so easy and friendly and satisfying.

Gift giving is not always so easy or appropriate. In my work with patients many intangible gifts were exchanged, but concrete gifts were infrequent and suspect. Some say that material gifts are always inappropriate in the therapeutic partnership. I sometimes felt that it was important for me and for the patient that I give something tangible, but what would be suitable? I developed a short list that included home grown or homemade things and paperback books. Home grown tomatoes and peppers, azalea and rhododendron plants grown from cuttings, trees grown from seeds and bread, cake and soup cooked in my kitchen all fit the bill for me. I disagree with the orthodoxy that criticizes such gifts and finds them inappropriate. Books that I enjoyed that included themes from our work together also seemed appropriate. Sometimes they were returned, but not often.

My children complain that it is difficult to find a gift for me. They do not know what I want or what I need. Carefully and clearly I told them that I wanted and needed a wristwatch with large numbers. They got me what they wanted me to have, an answering machine. Their choice has worked out very well and I bought the watch for myself. There is nothing the matter with giving someone what you want them to have, but it can be a problem if you subsequently charge them for it. Do not put that gift on your side of the balance in your score keeping system. Be open with yourself that the gift was for you.

It is gauche and obnoxious to be very open about keeping score in our relationships, but I contend that we are all keeping score. Much of the conflict people experience in their relationships is based on disparities in score keeping. When I feel I have been quite fair, even generous, you might feel that you have been shortchanged and that you have given much more than you have received. It is very unromantic and feels unfriendly if we get explicit about the value of various aspects of our arrangements. Clarity seems too businesslike and, worse yet, it makes it difficult to deceive yourself and others.

Mr. Jones was very depressed; he sat staring and crying all day. Mrs. Jones coaxed him into going for a walk. As they walked she pointed to various buildings and told him that they owned those buildings. Mr. J was incredulous and asked how it could be. She reminded him that each time he had sex with her she charged him ten dollars; she had invested the money in real estate. Mr. J sat down on the curb and sobbed loudly. Mrs. J asked why he was crying and he exclaimed, "If I had known what you were doing, I would have given you all of my business."

If a gift has a price perhaps it is not a gift at all.

Campaign finance reform has not had much action, but today the House of Representatives passed legislation to repeal the ban on assault weapons. The media mavens say it was a free vote; it repays the National Rifle Association, but will not lead to an actual repeal of the ban. We sure do a lot of pretending. So many of our deceits are transparent, but they persist.

I am still ruminating about the arrangements we make for ourselves and how often we deceive ourselves and others in those agreements. No doubt I am trying to decide about how I will proceed with my life.

We will never know whether Mr. and Mrs. Jones agreed prior to marriage that sex would cost ten dollars each incident and that Mr. J, not Mrs. J, would be the customer. Were they explicit about what the ten dollar price would include? Would there be ready availability? Did they agree that Mr. J would give Mrs. J all of his business? When we avoid the details it is likely that there will be divergent views about what to expect. Things are further complicated by the self-deception and outright fraud that goes into our compacts. Are there parts of the contract that are not renegotiable; is any of it open for change? What constitutes a good faith arrangement and what if you change your mind about what you want?

It is too difficult to anticipate all the details. Even when people get together in good faith it can be very tough to find friendly agreement about how to proceed; we tend to change our mind. The man who was attracted to his wife because she was such a good religious woman, complains that she spends too much time in church. Some marriages are little more than a joke. The rich ladies formed a group called Good Housekeepers; every time they got divorced they kept the house. When they marry is it understood that the marriage will end in divorce and they will keep the house?

It is unseemly that I am still so occupied with sex and women. Maybe it is just a symptom of my chronic prostatitis; excuses, excuses.

This morning I called Pat. She is enjoying her house on the verge of the tropics. All is well but her allergies are kicking up. She likes her work with a nurse practitioner. Her mother undergoes cataract surgery next week. Her garden grows.

This afternoon Wes and I were having a very nice game until I made a silly error. I did not see a card in the dummy and I failed to take the winning trick; very careless and costly. Maybe I have not yet seen the robins because of a similar inattentiveness; everyone else has seen them.

The candidates were well represented on the evening news. Most of what they are doing looks and sounds like theater. They seem moderate when the gurus from the radical right and the radical left promote major overhauls rather than fine tuning.

I set my internal alarm before falling asleep and it worked; I woke up in time to watch the final skaters in the women's world championship and then I watched the Saturday night fights. The top level athletes are awesome. Michelle Kwan's performance was beautiful and flawless; she won by a narrow margin. After she knew she had won, she was asked how long she had been seriously seeking the world championship. She responded, "Probably all of my life." It is both nature and nurture that makes us what we are.

Tim Russert is my favorite Sunday morning performer. He knows what he is talking about or he has me fooled. Every Sunday I enjoy his insights and predictions and his questions to the major players. Today his guests included Buchanan and Nader who described themselves as issue oriented and who are perceived as spoilers.

The Republicans keep saying that it is time to trust the people and let federal programs devolve to the states. It sounds reasonable, but I do not trust them; they seem not to want the programs that they would transfer away from the federal government. The most significant divergence between the parties, I believe, is about who deserves what. Although I am now affluent I still identify with the have-nots and I want to live in a society that tries to help them have more; I am a Democrat. The Republicans seem to believe that if you have, it is proof that you deserve to have. It is probably an extension of the notion that if you win it proves that God is on your side.

I am a double dipper. Since my sixtieth birthday I have received an Air Force pension and since this January I receive Social Security benefits. When I resigned from active duty in the United States Air Force in 1961 I had completed ten years of active duty. I remained in the reserves and completed ten good reserve years. That gave me the magical twenty good years that entitled me to a pension and all the benefits that go with being a retired military officer when I reached my sixtieth birthday. I estimate that if I live to be eighty-eight, as my father did, I will cost the American taxpayer over one million dollars. That is not so much compared to what many others will receive, but I still have that depression era mentality and it seems to me like a great deal of money.

Several years ago while Pat and I were having dinner with friends, two of our companions began to complain about excessive government expenditures. They felt we were being depleted by Welfare queens and other undeserving freeloaders. They reinforced each other and got moderately excited but their excitement approached agitation when I agreed with them and proclaimed that the first expenditure to be curtailed should be pensions. I had gored their ox; they were adamant that my notion was absurd and unfair. They had worked hard at a federal hospital and had fulfilled the contract that entitled them to their pension. I contended that they had been paid excessive salaries and that they should have been required to work for many more years before being eligible for such grand pensions; moreover, I thought they were against entitlements. No, they were only against unjustified entitlements, other people's entitlements. I enjoyed that exchange a lot. We never discussed it, but they are Republicans. I am a bleeding heart.

The government has already reneged on part of its contract with retired veterans; our guarantee of free medical care has been compromised. Even so, I am getting quite a bargain. No one has yet dared to suggest that I do not deserve my modest pension. The categories of people who are deemed undeserving never include veterans. It would be unpatriotic and, much worse, politically insupportable. The process of deciding what or who deserves support is often complex and murky.

Questions about deservedness often occur in medical practice. I am not referring to triage or allocation of scarce resources, but rather to feelings that the patient does not deserve treatment. When a condition is perceived as being wholly or partly self-inflicted, the patient may be viewed as disentitled. It is only a short step back to the notion that all illness is deserved punishment and an indication of wrong doing. People with psychiatric conditions are often subjected to this harsh formulation and neglected. I define clinical depression as a psychiatric condition that even Republicans think should be covered by health insurance.

There is easy agreement that it is better for us and for them, whether we view them as part of our family or not, if we teach them to fish rather than give them fish. The disagreement arises around what to do in the interim and what we will do with the slow learners, incompetents, cheats, delinquents, the unwilling and others who seem not to benefit from our good intentions and largess.

The backyard show yesterday included mourning doves, finch, sparrows, grackles, starling, cardinals, blue jays, mockingbirds and several species I did not recognize. The squirrels were very active. There were traces of yellow forsythia. Winter is over.

There is big news about the tobacco companies. Three scientists who worked for Philip Morris have submitted affidavits that will very likely speed up the process of making smoking less dangerous and less prevalent. Perhaps there will be indictments. It seemed like a joke when the tobacco company CEOs testified before Congress last year. Perhaps now they will be charged with perjury.

Cheating is pandemic; some is trivial and some is serious and very costly. The big, powerful cheaters are most likely to be tolerated and rationalized. We are used to corrupt authority and the unscrupulous exercise of power. Ideally the family teaches us to respect the rules and each other, but it is a difficult and imperfect process. When we divide into us and them, it may seem acceptable to cheat them.

Students are notorious cheaters. An appalling amount of cheating occurs in graduate school and professional school. Many find it acceptable to do whatever will give them an advantage while others cheat out of fear they will fail. The system seems to promote it. The same rationale can persist throughout life. I wonder if the flagrant cheaters in my medical school class have continued to cheat.

The parasitology course in my medical school had a set of slides for the various types of malaria. The slides were of very poor quality, but no one was willing to tell the professor that they were inadequate. I think everyone cheated on the exam; if anyone broke ranks it would have revealed what was happening. What an alarming arrangement.

I worked with an admirable and successful man whose career was focused on helping people in need. He told me about an episode in his boyhood. He very much wanted a special hat that he dared not ask for; he stole it. He kept it hidden; he dared not wear it; he threw it away because it seemed too likely it would be discovered. He wept while telling about it and then he told me that I had a very powerful position. I responded that he had given me great power. That is the way it works in our alliances, but it does not feel that way. It was startling to a mother when her three year old figured it out and said, "You can only make me do something if I decide to do it." So often we feel that we are in control or that we are being controlled when it is merely an arrangement we have made; it is mostly illusory.

People would often talk to me about their careers. They compete for promotions and express feeling about deserving a post or about being unfairly passed over. When someone told me he deserved a promotion because his credentials were superior to those of his rivals, I was likely to ask if he ever cheated in the pursuit of his credentials. Perhaps I have been selective about whom I asked that question; no one ever told me that they had never cheated. The fact that the person had cheated did not affect their standing out there in the world, but in my office it nullified any claim that their credentials made them best qualified. I wonder if my friends who deplored the cheating Welfare queens ever cheated in the course of earning their credentials. It is so easy to hold others to a more severe standard than the standard we impose on ourselves.

Dinner is almost ready. A cold front will come through this evening, but it is now in the 70s. Many goldfish survived the winter. The pond and yard await a cleanup; maybe I will do that tomorrow. I will be asleep soon after Deb leaves following dinner.

Deb and I righted and aligned the aqueduct that feeds the pond; it was a quick and easy two person job. Then, still before dinner, we inspected the property and I finally saw my first robin; one lone robin in the neighboring yard.

Dinner included a new addition to my cooking repertoire: chicken soup with large chunks of sautéed chicken added to the soup. We chatted about her work and about this journal. She left around 8 o'clock and I was asleep within minutes. I did not see the Academy Awards, again.

Edmund Muskie, former presidential candidate and Maine senator, has died. Senate majority leader, Bobby Joe Dole, gave a touching and emotional talk to his hometown constituency. He was choked up when he spoke and I had tears in my eyes when I read about it this morning. The polls show that there is much concern that Dole is too old to be president. That does not concern me; the many checks and balances will protect us if our president loses capacity. For his own sake I hope Dole does not stay on too long; he can still screw it up for himself and I think he might.

A defining moment in Ed Muskie's presidential campaign was when he cried on camera; it was all down hill from then on. I have always teared up about cornball things. When Big Joe Green accepted that Coke from an admiring kid and then threw him a souvenir towel, I teared up. Coke commercials and other tawdry efforts to pull at my heartstrings work. It is funny, at least it amuses me. It did not amuse me when I began to feel and show upset, especially at work, where my reaction might be counterproductive and not in keeping with my helper role. There is a big difference between a few tears in an innocuous situation and feeling shook up when serious circumstances require one's best effort. This increased emotionality was a big factor in my decision to retire from medical practice. Sometimes it is best to hold to a very high standard.

Perhaps Ed Muskie's emotional outburst during his campaign was an early symptom of deterioration; the public certainly reacted negatively. It was perceived as suspect and worrisome. Bob Dole's emotionality yesterday was not suspect; it was evidence of an admirable sentimentality and appreciation of his roots. I hope it does not help him too much.

Almost two hours of work in the side yard has cleaned things up considerably. Despite frost warnings for tonight, this is a glorious Maryland spring day; shirt sleeve weather. There is only a bit of growth showing. The forsythia is in full flower and the crab apple tree is showing small leaves. A few bulbs are up and that is it. A school of over fifty goldfish darted about as I dredged the pond with a rake and removed many dead leaves. The leaves of the willow oak look remarkably like baby goldfish. I kept thinking that I had removed goldfish but I quickly realized that I could use the wriggle test. If it wriggled it was a fish that I would return to the pond; if it did not wriggle it did not make any difference what it was. I found only one wriggler.

The Tuesday evening bridge game has been canceled because of a power failure at the Andrews Officers' Club. There is a game at the Washington Bridge Club, but it would keep me up too late. I'll read, write and watch TV this evening.

My very close friend, Elliott Schiffmann, and I spoke on the telephone this afternoon. Elliott retired from the National Institutes of

Health last year. He did important cancer research. I asked him if, in the course of obtaining his credentials, he ever cheated. He said, "No, I don't believe I ever cheated before or after getting my credentials." I told him he has always been eccentric. He is a wonderful guy.

The California presidential primary took place today. Bob Dole noticed and asked all Republicans, especially Pat Buchanan, to unite behind him to defeat Bill Clinton. He declared himself the Republican nominee.

It is below freezing this Wednesday morning; sleet is predicted for this evening. My day is unscheduled and I am very aware that I am not on call; I'm retired.

The big news yesterday was not the California primary. Mad cow disease, bovine spongioform encephalitis, was the top story and Muskie's death was a close second. An uncommon, fatal human disease is clearly related to the cow disease. The cow disease, BSE, occurs almost entirely in England, and for several years British beef has not been permitted into the United States. Several federal agencies have been involved in monitoring American cattle to protect both the public and the cattle industry. There have been no complaints from the Republicans about how the federal government has performed nor have they suggested that the work should devolve to the states. Imagine each of our fifty states bearing the responsibility for studying and regulating this threatening problem. The Republicans dare not criticize or devalue federal functions when a crisis points up the importance and effectiveness of federal programs. They dare not criticize the federal bureaucrat when the public is confronted with the dedication, industriousness and vigilance of our federal workers.

We are stuck with the reality that anything said by the politicos will have political consequences and that they are very aware of it. Of course they are trying to manipulate us. We hope they will tell us the truth, but we know that they sometimes lie to us and try to deceive us.

Edmund Muskie's obituaries support my recollection that his crying in his presidential campaign was crucial in his rejection. I did not realize that his upset was in response to a couple of Republican "dirty tricks." I wonder if it was Pat Buchanan who devised those particular dirty tricks.

I can just hear Buchanan laughing gleefully about the effectiveness of those tricks.

No one seems to have the high ground. Perhaps now that Dole is the Republican candidate, both parties can find the authenticity we claim we want. Maybe they know us better than we know ourselves. We think we want probity; perhaps we prefer deception and courting.

An unscheduled day can just slip by. I made two loaves of banana bread. While they were baking I called Teresa and Steven. They enjoyed their vacation. Steve and I have talked about going into the District together on a Wednesday, but we have not yet done it. I spent another two hours raking and clipping in the yard, undeterred by the muscle cramps I experienced after yesterday's work. A call from a patient who wanted to check up on me and hear my voice awakened me from an afternoon snooze. The mail included a newsletter from the University of Cincinnati Department of Psychiatry and a letter from the Cincinnati College of Medicine. The class of 51 will celebrate its forty-fifth reunion. Sixteen classmates have died; sixty-eight survive. We are a hardy bunch.

Ria and I attended the twenty-fifth reunion. We enjoyed it and we were impressed with how much the place had changed. The people seemed relatively unchanged and only a few had died. Most of us were in our prime twenty years ago.

When I initially went to Cincinnati, it was my first experience of living outside of my small parish in the big city of Newark, New Jersey. I had no idea of how parochial I was. I expected people to be wearing cowboy hats and found it amusing that Cincinnatians thought of themselves as easterners. They laughed at my "New York accent." When I went home my Jersey friends laughed at my strange Ohio accent. Now, after fifty years and traveling around the world, I suspect I am only a bit less parochial than I was then. Now, luckily, I can laugh at myself.

The snow line passed just north of here. It is cold and there has been drenching rain all day. I decided to drive, not walk, to the bridge game. It was so cold at the club that most of us wore our coats while we played.

There is political turmoil in England in reaction to the government's handling of mad cow disease. The risk to the public is not great, but the anxiety about a fatal human disease is very great. I wonder if the uproar is fueled by an underlying fear of AIDS. The world is in the midst of an epidemic that will kill millions of us. We are lucky that the human immunodeficiency virus is not very easily transmitted. Let's hope that luck holds up.

Our history is filled with periodic plagues and epidemics that have killed and terrified us. Plagues are probably an important part of the evolutionary process. Perhaps the dinosaurs succumbed to an easily transmitted dinosaur immunodeficiency virus.

When the entire species is at risk it is easy to overlook individual tragedies. The Holocaust Museum in Washington presents an overview of that terrible devastation while always staying focused on individual and family disruption and loss.

In the spring of 1986, two years after my neuromuscular disorder accelerated and six months after I underwent cancer surgery, I began serving as a volunteer psychiatrist available to see patients referred from the AIDS program of the Whitman Walker Clinic. People came to my office and were treated as private patients. I had about thirty referrals; mostly people with AIDS. I met and worked with some generous and talented people on the clinic staff. Most of the patients, staff and volunteers identified themselves as homosexual, but they were a very diverse group and I learned a lot from them. They felt much fear and anger. They attempted to find order, strength and meaning as they approached weakness and death. I was very lucky to have such important work during the last part of my medical practice.

Patients often complain that their doctor does not understand or have a feel for what the patient is experiencing; I know they are correct. I clearly remember when, as a young physician, I first experienced constipation and I thought, "So that's what they've been complaining about." Well, I know about fear; I smelled of fear for a couple of months around the time of my melanoma surgery and I remembered it distinctly while I worked with my patients. When that fear ended I felt that all the rest of my life was gravy.

Soon each of us will have a friend, relative or neighbor who is dead or dying of AIDS, but the big turmoil today is about the potential economic and health risk connected with mad cow disease. It is more than a bit weird.

The pond is overflowing. Puddles keep me from approaching to throw bread crumbs to the fish. They have not been fed since October; feeding them is much more for my amusement than for their sustenance. It was much too wet to walk to the food game, but after driving there I fed myself abundantly; much more for my amusement than for my sustenance.

Adam left a message that he and his family would be arriving in the Washington area early this evening. He will call me when they get close. I will offer to feed them. They will leave from Dulles Airport tomorrow morning for their ski vacation. He called again at 6 o'clock to say they were going directly to Saria's folks without stopping here. I accepted that with only a smidgen of disappointment in my voice. Deb came over and we had a full meal and a chat. Adam called from Saria's folks' house; we will get together Easter Sunday; Deb will take them to the airport tomorrow. Before going to sleep I called Steve and invited his family and Teresa's parents to join us for Easter buffet at the Andrews Club.

Several times each year the Washington Bridge League sponsors a tournament at the Silver Spring Armory. The big events are two session events that last from 2 in the afternoon until around 11, with a dinner break. I have been avoiding those events because I pay too heavily with pain and fatigue. My Obusforme portable back support helps a lot, but not enough. Today I will play in a one session seniors event with Wes. All players will be over fifty-five; most of us much over fifty-five. We will start playing at 10:30 and I will be home by 2:30, in time to watch the basketball semifinals.

Wes and I have had good luck in the seniors event; two first place overall wins in fifteen months. It is a skill game, but there is still a big luck factor. As in so many competitions, it is a game of errors and you are not likely to win unless your opponents make those errors. There are many excellent bridge players in the Washington area; I am not counted among them. That makes winning better and, at the same time, not so terrific. This game is very important and of absolutely no consequence. Perhaps the only part that matters is the partnership. Well, maybe it is also worthwhile to have a civilized way to blow off some of that primitive us against them stuff.

I awakened at 2:30; itched and scratched and ached and moaned until 4. The sky lightened at 5:30 and now at 6:30 it is a bright cloudless morning. It's spring. April is suicide month. The hibernation and cleansing period is over and now it is face up to it or give up on it time. It is time for birth and rebirth and for celebrating freedom and the prospect of the promised land. Let's go for it; I'm ready to rumble.

Our game at the tournament was not good enough to win; we were second. We beat forty-two other pairs, but no glory. Wes brought sandwiches, fruit, cookies and candy. That was very thoughtful of him. I enjoyed the unexpected lunch.

This evening Steven called to confirm that they and Teresa's parents will be joining us for Easter buffet. I made reservations for sixteen. I look forward to being with many of my most important connections.

At the game this morning, forty-four partnerships attempted to win an event. Each pair paid fourteen dollars to play and the two winners win about ten dollars each; the game is not about money. The winners win points and points are collected and recorded and are a measure of one's success at playing the game. One session of bridge requires thousands of decisions. It is intense mental activity. All those old folks, many of them more decrepit than I, sitting around, exercising their minds and often enjoying themselves. It is a wonderful opportunity for creative thinking, problem solving and partnership cooperation. It is a way to keep mentally fit and if you make a mistake no one cares, except perhaps you and your partner; it is of no consequence; it is just a game, unless you make more of it.

When I returned to playing bridge thirty years ago I had a moralistic view that there are workers and there are players, and workers are better than players. It took a few years for me to get past that inaccurate, uncharitable and self-serving view; it is wrongheaded. I was claiming that my activities were better than their activities. I worked it out. Some talented, creative players have done a lot to improve the quality of my life. Players often work harder than workers and too often work leads to deplorable results.

The players and the play this evening were excellent. Both basketball semifinal games were exciting entertainment. They kept me up well past my usual bedtime.

Sunday, the last of March; it is past 7 A.M. and still no newspaper. Every day I turn the pages of *The Washington Post* and read selectively. I like the Sunday book section best, next to the comics. I'm told *The New York Times* has no comics other than its editorials. The comic strip writers are the people who address the human condition. They are the philosophers who raise all the important issues while the rest of the newspaper reports and evaluates recent events. Most of the strange alliances we form and many of our frailties are portrayed in the funnies. Recurring themes include alcoholism, laziness, cowardice, corruption, insensitivity, arrogance, grandiosity and on and on. Zippy is one of my favorite comic characters and the strip also serves as an excellent eye chart. It was Zippy that took me to the optometrist and later to the ophthalmologist. Thank you, Bill Griffith.

Partnership activities are the best. My favorite individual activity is reading for pleasure. I was thirty-three when I began reading for the fun of it; not work related studying. No one told me that reading for the fun of it would be much better for me and for my work performance than studying. I avoid mysteries and science fiction; an old addict does well to avoid new addictions.

The FBI and the Justice Department have cordoned off a ranch in Montana that is occupied by a group that has declared itself free of local and federal laws. They call themselves freemen. The group is well known in its community; they are not intruders or strangers in that small society, they are part of it. It is reported that they are heavily armed and dug in. They have threatened judges and other officials and they are accused of illegal financial dealings involving millions of dollars. They are in default on their loans and refuse to leave the ranch they occupy so that it can be occupied by its legal owners.

It is a very risky situation. People may be killed and the reputation of the FBI and the Justice Department are at stake. The Bureau of Alcohol, Tobacco and Firearms has been deliberately excluded, but there is no way for the political candidates to exclude themselves from this brouhaha. It is important to establish that we, whoever we are, are the good guys and that they, the freemen, are not the good guys. There is plenty of disagreement about it; it is not clear-cut.

This highly covered drama cuts to the quick concerning our values and allegiances as Americans. Don't tread on me! I'm a rough and tough frontiersman who will not put up with unfair rules that disadvantage and restrict me. Give me liberty or give me death. My God tells me how to behave and God's word is sacrosanct. Bug off; leave me alone until I want you.

When this small dispute in Montana is over it might be the subject of a comic strip, but there already is a strip that covers this material. Barney Google first appeared in 1919 and his pal Snuffy Smith still runs daily in many newspapers. Billy DeBeck died in 1942, but his creation goes on. Snuffy Smith is a well known member of his sparsely inhabited rural community. He goes fishing and plays checkers with the sheriff, but he is known to be a chicken thief and card cheater and he has an illegal still. He is fiercely protective of his property and he is a lazy, lying, ignorant, unfair little squirt who somehow has persisted all these years. I think we hold on to him because he is so unfettered. We envy and admire that free spirit. We tend to feel caged in, and when we discover that the cage is of our own making, we feel scared. Even when he spends the night in jail Snuffy Smith is a free man.

Dinner was excessive. Deb says that her job on Monday evening is to eat too much; she did her job. While making dinner I started a vegetable stock and after Deborah left I strained it and added three pounds of split peas, sautéed bacon and lots of seasoning. I put it on simmer and planned to stir it every half hour until the peas were tender. The basketball game would start soon, but I fell asleep before it started and woke up in time to see the last ten minutes. Luckily the soup did not scorch. I finished it, left it on the stove to cool and went back to bed to watch the late news.

Of course I missed the news last night and although up briefly several times, I slept well and got up later than usual. Almost always I am up before dawn. There is one or more takeoff from Andrews Air Force Base just before dawn and I am usually up and anticipating that announcement of impending sunrise; not today.

Five quarts of very thick pea soup are in the freezer.

This afternoon I peeled and thin sliced about a pound of fresh ginger, put it in vinegar, added liquefied hot peppers and cooked it briefly in the microwave. I am hoping it will turn out similar to the pink Japanese pickled ginger.

Next I made my first chocolate pecan pies, primarily to use the pecans that I bought in December. I toasted the nuts in the oven and let them cool. Next I prepared the batter for my favorite brownies, but I left out one third of the flour and I added about an ounce of corn syrup. I mixed the nuts into the batter and poured it into two chocolate cookie crumb crusts. The brownie recipe calls for baking thirty-five minutes at 375 degrees. I baked these pies for twenty-two minutes; undercooked is much better than overcooked. I hope they are baked enough. I filled the ready-made crusts to the very brim to avoid having them burn. These pies will probably be superb; I' m a creative cook.

Since my retirement I have had occasional telephone contact with several of my patients; I had invited them to check up on me periodically. People call to ask and to tell. I have turned down several lunch invitations; I don' t do lunch, but I welcome telephone calls. I' m missed and I miss.

Parting was particularly difficult with one person I had worked with for many years. She made it clear that it was unacceptable to her that she be the one to initiate all of our contacts. She asked me to reconsider my position; she knew I would. She found an excuse for making the first call and we have alternated calls every four or five weeks. For several years she told me about her computers. She tried to give me one of hers and she encouraged me to give up my low tech lifestyle. Now she knows that I am writing this journal and that I am ready for a word processor. She wants to research it and advise me. It is likely that I will follow her advice. Early in our work together she saw me as a potential conquest. Our partnership became constructive and benefited both of us greatly.

Kitch and I played in the Tuesday evening game at Andrews. I yawned a lot and played very poorly; too tired to think straight. Kitch's husband, Dick, died at a bridge game a couple of years ago. I attempted, without success, to resuscitate him and I have revisited that failure repeatedly. On the one hand I rationalize that it was amazing that I could get down on the floor and bend over him; on the other hand I failed him miserably. It shook me and reinforced my decision to retire.

Archie Moore was chopping away at his French–Canadian opponent who was standing helplessly, paralyzed, in the middle of the ring. I thought the referee should stop the fight or the corner men should throw in the towel. The poor guy was taking terrible head and body blows. This was not an anxiety dream, yet I awakened while dreaming. This dream tells me about an aspect of myself that I do not feel. I am not ready to throw in the towel. It won't be tragic when my fight is over, but I am prepared to continue and to enjoy my big event; I can go at least a few more rounds.

Today is overscheduled; most unusual for a Wednesday. Wes asked me to play bridge this morning. Between going to the game and going to the first seder at the home of Iris and Murray Kivitz this evening, I will drive over one hundred miles today.

It was near freezing this morning, but it is quite warm this afternoon and the drive around the Beltway shows signs of spring; many buds and blossoms. This is cherry blossom week. The tidal basin will be in full bloom before the week ends.

My game with Wes was fun. If I had played as well as he did we would have won.

There were several calls, none satisfactorily completed, concerning my computer needs. Steven may have something available for me and Deb tells me I do not need a printer. I wonder if I will stop writing longhand when I have a computer.

The Passover holiday celebrates freedom from slavery. God pressured Pharaoh by imposing ten plagues on the Egyptians. Each spring we remember and celebrate our quick getaway and we identify with all oppressed people. Since Ria and I separated, the Kivitzes have made me a part of their traditional celebrations. The ceremony centers around the evening meal. There were sixteen at the table, family and friends. It is a lot of work for Iris; she smiles through it. I greatly appreciate the way they have taken me in. I enjoy the closeness, rituals and good food; Iris is a wonderful cook. We end up with jokes and reminiscing.

Four generations were represented at last night's celebration of freedom and rebirth. It is the connections between the generations and all of my important connections that I celebrate. That is what gives my life meaning. God is not required, but I sometimes like the ritual. Life is a partnership game.

Steven and Teresa are married eight years today. My playboy son is now well settled down and he has established many connections that I can enjoy; how lucky.

Once upon a time if I slept in the afternoon I was ill or about to become ill. Today, after walking to and from the Andrews bridge game, I got into bed and slept for more than two hours. I am not ill but I get very tired.

The television news tonight is filled with religious expression. Panegyrics for Ron Brown, Secretary of Commerce, who died in a plane crash today with thirty-four others, make frequent references to prayer and to God. A long segment with four panelists considered the forty major versions of the Bible and why new versions are still being written; some to separate and divide us, some to unite us. An hour long program explained Passover and its rituals.

Most voters in the United States claim that they believe in God. Many believe that they are obligated to advertise and promote their version of religious truth. What we believe, including our religious, moral and ethical views, will tell us what lever to pull in November. President Clinton said all the politically correct and pious words that were expected today. He sounded sincere, but he did not look pained. I thought he might be smirking. Perhaps he is on to something; Dole's serious mien may be passé.

Good Friday is sunny, windy, cold and just right for my walk to and from the game. It is snowing in Texas and snow is expected in D.C. on Easter Sunday. At bridge the food included matzos and homemade candy Easter eggs. I was asked about the meaning of Passover and the correct pronunciation of seder. We are one nation, under God. A reenactment of the crucifixion took place on public ground today and the same group plans to reenact the resurrection on Sunday.

Repeatedly I was called Father while I listened. Occasionally, with mock seriousness, I would grant forgiveness and we would laugh together because I lacked authority to forgive sins and I did not think of their acts as sins. My views were not entirely concealed and I might reveal my feelings that an act was wrong, bad, criminal, awful or unwise and undesirable—but no authority to forgive sins.

Tell me a secret and I will keep it. I might reject receipt of a secret, but if I accept it, don't depend on me to broadcast your stuff. I have a couple of friends who are broadcasters. There is no need to advertise; just tell them and they will spread it around. These yentas tell tales even when it might lead to unwanted and disruptive confrontations.

Often secrets are feigned; devices that help us to go on together rather than be torn apart. When we are ready to go forward apart or to repair the arrangements and stay together, then we can dispense with our secrets.

Only once was I accused of telling someone's secret. Somehow, without intending to and without realizing it, my manner revealed that I already knew a secret that I was not supposed to know. It was very disruptive and it took a long time to repair the partnership.

The secrets I keep from myself are the secrets I worry about. What are they?

This afternoon President Clinton sermonized. Perhaps all of this writing is sermonizing.

At least three of us were seated at a round table with a heavy white tablecloth. It seemed like a high quality restaurant. Two men sat to my left. We were eating a dish, probably an appetizer, that contained pineapple. I took credit for its formula and tried to sell it to the others as a superior product that they should choose for the success of their own enterprises. I felt confident about the dish, but I was clearly acting as a high-pressure salesman. The table was cleared and a tureen appeared. The man on my left, wearing a special glove, began to ladle the tureen's contents into a soup bowl. The tureen contained a very viscous consommé. He acted with confidence and skill. I was glad he had proceeded because I did not know how to properly do what he was doing.

This dream tells some of the secrets that I keep from myself. What happened in the dream and how did I feel? In the beginning I am confidently and aggressively pushing my stuff, but I soon find myself lacking the knowledge and skill to go on and I am relieved that another has taken over.

Distinguished medical ethicists discuss the tension that exists between professionalism and entrepreneurship. Physicians have been under intense pressure to be more businesslike and yet the public wants professionalism, not entrepreneurship. The consummate professional (consommé professional?) always puts the client first and the professional undertaking second. Even when the professional acts as a salesperson, the focus remains on serving the client well. So, perhaps the dream is partly about my decision to retire, my relief that competent people are there to take over and my uneasiness about being self-serving. These writings must be significantly self-serving.

Last night I was awakened by a call from Adam. The vacation went well and they are safely back and looking forward to the Easter Sunday buffet. I asked about their plans for today, Saturday, and they will be going to see the cherry blossoms and then visiting with friends. There was no hint of an invitation. I remind myself about how little enthusiasm I felt about spending time with my parents.

My neighbor called to tell me that blackbirds are nesting in my attic. Deborah and I will investigate that soon. There are many blackbirds in the yard this morning and very few robins. I wonder if they are in competition.

My life is changed; there is a computer in my house and it feels like an elephant. M delivered the goods this morning and gave me a brief lesson and a large book on Word Perfect, the computer program I'll be using. (A slip of the pen reveals my uneasiness about it; I wrote ill, not

I'll.) The bill was quite small; I think she gave me one of her printers. I thanked her, paid her and gave her four soups, red cabbage and bread. We maintain our connection.

Deb asked if I would feed her if she came over this evening. I was pleased to have her look at the computer and give me further instructions after we ate our dinner. Soon after she left I was in trouble; nothing worked. I was sure I had lost all the tedious two finger typing I had done.

Easter Sunday, April 7, 1996; daylight savings time, cold and windy, but none of the predicted snow or sleet. A long sit down at the computer, before the newspaper arrived, proved very frustrating and I was ready to trash the whole thing, but I noticed that my two finger typing was much faster and I felt pretty sure I would eventually learn how to avoid losing everything I had entered. Deb arrived before noon and was able to retrieve what I thought I had lost. She provided me with further instructions and ran a spell check on the little I had done. Many errors were corrected.

The crowd arrived on schedule and only Saria's brother Floyd was missing. We drove to Andrews in three cars and with little hassle we were ready to enjoy a very good buffet dinner. It was a very pleasant afternoon for me and I think all the cooks and dishwashers in our group were glad to have done it the easy way. Saria brought me a special flexible spatula and several of us were given large weird hats that Adam and Saria brought back from their ski trip. I gave Easter baskets to my grandchildren. Everyone was gone by 5 o'clock and I went right to the computer.

Entering what I have written into the computer keeps me from writing. Soon, I hope, I will be able to write directly with it. The elephant is shrinking.

The computer kept me occupied for many hours yesterday; the first day since early March that I failed to make a journal entry. I have become a typist. Some important things happened that will have impact on the political process and the world goes on while I am held hostage by a beast-like electronic device. I have survived only because Computer Woman Deborah has rescued me repeatedly.

Senator Robert C. Byrd speechified mightily against but refused to block the line item veto bill that President Clinton signed yesterday. The president, by agreement, will not use this new power until January. Isn't that cozy.

It is only two hundred years ago that there were serious discussions about how many angels could dance on the head of a pin. Yesterday, in the Easter spirit, Supreme Court Justice Scalia affirmed his belief in miracles and offered encouragement to others to reaffirm their own belief in miracles. Perhaps belief in miracles will become a litmus test for appointment as a federal judge.

I called my brother, Fred, and wished him a happy birthday; he is sixty-four tomorrow. I told him about my computer. Fred teaches computer studies in junior high school. He laughed when I told him the computer does not do what it is supposed to do after I have carefully followed instructions. He hears that a lot.

A fierce snow storm brushed the East coast today. It dumped eight inches of snow on Atlantic City, but it only dusted Maryland and Fred said there was little accumulation in northern New Jersey. I hope it is winter's last gasp.

An hour at the computer is similar to driving for an hour. I have been overdoing it and I felt it today when I walked to and from the Andrews game; my body hurts. Bill and I had a big game; he is a skilled player and a good partner.

President Clinton vetoed the so-called partial birth abortion ban bill today; very political stuff. He proposed a new retirement savings plan for middle class workers. Every move by every major player has powerful political overtones. Every little movement has a meaning of its own.

The Kennedy–Kassebaum medical insurance bill seems to be on a back burner. The bill would require insurability and insurance portability. I think it is likely that the outcome of the election will be determined by issues around medical care and abortion.

Snow yesterday, in the 80s tomorrow; it must be spring.

My dream this morning was nasty. I was picking my nose (brains) and extracted vermin (unpleasant dirty stuff) that flew away before I could examine it. The dream suggests to me that I have been writing about the easy part and avoiding an unpleasant, dark aspect of myself that remains unexamined. Perhaps the computer has given me a respite from the difficult part. I have been generous with myself. I have not lied, but I have presented an incomplete view of my motives and behavior.

The yeast was working in the bread sponge all night. This morning I will shape one loaf and bake it in time for the Friday morning bridge game; later I will complete the rest of the batter and will fill the small freezer with fresh bread; Passover has ended.

What dirt am I aware of that I have withheld? I have avoided sleaze; that still seems best and need not keep me from an honest presentation. What comes to mind is that exchange with Ria in August 1982. In that interaction Ria was strong; she firmly stated her position. I have wondered what would have happened if she had played weak or less strong. We probably would have stayed together in the same unsatisfactory manner. If she had cried I would have tried to comfort her and, again, we would not have parted. I would probably have taken her to bed; that is what I had in mind when I kissed her. Maybe the dirt I have avoided is the extent to which I have made decisions based on my sexuality, but that does not feel like dirt and I have already alluded to it. The dream raises questions, but does not provide answers.

It was hot as summer as I walked home from the bridge game. The large tulip magnolia tree behind my pond is not yet in full bloom, but many similar trees are in full flower and the star magnolias are already past their prime. It is a grand reawakening. I noticed several dead animals: birds, a rabbit, a squirrel and a rat; not all survive into the new cycle. I counted sixty goldfish in the pond and noticed small leaves forming in the water lily pots.

M called and expressed disappointment that I had not called her about the computer. I explained that I have been relying on Deb and then I gave her a detailed account of what I have done so far. She clarified that she has loaned, not given me, the printer. I was pleased and relieved about that. She did give me some software; I think I know what that means; it is a whole new language. She would like me to contact her more often; it does not feel appropriate.

Dinner this evening was a large bowl of bean and ham soup cooked by Alice Behre. Last week and again this morning, Alice has brought soup to the bridge game for me. I guess it is in response to the food I brought to her and Herb a few weeks ago. The soup and a thick slice of bread were satisfying and delicious.

The bread did not get baked until after midnight. I was groggy with fatigue and went to bed.

First thing this morning I filled the small freezer with bread and I went right to the computer for a two hour stint. When I went out for the newspaper I saw a glorious day. Things are changing so quickly; if you turn away for more than a moment the scene has been transformed. Yesterday's cherry blossoms on the tree next door are now petals on my lawn. The tulip magnolia blossomed before my eyes. The ornamental crab apple tree changed throughout the day. The scene around the Beltway seemed the same going and coming, but I was keeping my eyes on the road.

The day went so well; almost perfect except that I overbaked the banana bread. I'll call Pat before going to sleep.

Pat is creating a bit of southern India in central Florida. She excitedly told me that she had found a special tree at a garden show in Tampa. I correctly guessed that it was a custard apple tree. She has spoken several times about the custard apple. She also bought a jackfruit tree.

I spoke to Mrs. Bush, Pat's mother. She is recovering from cataract surgery, can't read, is bored and is looking forward to being in Maryland in May on her way to Canada where she will spend several months with her daughter Joy. I will surely see her then. She is eighty-eight and she suspects that every meeting may be the final meeting. I like her a lot. She and Deborah are each other's fan.

There is nothing, surprisingly, of great political interest in the Sunday newspaper or the morning TV shows. The commentators are digging deep to earn their pay. Every little movement is examined and there is speculation about its meaning. This week the President has gained one ethnic group and alienated another; maybe.

Tomorrow is dreaded April 15. I put a check in the mail to the state of Maryland yesterday. My accountant made an error and a small refund became a medium small tax due. A call from a friend in trouble was easy to handle. He needed help to tide him over and I wrote a check. I wish every request from a friend was so easy to meet.

Many great athletes are competing today. Augusta is in full bloom for the Masters' Tournament. Maryland is about ten days behind Georgia so the azaleas, dogwoods and rhododendron will soon be in bloom here. Augusta looks like an artist's palate; that is the way my side yard will look soon.

Golf teaches discipline and humility.

There has been a lot of psychobabble in connection with the capture of the "Unibomber" at a remote Montana cabin. His brother realized that he is the perpetrator, and his brother and mother told the FBI. There is much interest and speculation about how a mathematics genius turns into a moralistic killer who does not bathe. We want the killing to stop and we want to punish and to deter, but we also look for reassurance that we ourselves will not become dangerous and destructive.

Our system considers mitigation. If a destructive act is committed during a febrile delirium it is probably not a crime at all. If behavior is deemed to be secondary to a brain tumor, we offer sympathy and treatment, not trial and punishment. When destructive behavior is deemed to be a manifestation of psychological illness, there is often much confusion and ambivalence about how to deal with it. Juries often ignore uncontradicted expert testimony, find guilt and ask the court to impose punishment. We tend to be much more forgiving when there is an organic condition. A condition, even a psychological condition, is much more likely to be found mitigating than is an explanation. Similar thinking extends to the provision of health care. There is less sympathy and less willingness to provide care when a condition is labeled psychological. That, in part, is why there is now so much emphasis on the organic underpinnings of psychiatric conditions. It is always nature and nurture; no mind without body.

The tendency to give greater respect for the organic is shared by physicians, including psychiatrists. If it is just in your mind, you may get short shrift. When the perception is that the patient has participated in bringing on the condition, it is too easy to decide that the condition is deserved. It is very close to the old notion that all illness is justified punishment and shameful; it is your fault or your parents' fault or your grandparents' fault. Addictions, venereal diseases and mental conditions are still often put in this category of being deserved and undeserving.

One of the first patients I saw when I arrived in Washington in 1957 was a sixteen year old young woman who was brought to the hospital by her mother. She showed very peculiar face and mouth movements including repeatedly and slowly protruding her tongue. It looked bizarre, mysterious and perhaps hysterical. A careful history revealed that the mother had given her daughter some of mother's prescription. The symptoms were a complication of the medication. It was new information in 1957 that the phenothiazines, antipsychotic medications, sometimes led to these strange dystonic reactions. It was easy and effective to explain what had happened and to try to insure that the young woman would not again ingest her mother's medications. It was so nice and neat.

A few weeks later I saw a woman who had the misfortune of having a dystonic reaction before it was well known that this could occur as a complication of phenothiazines. She was a patient at a prestigious hospital where she had responded very well to treatment. Her doctors had increased her medication and discharge plans were begun, when she began to experience unusual movements of her head, neck and mouth. Her doctors thought she was resisting discharge. Whether it was a hysterical reaction or malingering, when she did not give up her symptoms the staff became angry and punitive. They finally kicked her out of the hospital. Fortunately they gave her insufficient medication; she reduced her dosage and her movement disorder stopped. It was a year later that the episode was understandable. She had experienced an organic syndrome called a dystonic reaction, but her medical helpers thought that her symptoms were psychological and manipulative. They reacted with anger, devalued her and punished and rejected her. Well, we are all only human; nobody is perfect.

Deb was in a hurry last night; she is busy with work and taxes. After we enjoyed dinner, she checked the attic—no birds or squirrels—and then she tried to find what I had lost in the computer. She was not able to find my efforts; they are lost forever and we have little notion of how it happened. The computer ate my homework.

The gods were bowling all night and the cacophony awakened me repeatedly; I'm groggy this morning. There were heavy rains and nearby tornadoes. It is much greener today. Most of the tulip magnolia blossoms survived the rain. The big black cherry tree has started to leaf. Quick changes continue.

Congress passed a watered down version of an anti-terrorist bill. It was a compromise that tries to protect the public without eroding individual rights. Our history is replete with examples of excessive curtailment of individual rights in the name of public safety. The internment of Japanese–Americans during World War II is an egregious example of such excess. A similar tension often occurs concerning medical matters. There can be a fine balance without an unambiguous right and wrong. Vaccination and quarantine are imposed on individuals to protect the community. Effective but unwanted treatments are sometimes imposed over an individual's protests. Drugs that people want are declared illegal or are carefully controlled. Dangerous behavior such as cigarette smoking or driving without using safety devices is considered in the context of this tension between individual rights and what is best for the group. In surprising ways, conservatives and liberals tend to take opposite sides on these issues. Even stranger are some of the coalitions that form.

This afternoon I read a slender, pithy science fiction novel that Steven gave to me on Easter Sunday. *The Dechronization of Sam Magruder* was written by George Gaylord Simpson, a great paleontologist, and was published after his death through his daughter's efforts. The novel is introduced by Arthur C. Clarke, a famous science fiction writer, and an afterword is by Steven Jay Gould who greatly admired Simpson, his colleague and teacher. My son was very impressed with this book and so was I. The author tells so much about himself and his scientific ideas and he does it so concisely and without being pedagogical. He was a talented, enviable man, but, with all his attachments, he was, in his heart, man alone. I suspect that man alone is my primary theme; man alone and what he does about it.

I walked to the evening game in full daylight and solicited a ride home. It was a very pleasant day.

It is blustery and cold again. A quick walk around the house revealed many blossoms on the two Granny Smith apple trees. Eight out of twenty rhododendron cuttings look alive. The deep red crab apple blossoms are about to open. A hundred dandelions have flowered and dot the lawn. All of my neighbors have mowed; I will soon. The main feature is the tulip magnolia tree in full flower.

The bean and ham soup that Alice gave me last week has inspired me to try something similar. I will start it today and finish it tomorrow.

I spent the morning at the hospital having my pre-admission work done for cataract surgery next Tuesday. I walked both ways. It was too warm for a jacket.

The bean soup has turned into a delicious cassoulet. Cooking is so forgiving; mistakes turn into excellent new recipes.

Politics abounds. So much of it is manifested in violence. Tomorrow is the anniversary of the Oklahoma City bombing. Today Israeli shells killed seventy-five Lebanese refugees in a United Nations camp in Lebanon. Representatives of Lebanon and Israel have very different views about the sequence of events and about underlying motives. Denials of political motives ring hollow. Maybe forthright politician is an oxymoron.

Senator Dole proposed an amendment to the Kennedy–Kassebaum medical insurance bill. It was defeated and there is hope that the Senate will pass the bill soon. It is a moderate compromise that addresses limited but important issues about the availability of medical care. Another compromise bill, an anti-terrorist bill, will probably reach the President soon and he is expected to sign it. This spate of cooperative compromise does not feel very satisfying, but it is overdue and welcome.

The whole country is observing the first anniversary of the Oklahoma City bombing that killed one hundred and sixty-eight people. Shells continue to fall on Lebanon and Israel. President Clinton's plea that all sides observe a cease fire has not yet affected the killing exchange.

A lot of musculoskeletal discomfort did not keep me from enjoying my walk. I walked carefully and was especially attentive while crossing the dangerous, disrupted intersection. There were several fresh carcasses strewn amongst the new growth. I am occupied with life and death.

It is almost full green; the view from the kitchen window is now partly obscured. The progression of new and fading blossoms continues. The magnolia no longer looks grand, but the crab apple does and many other species are close behind.

A very relaxed morning and early afternoon were spoiled by the mail. A check I wrote to help a friend with his taxes was returned for insufficient funds; the first time I have ever bounced a check. I quickly transferred money into that account and called my friend who was not aware of what had happened. I am embarrassed and upset about my miscalculation. I hope it does not cause a lot of trouble.

At the Oklahoma City memorial service Vice President Gore said that we will not be defeated by terrorism and violence because we are a nation that settles things through dialogue. What a nice idea.

I was pleased to read that Dole has attacked the liberal, Democratic federal judiciary. It is that kind of deceitful pandering that will erode his portrait of probity.

Three tedious hours at the computer produced little except problems. I brush a key and terrible things happen; things disappear. Some text is out of order. It takes me forever to get it going right again even after telephone help from Deb and M. I have asked Deb to come over for dinner and help me get it back on track.

Thirty minutes mowing and thirty minutes raking were more than I needed, but it gave me a chance to look the place over and I do like that. The surviving double blossom Japanese cherry tree in the front yard will be in full bloom in one or two days. The dogwoods are getting close. The pond surface is covered with petals from the magnolia tree and the petals fall as quickly as I rake them. I will complete that job tomorrow. The fragrance of magnolia and lilac was strong and pleasant. I had to go to the street side to find the lilac to break off a sprig for the dinner table. The red bud tree is close as are many of the azaleas. The miniature leaf Japanese maple tree that I grew from a seed ten years ago has died.

Sunday morning is politics time. Almost every important event is given political spin. Three new books were reviewed or excerpted concerning our political system, past and present. Ross Perot showed up for a full hour on "Meet the Press." Very little is new; nothing much gets clarified. The noncandidates may be trying to tell the truth and clarify the issues. I wonder if the truth gets anyone to change his mind. I feel stuck in my political stance. It would take something extraordinary to get me to vote Republican.

A robin struggled mightily, but unsuccessfully, in the back yard to gather nesting material. I went out with the hedge clipper to ease her efforts. The neighbor's bird feeder is now entirely obscured by new leaves. A very yellow bird appeared that I had never seen in the wild. It looked like a canary or parakeet.

We have had several deluges this April, but few spring showers. Today there is a fine drizzle; the smell is very welcome. I bought lettuce, strawberries, corn and asparagus, all grown elsewhere, but making my mouth water about what will soon happen here.

What is so rare as a day in June in April? It neared ninety this afternoon and I drove home from the Bridge Center with the air conditioner on. I raked the magnolia petals while in a flurry of crab apple petals that are too fragile to require raking. One small purple azalea has bloomed. The place will be a riot of color by the end of the week.

Late in the afternoon I received a call from the hospital; they neglected to do an important measurement to determine what lens will be implanted after my defective lens is removed tomorrow. I was there in ten minutes and back home in time for dinner with Deb. I will walk to the hospital and be there by 6:30 tomorrow morning. Deb will bring me home in the afternoon. I will be seeing the world with both eyes again, but not for a few days.

Tuesday, April 23. The clock radio alarm was set for the first time in over a decade; insurance against oversleeping. I awakened at 3 A.M. after five hours of deep sleep and my nose was up and running soon after, so here I am at the computer. I have caught up on my typing and now, for the first time in my life, I am writing on the computer. That sentence does not sound right but I do not know how else to express it. I obtained this beast to use it as a word processor; it feels like writing. The beast has got me trained, almost. If I am very obedient, it will often reward me. Now, finally, after all these years, my handwriting is legible.

My medical history is as long as I am old. I have had many surgeries. There is some danger and it takes special trust to put oneself so completely in the hands of a bunch of strangers, but I have been lucky so far and I am hopeful that all will go well today.

More than six days have passed since I walked to the hospital last Tuesday. I walked slowly and arrived on time. The bunch of strangers at the hospital were divided into teams of well trained, highly competent, kindly, efficient care givers; that was not enough to avoid difficulties. An emergency case tied up the operating room and delayed my surgery almost six hours. During the later part of my surgery the local anesthetic began to wear off and I experienced intense pain. When my lens was removed the capsule ruptured, exposing the posterior chamber of my eye and requiring removal of vitreous, thus prolonging the procedure and increasing the risk of further complications. I felt depleted after the procedure, but I was not in pain and three hours later I was at home in my own bed.

Except for visits to the doctor on Wednesday, Friday and today, Monday, I have spent most of my time in bed, listening to television with my eyes closed. As directed I have applied three eye drops every four hours and I took an antibiotic twice a day for three days. When I started using my right eye a bit two days ago my vision was quite limited, but I was aware that I sometimes have double vision so it is likely that I also have a muscle weakness or paralysis. Although I continue to feel spent, it is clear that I am improving and I hope to play bridge tomorrow evening.

Deborah has provided concrete help and emotional support throughout this ordeal. It would have been very difficult without her. We planned to go to celebrate Kelly's fourth birthday yesterday, but I decided to be conservative and rest at home; I tire so easily. Adam drove up from southern Virginia and we had a good visit. This evening Deb and I will have our regular Monday evening dinner, but I do not feel regular yet.

While I have holed up to recuperate, things have kept right on happening. Each day I have glanced out at the yard to note the progression. Now everything that is alive, except the crape myrtle, is in leaf and almost everything has flowered. A few azaleas and the rhododendron will bloom soon and the big black cherry tree has formed its racemes, but the tiny blossoms are not yet open.

It has been politics as usual. A cease fire that is not a cease fire is in effect in Lebanon and Israel. A federal budget has been passed, but it extends only until the end of this fiscal year and in no way resolves the budget dispute that both parties will use to electioneer. The Kennedy–Kassebaum health care bill was passed by the Senate, but it accomplishes very little and it will probably be destroyed in committee.

A huge amount of time and space were used to cover the auction of the millennium, the things left by Jacqueline Kennedy Onassis. Things sold for many times their estimated value. It is both sad and laughable.

It is one week since I underwent surgery and it is the first day that I feel confident about full recovery and hopeful about a very good result. Now I can look at my right eye with my left eye and see that the external appearance is near normal. There is considerable ecchymosis below the eye but I have had a black eye before. Some hemorrhage remains under the conjunctiva, but the globe no longer looks shrunken and soft. As my eye has improved I have become increasingly aware of my head movements and of the tension and discomfort in my neck and my right shoulder. One thing distracts from another.

A recent snapshot reinforced my awareness of how I now closely resemble my father's appearance in his old age; I am beginning to believe it. It was my good fortune to be viewed as conventionally good looking in my youth and middle years. I was always aware of that, but tended not to confront it. Now it strikes me as suspiciously seductive when a woman says anything complimentary about my appearance. My concern about appearance may now be as great as it has ever been and it feels inappropriate and unbecoming.

I view myself and others as always, even when naked, in costume. How I choose to present myself is a complicated matter that I understand incompletely. It is not always clear that I am being authentic when I think I want to be authentic. Often my preference is to be humorous rather than authentic; funny hats suit me. I often stir up a little lighthearted trouble by refusing to go along with the gag. The first time I went with Ria to meet her best friends at a sorority dance, I wore wax buck teeth throughout the evening. That is probably how I would have looked without the expensive orthodontia treatments I had, but I was not trying to be authentic, I was refusing to go along with being presented as the handsome new boyfriend. I wonder if I would have found it amusing and admirable if Ria had pulled that stunt; probably not.

It makes no sense to be fraudulent in our most important relationships and yet it is often tempting to misrepresent out of fear that authenticity will lead to rejection. When you present yourself accurately and it leads to rejection, you have saved yourself a lot of time and energy that can be used in more worthwhile pursuits. A fraudulent presentation is always a loser, authenticity has a chance. If I am correct it is important that I figure out much more about myself; who is the authentic me.

I suspect that what I have written today is connected with two dream fragments that I remembered this morning. A day or two after the surgery I awakened with the end of a dream. I was leaving a building with several men walking behind me and I became aware that I was wearing my good overcoat, but that it had a large moth hole in its lapel. The second dream occurred this morning. A man was in a hotel room looking out of a large picture window at some skyscrapers. Several men were in the room with him and they were fugitives or criminals or in hiding. The man telephoned a woman and described his view, including a mud colored building. Whether he did it on purpose or stupidly, he had jeopardized their hiding place and it was clear to all that they had better move quickly to avoid being caught.

A dream is just a dream, but these dreams remind me of my concerns about seeing and about being seen. A question is raised about whether I want to be located or caught. I wonder who the woman was. My ambivalence is showing. I am not certain that I want my position known; so many questions and so few answers.

The day has been gray and windy, but fragrant with the smell of spring rain. The front lawn is a disgrace; long and full of dandelions. I have multiple excuses for neglecting it.

Fatigue and intermittent double vision persist, but I am feeling much stronger and I enjoyed playing bridge last night. People were solicitous and seemed pleased to have me back. Most of the players are seniors and they have many health problems. We are the big entitlement folks: pensions, Social Security and health care. Are we deserving? Maybe that is not the best question to ask; it might be decided that we are deserving, but not affordable. My surgery was paid for by the taxpayer and my supplemental health insurance; I got less than I was originally promised, but still quite a lot. Even when I'm feeling very deserving I'm quite aware of what a lucky, cushy arrangement I have.

So I am back to the most important political issue: who deserves what and how it can best be provided. The people who know they are deserving, but have a great tendency to doubt that others have a similar legitimate claim, are called Republicans. Just listen to them; they will reveal themselves over and over again. God is on their side. God seems to choose sides a lot.

Now is the time for me to reveal my plan for providing high quality health care for all who deserve it—that includes almost everyone during an election year—at a price we can afford. Well, I do not know enough about it to construct such a plan, but do not despair, I have some ideas; I will elaborate. Some of our most financially successful citizens have been, pure and simple, insurance salesmen; insurance pays well; pays the insurance companies and insurance salesmen well. Eventually we will have a system that eliminates those insurance costs; a single payer, self-insurance arrangement. Services will be provided by nuns or nun-like people who are medically trained, low paid, service oriented, highly professional people who lack avarice and are ambitious to do good work and relieve suffering. Of course, the very wealthy will continue to secure the professional services of people more like those who currently do the job and the politically powerful will arrange to have something special although not necessarily better. Now, that was not so difficult, was it? I almost forgot rationing of services; we will continue to pretend that we do not do that.

It is the pretending that is so strikingly apparent this political year. It is a mistake to take anything at face value and everyone who is paying attention seems to know it. What would happen if the truth was told; would it be believed; would the truth teller be ignored, ridiculed, stoned, expelled or perhaps just resented for disrupting the political process? We know we are lied to, but we are in collusion with the liars and seem to agree with them that it is for our own good. We are not prepared to deal with the truth; the truth would drive us wild. If we were given a steady diet of truth, we would learn to live with it and we would learn to like it.

May Day started with frost all around the area. It has evolved into a delightful, warm and sunny day. A cattail plant extends nearly a foot out of the water and many water lily leaves have surfaced. Just to the left of the pond is an azalea that I grew from a cutting; it is six feet high, about eight feet wide and is covered with brilliant, pink blossoms. The place would look just right if the front lawn was mowed. Slowly, carefully and with my eyes protected by my special postoperative sun glasses, I mowed.

There were no oneiric disclosures this morning. I awakened playing old bridge hands; this time I got them right. One hand in particular keeps coming back to remind me that I failed to figure it out when it counted. My partner made an excellent bid and I let her down. Gerda and I would have won our section in a big tournament if I had been effective. It has importance only to the extent that I endow it with significance about myself. My partner was generous; more generous than I.

Generosity is so becoming. I wish I had shown more of it and I have some hope that I will do better in the future. When the chips are down, I tend to be mean rather than giving. It is only after the fact that I realize how I have missed an opportunity to be more the way I tell myself I want to be. Things happen so quickly and my spontaneous response reveals my selfishness. I do better when I anticipate the opportunity, and I was at my best when at work, clearly focused on the therapeutic partnership. I no longer have the lame excuse of having exhausted my best stuff at the office. I would like to be more terrific; all it takes is terrific behavior; I'm trying to talk myself into it. It is too easy to be lazy and inattentive.

When I treated my in-laws with affection and respect, I was being disingenuous; I actively disliked them and resented the way they used their power over my wife. My goal was to have them feel pleased so they would let up on their daughter; it worked. All of us felt more at ease and benefited from the reduced tension. My distrust of them persisted, but they were responsive to generous behavior and, in a strange way, I think they deserved it for it made it much easier for them to behave better. It is that kind of constructive interaction that too often eludes me when I am not paying sufficient attention.

There was a celebration party at bridge this morning. Donna made life master. Making life master does not make one a master of life, but it is an important event for bridge players; it recognizes a level of achievement that eludes many players. It was a great excuse for the ingestion of large quantities of homemade food, especially pies and cakes, for me. Before the game I stopped at a nearby nursery and bought forty-eight tomato plants, but when I got home after the game I was so full and so tired that I barely had the energy to take the plants out of the car; I plopped into bed and slept for almost two hours.

The mail contained a bill. My Medicare supplemental health insurance rejected the claim submitted by the Air Force hospital concerning my recent surgery. It seems I will have to pay for the box lunch I received about an hour before I left the hospital; $4.75. I wonder how much it cost all of us for that bureaucratic process to occur, and it is not over yet.

The political struggles this week have been more internecine than interparty. Senator Dole's poor showing in current polls has mobilized many Republican voices; they want change—change in the discouraging numbers. Every statement about substance has strong strategic overtones and the bad numbers have stirred up some strategies that seem directed toward next time, not this time. Maybe there are knowledgeable insiders who can accurately predict election results well in advance. It was recently reported that George Bush knew he would be defeated two months before the election. Why wasn't I told? Maybe it is as with all tout sheets, you must buy the information.

The minimum wage, legal and illegal immigration, Welfare reform, abortion policy and entitlements were all in the news, but none was as important as the rise in gasoline prices; that provided an opportunity for Dole to thrust and for Clinton to parry. Anticipation and quick response is the President's game and, although it makes sense, the game itself takes precedence over the substance. That cannot be best for anyone. Cynicism prevails.

Public Television aired a two hour special, "Who Plays God," last evening. It dealt with several important, difficult dilemmas and contradictions in our current health care system. None of the distinguished panelists is running for office, but all are deeply involved in trying to define the important issues and provide sensible, ethical directions. We have the most expensive health care system in the world, yet it is seriously flawed. I was pleased that the program clearly recognized the current rationing of care and the inappropriate emphasis on treatment rather than prevention. Our system often provides millions of dollars for the treatment of a condition that could have been avoided for peanuts, but no peanut money was available. The lack of a sensible approach has to do with vested interest and politics. Our willingness to accept the obvious is impeded by a combination of moralistic and selfish interests.

The program also dealt with some of the difficult decisions that patients, doctors and families are faced with when care is available and when it is not available or available only at very great financial and emotional cost. There are many slippery slope problems. The right to die might be the precursor of the obligation to die. The provision of adequate nutrition and health care to a pregnant woman might usher in a socialistic state that does not adequately reward individual discipline and effort. These concerns are so important in determining our political identity; the bleeding hearts versus the heartless.

The spring rain ended early and the ground dried sufficiently to allow some spring planting. I am not supposed to do any hard work, nor am I supposed to bend over. I cheated a little but Deb came over and did most of the job; twenty-three tomato plants were planted. We were both too tired to finish but that is about half the vegetable garden; a few more tomatoes, some hot peppers and a row of squash will go in on another day. We enjoyed a steak stir-fry and fresh strawberries, corn on the cob and asparagus.

I was quite comfortable while working in the garden and during dinner, but now my neck and back are severely twisted and uncomfortable. I'll go to sleep very soon.

The spasm and twisting are just beginning. It is early Sunday morning but I have been up and feeling very comfortable for over an hour. My vision has changed little these past few days, but I am confident that things are progressing as expected. So much can go wrong and often does. That is why it seems so miraculous when things go well. There must be a master plan, a guiding hand, an immovable mover. If I say maybe, I move away from my atheistic stance and toward the agnostic. My father, in his final years, expressed himself as a believer; I felt he was playing it safe, just in case he was wrong in his conviction that when you die you are dead and that's that.

Cataracts are like kidney stones; when you have one you learn that most of the people you know have had one or more. At the bridge tournament, yesterday morning, I wore my Solar Shield glasses and was approached by many old geezers who provided me with details of their cataract experience. Some of them had a difficult time, but every story had a happy ending. I did not ask any of them who paid for their surgery. There were about two hundred of us playing in the senior pairs event and most of us have someone who loves us, but no matter how lovable we are, we are a very expensive bunch.

During my first ten years after graduation from medical school I did no fee for service work. When I began part-time private practice in the District of Columbia in 1961, the medical community was hungry for psychiatric consultants and a competent, reliable psychiatrist could expect to have a thriving practice. Early on I associated myself with a small group of internists and I maintained that relationship until my retirement. All of us have had conventionally successful professional lives and none of us focused on earning big bucks, but I think all have been financially prosperous. Not all physicians are so reasonable about money. People who are very interested in lucrative medical practice tend to go into specialties that generate large fees; statistics are available to guide them. Others will develop their practice in ways that are guided more by financial considerations than by an effort to provide excellent care in an ethical manner.

Soon after I started private practice I met an internist whom I knew in undergraduate school; our offices were in the same building. Referring physicians often have a characteristic style and interest and as the receiving consultant I could often accurately guess a lot about the patient and the patient's problems before the patient arrived. It soon became apparent that patients referred by this fellow were people he wanted to get rid of or people who might expect special treatment. I think that he rarely referred anyone when he might benefit financially by not making the referral. When he referred a relative who very openly asked me to cheat on my billings to his insurance company, I began to think of him as a crook and solved the problem with his relative by seeing him without expectation of payment. Most of his referrals were deadbeats or freebies. I do not know what I would have done if he had not died; good riddance. Such convenient deaths do not usually occur; it is very difficult to deal with such unsavory individuals and hard to protect the integrity of the system from their avarice and second rate medical care.

In all aspects of life we take the bitter with the sweet. One of the people referred to me by that internist was a medical student whom I saw off and on for many years without charge. In the last decade of my practice she referred many interesting patients to me. They were very appropriate referrals and they came at a time when I needed the work and welcomed it. I like to think that I did well by doing good.

Whatever new or modified system of health care is put in place, it will have both care givers and users who will use it unfairly to advantage themselves. There are many difficult compromises ahead. It is my hope that more effort will be made to attract people interested in serving, and I think that can only be accomplished by insuring that those who serve will receive modest financial compensation. In some ways medical care may be less adequate, but in the overall the public will be better served, at less cost and with much more emphasis on prevention rather than treatment. There are existing models of such care in the United States; I am pleased with the care I received at the Air Force hospital last week and I admire the people who serve there; they served me very well.

This has been an excellent day for me. An early morning rain watered the garden and left the ground just right for planting the remaining tomato plants and preparing the beds for squash and peppers; Deb came over and worked with me for over an hour in the early afternoon. I worked hard, but only a little at a time and without bending over very much, good patient that I am. It was sunny and warm and while we were in the back yard, magically, two rhododendron flowers burst into bloom followed by an explosion of fragrance from the black cherry tree. All of this happens every year, but never before have I observed it with such deliberateness and awareness. Before Deb left we looked at the pond. Many blossoms from the big azalea were floating as water lilies; it was grand.

It is difficult to believe that the cynicism level could increase, but it has. The mavens are wondering if the important issues will be dealt with before the election. They suspect we may be faced with a series of petty attempts to gain or maintain advantage. I'm told and I believe that we have the world's best system of government.

This week I have been impressed with the degree to which a role reversal has occurred between me and my kids. They now correctly perceive me as needy; they check up on me rather than dutifully reporting in to meet my expectations. Deb is gentle in how she expresses it, but it is clear to me that she is concerned that I will hurt myself because I will fail to recognize some decreased capacity or I will use poor judgment. I try to strike a reasonable balance; I gave away my electric chain saw years ago.

Yesterday, before she came over for our regular Monday evening dinner, Deb spent most of the day chasing around with insurance adjusters concerning repairs for her car. Last Thursday she was in Richmond on business and as she left her customer's parking lot, one of the employees pulled out and raked the side of her car. It was a low speed affair with no injuries, but with resulting hassle. She was distressed that her almost new

Millennium was scarred, but she was pleased with her efforts at getting things rectified. When she arrived here I told her we had garden work to do before dinner. I had taken a thin tomato stake and poked eight holes in the earth. It was Deborah's job to drop a squash seed in each of those holes; that took care of her preprandial garden work. It was my way of saying, "See what a good boy I am; I did some garden work, but I followed the doctor's orders and did not bend over."

After dinner and the dishes I got into my reclining position and Deb, instead of going to her chair, cut and filed my toenails. I am able to cut them myself, but only with great difficulty, my body is so inflexible, and risk that I will strain my back; so I am needy and I try to be balanced about doing for myself and asking for help.

Deb left at seven and I turned on the television. A phone call at nine awakened me. I was groggy. On reconstructing things I realized I had fallen asleep very soon after Deb left. I think what happens is that I get such great relief from my dystonia when I start to fall asleep that it tends to predispose me to sleep. It is a dramatic change from the way I used to be.

This is a gray, cool day, just right for cooking. A large pot of split pea and lentil soup is on the stove and almost done. Next I will make a potato pudding in preparation for Mrs. Bush's arrival. Her grandson, Brian, will have a graduation party on June 2 and I'm looking forward to seeing her and all of the Smith family then. If I have energy left perhaps I'll try a pineapple cake; I'll follow the banana cake recipe but substitute pineapple; we'll see; it will probably work.

Two out of three is not bad; I cooked the soup and the potato pudding but ran out of time and went off to the bridge game. My fatigue is so great in the evening that it impairs my ability to play, and last night I also was irritable and critical. Kitch was patient with me. I think we had a below average game. I did not wear the Solar Shield glasses last night.

This morning I created a sweet potato and pineapple loaf cake that has not yet cooled and I started a new batch of bread that won't be baked until tomorrow or Friday. Tuesdays and Wednesdays seem to have become cooking days; I hope it doesn't stay that way; I plan to diversify.

The role reversal that I spoke of feels mostly comfortable. The children have been benevolent and gentle with me. Ria's death hit them hard and I think it is now less important to them that they assert their independence. Asserting independence was my issue and it kept me from greater closeness with my parents. I did not trust my mother's ability to conceal her views or my ability to be objective and be unaffected by what I thought she thought. Now I am amused at how often my behavior is in line with what I think she wished to impose on me. Mother would be pleased; so am I.

The children viewed me as the person in charge. It is likely that Ria felt that and communicated it to them. Deb tells me that she always knew she was expected to be a certain way, but that she did not know what that way was and that she was supposed to figure it out rather than ask; we were not going to tell her. I suspect that was the result of my cockamamie effort to be laissez-faire with my children, in contrast to the intrusive techniques I felt subjected to in my childhood.

When I was a child I was often told to go to bed and go to sleep; Ria had that experience also. We discussed it and agreed that we might tell our kids to go to bed, to get them out of our hair, but we would carefully avoid telling them to go to sleep. They could read or play in their room and I remember that they were often still up when we went to bed. A few years ago I mentioned to the children that Ria and I followed that house rule strictly. They laughed and were vehement that we always told them to go to sleep. All of us are telling the truth; it could be that all of us are also correct. Words: what we communicate and what we mean to communicate.

How do you regard me? That is the question. No one taught me about that in my training. There was talk about respecting the underlying good core in each of us and about the therapeutic alliance. Transference and countertransference are important concepts that were frequently considered. No one ever directly addressed the issue of lying in psychotherapy. There was a joke told about the concerned spouse, whose wife was dying, who asked if the doctors practiced psychosomatic medicine and was pleased that they did because it meant that they could lie to his wife. The joke is about patient naiveté, not the appropriateness or inappropriateness of lying.

Soon after I finished my training I lied to a patient. She had made some strong anti-Semitic statements and I felt distressed but said nothing. In a later meeting I told her that I am a Jew. She asked me if I had been offended and I lied; I denied that I had felt offended. She became outraged that I had so little regard for her that I had not been upset by her statements. I tried very hard to avoid lying after that; she taught me a very valuable lesson: do not lie for your own sake. That is not the same as not lying at all, but it is in the right direction.

My appointment with Dr. Tran, the ophthalmologist who performed my surgery, was his first appointment of the morning. I arrived at 7:30 and was there until 9:30. He was pleased with my recovery and discontinued the eye drops to see how I will recover without them. Colors are still distorted, but my near vision is much improved; far vision not as sharp as it was before surgery. Things are still settling down. He said little about it, but it is clear that he feels my dystonia is aggravated by and perhaps partly caused by an eye muscle imbalance and that surgical intervention may be indicated. I asked him to please communicate his findings to my neurologist, Dr. Greenberg.

The bridge game was one minute from the hospital so I was there with time to spare. It is a cold, rainy day and it was freezing at the club. I played without glasses, but needed glasses to keep score; a big improvement during the last two or three days. It has been another easy, relaxed day. Calls keep coming in from patients, but without pressure for me to perform. The oven is full of baking bread and I'll bake another batch in the morning so the bridge players at the food game can ooh and ah about the aroma and flavor of bread straight from the oven.

The candidates have been exceptionally visible and active the past day or two. Dole is on the attack and trying hard to assert substantial differences between his views and current policy. He is doing what his advocates insist is required if he is to catch up in the polls and have a reasonable shot at winning in November. President Clinton is projecting a cool eagerness to compromise and cooperate to achieve important bipartisan results. All of it is glaringly theatrical and choreographed. The phoniness does not mean that gridlock will result; some good legislation might come out of all this maneuvering; let us pray.

What does it take to get someone to change his or, in this case, her mind? It must be very similar to giving someone insight; it cannot be done. The ground can be prepared, information given and further consideration encouraged, but insight is not given, it happens. It is the women who seem most aware of how meanspirited the Republicans have been and they make the margin of difference. Senator Dole does not seem to be courting their vote at all; he persists with the stuff that turns them, and me, away. I suspect that the authentic Dole is not as ugly as the Dole he is projecting. It must be a problem of constituencies; how to win one without alienating another.

I am disappointed with the repetitive, nothing new, quality of the debate; it is hardly a debate. The Friday evening shows are often enlightening and entertaining; not tonight. Everyone digs deep for something to ward off boredom, but with little success. I was hoping to maintain a high level of enthusiasm right up to the election.

The air was heavily perfumed this morning. I traced the odor to the showy rhododendron in the back yard; that seemed so unlikely. Everything but it and the azaleas has faded. The tomato plants have been fertilized by myriad tiny black cherry tree petals.

Last evening Deb called and asked me to feed her tonight; my pleasure. I decided to cancel this afternoon's bridge game and, instead, mow the front lawn and watch the basketball playoffs. Steven called while I was at the commissary and invited me to join them tomorrow, Mothers' Day. I declined but he, Teresa, Kelly and David will join us for dinner this evening; there is enough for all of us. A routine day has turned into something special. Dinner is cooked except for heating things and microwaving the corn.

Grapefruit with strawberries
Salad with spicy red cabbage and asparagus
Split pea and lentil soup
Corn on the cob
Lamb with seasoned rice and mint jelly
Prune cake   Nut loaf cookies
Pineapple and sweet potato loaf

I think I'm showing off; it's fun. The house and breezeway are a little messy but the front lawn sure looks nice. Kelly and Dave will get to feed the fish and we will all be happy.

All have come and gone. Dinner was good and we had a pleasant indoor exchange; a fierce thunderstorm began before they arrived and was still going strong when they left. We played guessing games and Deb figured out that I was thinking of bellybutton lint. I am a known quantity; crystal clear.

I forgot to serve the mint jelly.

Once again politics is delayed by the national interest in sudden death. A bizarre clinical trial by illegal drug dealers has resulted in hundreds of severe reactions and at least a dozen deaths. They created a new concoction and sold it to their usual customers to see how it would work; it worked lethally. Fatal air crashes occurred on successive days; fourteen marines killed in a helicopter collision and one hundred and nine presumed dead in a crash near Miami. These events get first billing with prolonged, curious inquiry; over and over.

The dance goes on. Senator Dole's heroic behavior and severe war injuries were detailed to impress us with his firsthand experience with intense suffering and neediness; he must be compassionate and eager to assist the (deserving) needy. It is not easy for him to be all that he must be to win the constituencies he needs to become president.

The secondary players rehashed things on the political shows. The Republicans deny that the gender gap is the result of their policies; it is just a public relations problem that requires improved communication.

India's recent elections kicked out the long dominant Congress Party. Secessionist movements are everywhere. Religious and cultural conflict underlie these movements. Minority groups feel denied and oppressed; they have little hope that they will be dealt with fairly. There is much to support their discontent. If they gain independence and autonomy it is all too likely they will do unto others what they feel has been done to them.

The us against them stuff appears to have very strong biological underpinnings. We are, as competing prides of lions, not very civilized. We distrust and derogate difference while proclaiming our superiority and our righteousness. Our language is replete with examples: The sinister, louche, Indian-giver gypped, jewed and welshed. It is not safe to be different, in the minority or a stranger.

Weather records show no frost in Maryland after May 15. There are frost warnings for tonight and tomorrow night. A heavy frost would cost the area many millions of dollars and would kill my tomato plants.

The area has dodged the bullet the past several days; frost all around us, but no great damage to vegetation. Nearby farmers and orchardists used their special techniques to protect vulnerable blossoms from the record setting mid-May low temperatures. My tomato plants went unscathed without my taking special precautions. We are led to expect several more very cool nights followed by months of summertime temperatures.

Things can feel so sudden even when they are preceded by prolonged anticipation, expectation and preparation. A child leaves home, suddenly, after fifteen to thirty years of preparation and prodding. I worked in a psychotherapy group where one of the members was thought of as characteristically impulsive even though his behavior was well planned. Over many weeks, another participant discussed her indecision about marrying a friend, yet the group was dismayed when she "ever so suddenly" announced her wedding date. Soon it will suddenly be summer. The whole megillah is so very sudden; over in a flash; just a flicker. It does not feel so while the kidney stone passes.

A long session with Dr. Tran went very well this morning. Suddenly my corrected vision is 20/20. There are no complications to the surgery. He did an extensive evaluation of my strabismus and concluded that he wanted consultation from an expert at Walter Reed Army Hospital. That is being arranged.

Before I left the hospital I went to the neurology clinic and was able to secure an appointment next week with Dr. Greenberg. My neck has been painful and severely twisted. I think there is considerable new hypertrophy of my trapezius muscle on the right side. If that is correct there is a likelihood that botulism toxin injections into that muscle will be very helpful. I am also interested in what Dr. Greenberg will think about the notion that the dystonia might be relieved by eye muscle surgery. Many people with spasmodic torticollis experience increased symptoms associated with visual activity and they often, as I have, develop visual tricks to make activities less uncomfortable and easier to perform. It is much easier for me to walk if I look up and to the right frequently and, in addition, alternately close one eye and then the other. I almost always wear sun glasses while I walk in an effort to conceal these antics and avoid looking too bizarre. I used to joke that I was not very peculiar, for a psychiatrist. Now I am peculiar, even for a psychiatrist.

Big political news is about to break so, of course, it has been leaked and discussed elaborately prior to its expected announcement later today. Bob Dole will resign from the Senate and devote himself exclusively to his campaign for the presidency. We knew he was behind, but I did not know he was that desperate. This move breaks the ennui and raises the specter of the resurrection of Republican hopes. Well, I have been complaining about the boredom; I better not complain about the exciting uncertainty. It is just what I said I wanted; an exciting political year.

Are you bored? Do things seem stable and predictable? Has your partnership lost intensity? Are you being taken for granted? Shake things up! Don't be a sure thing. Destabilize—it creates excitement. If you want to be in love, remember that the intensity required thrives on uncertainty. Stability is not exciting. Candidate Dole is going to try to have a love affair with the American people. It is one version of family values. I hope no one gets pregnant. Billets doux will follow. Keep your barf bag handy. Drama, suspense and uncertainty will ward off torpor and keep hope alive.

Yesterday I went into town as a tourist for the first time since December. The West Building of The National Gallery of Art is a wonderful place. I looked at beautiful things for almost three hours and would have stayed longer but my discomfort was too great. A collection of Jan Steen paintings is outstanding; the permanent collection is even better. This is a great place to live; the vital center of our government in a most beautiful city. What good luck.

Senator Dole has declared his love for us by disclosing the great sacrifices he is making to win us. He has resigned from his position of power, given up the work by which he has identified himself, to devote himself to courting us full time; devoting himself to de vote. He was properly and, I think, authentically emotional at the news conference. The mavens say he had to do something to avoid being dead in the water. The curtain is up for the next act. We await the performance; he has new life. He has put something of a burden on us; he has no place to go now but the White House or back home. It is up to us to choose him or send him away to oblivion, after all he has done for us. I like it. I hope it does not work.

Last night I dreamed I was arranging office space to continue my psychiatric practice. Yesterday, while I was with Dr. Tran, a young family practitioner came in to observe. She asked me if I still practiced and I gave my usual spiel; I am recently retired and I retired because I thought I should, not because I wanted to experience retirement. Still, the dream surprises me; I am growing accustomed to retirement and I like it. Now, much more than when I was in practice, I am aware of how stressful it was to be continuously on call and available to people who relied heavily on me. It was wonderful, fulfilling, rewarding and lots more good stuff, but it is clear that it was becoming too difficult for me. It is, indeed, a dream to think about going back to it.

While I played bridge, ate chili and enjoyed myself, the Chief of Naval Operations committed suicide and Bob Dole went on the offensive by proclaiming that his side stands for decency in America combined with compassion. Dole emphasized that he has always had to do it the hard way and he was prepared to go that route again to win the election. The contents of Admiral Boorda's suicide note have not yet been revealed, but the brief biography that was presented on the news made it clear that he did life the hard way and seemed very successful at it until the last moment. The gory details will be revealed soon. He was the first enlisted man to rise through the ranks and become CNO. He was a young high school drop out when he enlisted; the American dream realized, almost.

V is for valor. Last year Admiral Boorda stopped wearing the V on his Vietnam service ribbon when questions were raised about his right to that honor. The V is authorized only when an individual has been in danger from enemy attack and he had not been in the required battle situation. His wearing the V was similar to lying on one's resume. We do not know if he had deliberately misrepresented his military activities. Someone called attention to the fact that he had not earned that award and when he found out about it he removed the V from his ribbon. The matter was not dropped and was soon to be made public. He chose death before dishonor. That is the story that is being told; maybe it's correct. We may never understand why a mustang who rose from the lowest rank to the very top of the hierarchy would need to engage in puffery. His achievements were so very great and had been rewarded abundantly. How could there be a need to embellish such a record? Perhaps additional pertinent information will help us to understand this tragedy; I hope so. A thousand gnat bites can do a person in.

Armed Forces Day is appropriately funereal; gloomy and drizzling. Admiral Boorda's interment occurs tomorrow while today the show will go on. The Blue Angels will be a big part of that show here at Andrews Air Force Base. They will fly over my house, so close that I might reach up and touch them.

There is dispute about whether the CNO was entitled to wear the V. His supporters claim his battle experience in Vietnam entitled him to the V. His critics state that the V was not authorized and he should have known that when it has not been authorized it is not to be worn. How surprising that the matter could be so unclear. The criticism was a final straw; he succumbed.

Last night I called Pat and we talked about her garden, her job, her knee and, for the first time, some of her discontent. She did not know about recent events and it turns out that she has not been reading the newspaper or listening to the radio or television. Her mother has been very feeble and Pat has felt confined, except for going to work, and unhappy about her work situation. She is waiting for her mother to come north, the end of this month, before she seeks new employment. Pat has always made new friends easily and it is likely she will do so again but as of now she seems dispirited and lonely. Her garden continues to occupy her and give her pleasure. She was discontent here and now she is discontent there. How do you regard me?

No bridge today. Deb called to say hello and she accepted my invitation for dinner. Dinner will include a new item, eggplant parmigiana. I am slowly increasing my repertoire. Yesterday, after bridge, I cooked the eggplant and also made baked apples. Rome apples look so perfect that I repeatedly get them for baking; that is all they are good for. The fresh fruits and vegetables have been superb; it's a pleasure to consume the recommended five or more each day. The asparagus has been better than ever.

My vegetable garden is started, but shows no action. All thirty-six tomato plants are still alive; that is lucky. None of the squash seeds has sprouted yet. I plan to plant the squash seeds in stages and stage two awaits the appearance of stage one. Eight peat pots contain flimsy seedlings of habanero peppers that I started from seeds collected from dried peppers grown last year. Garden tomatoes and squash make sense since the fruits are better than what is available in the markets, but everything else is just for the fun of it. I've gone back to the land before I go back to the land.

The sun is out brightly in time for the air show. Except for the flybys it has been very quiet around the house. There are many thousands of visitors at Andrews, just one mile from here, but I see no sign of the activity.

My mother was born on this day in 1900.

The temperature around here has ranged from below freezing to near one hundred in one week; as predicted. It has been quiet again except for the low flybys on this second day of the air show. My usual Sunday routine was restful and easy on my neck since I was reclining in bed most of the day. My rheumy right eye looks worse, but sees better. If it doesn't look better soon it will concern me.

I'm losing things. The garden gloves are not where I left them and an insert from the Sunday paper has disappeared. It is unlikely that someone took the gloves, but I considered that possibility. I recently found a booklet in my magazine rack that I do not recollect having seen before; an interesting item that I ought to remember. Well, my memory has always been selective.

Pundits and mavens did their Sunday thing but it was another boring rehash. The athletes were much more talented and interesting.

A couple of squash sprouts have broken out, several rhododendron cuttings will probably survive, the fish now expect to be fed and the weigela and rhododendron are in full blossom. It is too soon to speculate about the survival of the dogwood and miniature leaf Japanese maple seeds that I planted last fall.

The Supreme Court announced several decisions yesterday. One decision has been characterized as a victory for gay rights. The conservative three wrote a dissenting minority opinion. It will add fuel to the campaign shenanigans. Dole has been emphasizing the importance of preventing the appointment of any more liberal federal judges. Conservative politicians have quickly reacted; they decry the undermining of traditional American values. The right wing of the Republican Party wants a theocracy. We might wind up with Scalia, the miracle man, as the grand inquisitor; crusades and inquisitions to follow; repent and conform or die and go to hell.

A telephone call today confronted me with some surprisingly wistful feelings for my working days. The partner of a former patient asked me to be psychiatric consultant to their psychotherapy practice. I told her I am retired, gave her three names and asked her to give my best regards to her partner; I last saw him over twenty years ago. These feelings of longing for the old involvement are unexpected and fleeting, but they are there while I am awake and while I sleep. Perhaps they are induced by the slow but steady stream of calls from and requests about patients.

It would be all too easy to become a full-time patient. If it's not one thing it's another for which I might seek medical evaluation, advice or treatment. I have not, as a patient, seen my civilian primary physician for a very long time; he has chided me about my absence. The Air Force neurologist, Dr. Greenberg, is the closest thing to a primary physician that I have at Malcolm Grow Medical Center, Andrews Air Force Base. I have had an appointment with Dr. Greenberg every two to three months for about two years. He has treated me and made needed referrals to other specialists.

For nearly two years Dr. Greenberg has injected selected overactive muscles in my neck and shoulder with botulism toxin. The toxin permanently blocks the function of muscle fibers with which it comes in contact; the muscle is weakened and that is the desired effect. The body, including the dysfunctional body, is a wonderfully adaptive machine; when the overactive muscle is weakened, new muscle fibers grow and different muscles become overactive to recreate the dysfunction that was treated. So, the treatment works somewhat, but not for long. The etiology and pathology of the dystonias is unclear. When I die my brain will go to the Brain Tissue Resource Center at McLean Hospital where they are trying to work it all out.

This morning I had an early appointment with Dr. G. I presented my red herrings: I slipped on the ice soon after the previous injection, with resulting thoracic bruise and head thunk, and Dr. Tran thinks I may have a trochlear nerve defect that is a factor in the dystonia. That out of the way, I told him how uncomfortable I have been and showed him where I hurt. He was interested in my fall and wanted to try a nerve block, but I declined and he agreed to wait and see. He then proceeded to inject massive amounts (I'm just kidding) of botulism toxin into my body. The needle was dull, but even so it hurt only a bit. It will take a week or so to assess the degree of relief that will be achieved.

Next I went to the ophthalmology clinic, without an appointment, and asked to be seen because of the increasing irritation and catarrh of my right eye. I received prompt attention; Dr. Tran removed a stitch and prescribed two days of antibiotic and steroid eye drops. When I left the hospital it was time for lunch.

I am a cheapskate and I view the government's money as my money; I try not to waste it. The best, most cost effective course is the one I choose when I can figure it out. It is likely that it costs us less when I get my medical care through the military; probably; there is room for argument. My big cancer surgery occurred prior to my sixtieth birthday, before I was entitled to medical care through the military. Since then, with rare exception, I have chosen military medical care and have found myself more critical of the private sector. It has become too difficult for the private practitioner to avoid being a businessman; he is pressured and encouraged to be a businessman. The many women physicians are subjected to the same forces and are all too much like the men. The public and the practitioners are very ambivalent about what they want. Socialism is a dirty word and free enterprise is the American way. Once again I suggest that it is important to take the money out of medicine. It will then attract different, not necessarily better or worse, people who can avoid entrepreneurship.

Even without the profit motive, it would have cost us—all of us—several thousand dollars if I had gone to the hospital after I slipped on the ice. Current standards and technology are very expensive. I saved us a bundle.

Medical care is so important, expensive and out of control. My views are not popular or likely to prevail in the near future, but of course, I have it right and it will happen down the line. Don't forget how much I saved you—I mean us.

The patient complained to the doctor that no matter where on his body he pressed, he felt pain. He had a broken finger. Some diagnoses are easier to make than others; the cost depends on the skill and motivation of the physician and the system in which the care is delivered.

A few good laughs made yesterday much more than a day at the hospital. I saw one of the world's funniest commercials on television; Father Guido Sarducci did one of his shticks advertising a department store sale; I almost fell off the bed laughing. Public Television had an hour long program showing Mike Nichols and Elaine May doing their hilarious routines; they ended their partnership in 1962. The program did not deal with the considerable success they had independent of each other following their partnership. One routine was shown in its entirety and I remembered it well, but incorrectly. It was even funnier than I remembered.

Nothing beats a good hearty laugh. The Marx brothers and the Ritz brothers were worth their weight in gold. I remember with great pleasure some of the laughs I have enjoyed. Writers and performers have greatly improved the quality of my life. When Steve Allen broke up during one of his shows he carried me and a million others to the brink of ecstasy; I am indebted to him. Robin Williams deserves every cent he gets for his creative antics.

During my teens and early twenties I was frequently at my friend Jerry's house where one of the regular attenders was his brother Morton. Starting around Thanksgiving Morton, Mutt, would wait for a small group to gather in the living room and then he would begin to chant, "Ho, ho, ho; I'm Santa Claus." He would repeat the chant until we would laugh and he would stop when we were all in tears with our laughter; only then would he stop. When we had calmed down he was likely to start up again. What a wonderful power to have.

Illness, hospitals and medical care are very serious business and yet full of humor. Psychotherapy often includes funny, not crazy, stuff. What you find funny can tell you a lot about yourself. My favorite jokes are irreverent or suspenseful. The learning process in medicine is fraught with potential danger for everyone involved, but still full of humor. Many dreams are similar to jokes or a play on words. The serious business of life can be a lot of fun. It is especially valuable to be able to make fun of oneself and enjoy it. I'm working on it.

Was it a dream or did it happen? Does this place exist; have I been there? Have I dreamed it repeatedly or only once and then remembered it recurrently? I go to this dingy room that is up a hill past a high concrete retaining wall. The room is mine; perhaps I live there. (A typing error; I typed lie, not live.) The room reminds me of a room I lived in when I worked as an extern during my sophomore and junior years in medical school.

The externs at William Booth Memorial Hospital in Covington, Kentucky, worked every fifth day from late afternoon until morning and their duties included doing a history and physical exam on all new admissions to the hospital, examining and treating patients who came to the emergency room and being available to assist in emergency procedures. In return for this work they gained clinical experience, exposure to the workings of a small nonteaching hospital, great fatigue, room and board, free laundry and fifty dollars a month. For the first time in my life I was more or less self-supporting; I was twenty-one. It was a heady time for me.

The living quarters for the externs were behind the hospital and up a small hill; perhaps there was a concrete retaining wall. The house was the boyhood home of the founder of the Boy Scouts. The chief nurse and her husband lived on the first floor and the externs occupied the top floor. Two of us lived there nightly while the others were local students who used their rooms only when on duty. The rooms were dingy and each had a smelly gas heater. I viewed it as a vast improvement over the very nice room I had occupied in a private home near the medical school during my freshman year.

The Salvation Army nurses who administered the hospital were stiffly starched women who were apparent only when there was trouble. All others seemed friendly and helpful. The emergency room nurse was a peach who knew her stuff and was always aware that the externs, and others, needed her guidance and assistance. She was always in good humor and I thought she was unflappable. Early one morning she called me to the emergency room and I knew something was amiss when she seemed flustered and unclear about what she wanted. A woman was on the examining table in the lithotomy position, supine with her legs in stirrups, and her face was covered by her arms. Finally it was made clear that there was embarrassment and confusion. The embarrassment was that the woman had intercourse with a tampon in her vagina and the tampon was stuck behind her cervix; I was to remove it. The confusion was that the nurse thought I had experience using a vaginal speculum, I had not, but she thought I did not know what a tampon was. We worked it out. When it was out, we three relaxed and laughed; medical humor.

Some of the nurses at the hospital were extremely friendly and giving. I looked ever so needy and one of them helped me a lot. It was a very exciting time and it distracted me somewhat from my primary task. I met Ria just before I began my work as an extern; we were seriously interested in each other. Even then, at the height of my horniness, I was inclined to stick with one partner and become quite attached to her. My extracurricular activity at the hospital was probably noted; I was not asked to continue there during my senior year. Ria and I married before my final year in medical school began.

During my senior year I filled in a couple of times at that hospital and I became aware that the nurse I had been seeing was having a hard time. She had developed anxiety symptoms and gained a lot of weight. She was much older than I and married. Nevertheless it is likely that she was adversely affected by our relationship and I remember that with chagrin.

Too often my partners have been more generous than I.

Memorial Day weekend, with its flurry of vacation travel and brief moments of solemnity, is in process. Next to Thanksgiving weekend it is the very best time to stay close to home and listen to the horrific traffic reports. Dirty campaigning has begun in earnest with emphasis on personal attack. The character issue looms large. From my Democrats' point of view that is where the President is most vulnerable; we have the advantage on substance. The Republicans are stuck with raising doubts in all other areas. Every move will be taken as an opportunity for attack and counterattack. If the President provides the opening, they will try to cold-cock him; if not, they will pepper him with blows in an attempt to gradually weaken him. It has become more interesting, uncertain, again.

Special, for Memorial Day, the Republicans are running a television spot that claims the President is using "military service" to put off a pending trial. The spot questions his patriotism and reminds us that he avoided military service during the Vietnam war. It is a very clever ad that never mentions Dole and will not be charged to Dole's campaign. Senator Dole's patriotism is unassailable; a Democratic ad unwisely calls Dole a quitter and a double-talker for resigning from the Senate to devote himself to the pursuit of the presidency. Both parties are in dire need of some of the topnotch comedy writers who are standing on the sidelines, observing and describing the frailties of the candidates and the parties. I wonder what Nichols and May would charge; no doubt they would only work for the Democrats; this is a great opportunity for them to renew their partnership.

We who are dyed-in-the-wool are unlikely to be moved by the infighting of the next few months and we are not the ones they are trying to influence. The professional influencers are in charge now. Some of them are unscrupulous; they are for sale and will do their best as hired guns. The candidates probably had veto power, but today's efforts to win the voter were devised by influence specialists who reveal their opinions about the undecided citizens through the ways in which they go after them. Their appeals suggest they don't have great respect for their intended audience; frighteningly, they may be correct in their assessment. Fear and prejudice have worked well in the past, why not again? Waving the flag and proclaiming moral superiority are not likely to lose much.

No one is going to win an election by proposing that we are one human race living in one world; we are not ready for such notions even though they were more or less proposed by a Republican presidential candidate over fifty years ago. Even an attack from outer space might not be sufficient to give us such unity and identification with each other.

I had a dream (no I didn't) that Mickey Rooney and Elizabeth Taylor got married to set a new world's record for the couple with the most intense belief in the sanctity of traditional marriage. Somebody put him up to it. This week the President indicated he would sign, not veto, a bill that would permit states not to honor same sex marriages that were sanctioned in another state. It was a disappointing political decision that is understood but regretted. A Republican congressman, who was advocating the need to prevent same sex marriage in order to maintain the sanctity of the traditional marriage, took umbrage when his lesbian opponent asked him which of his three marriages he viewed as most sanctified.

In this age of instant information it is difficult to maintain illusions. Senator Dole delivered an excellent speech and almost before the words were out of his mouth we were told which famous novelist had written those words for him and we were alerted to how unlike Dole Dole had been while delivering that famous novelist's words. It is not realistic to expect the candidates to write their own speeches, but someone ought to have enough good sense to avoid giving the job to some publicity hound who will nullify the intended effect of his work and make the process appear ridiculous.

Does Welfare promote dependency? My goldfish expect to be fed. I cast bread upon the water, in crumb form, and they come running. They swarm near the surface when I appear, in anticipation of an impending meal. They are growing much faster than if left on their own, but it is more likely that they will expect that the neighborhood cats are providers rather than predators. If they breed this spring as they did last year, there will be a million fish in the pond. Birth control may become essential to avoid overpopulation and severe neurosis. I may institute a new regime that requires them to work for their victuals; no more manna from heaven. Chances are they will be hungry but survive if I stop feeding them; they might eat each other. They are goldfish, not sole. It is a known fact that fish do not have soles. While I'm playing god with those poor fish, I might feed them sole food until they develop soles. A sole would fit nicely on the end of each ventral fin. I feed them much more for my pleasure than for their sustenance.

There were several dead birds around the house last week. Two fledgling were alive on the ground when I first noticed them. I don't think the neighborhood cats killed them; they were somehow displaced from their nest too soon and could not fend for themselves. There are numerous robins nesting nearby; they make it clear that this is their territory; we tolerate each other very well; they know me. The rabbit—I see only one at a time—that lives under the big evergreen in the front yard is either sick or foolishly secure about his situation; he sits quietly on the lawn and does not stir when I go in and out. The cats will get him; they got one rabbit last year. I have never complained to my neighbor about her cats. Only last year did I discover that they were not feral and that they live with her. They do much of their stalking on my side of the street. I am not friendly toward them. I will check with the county animal control department about local rules and then, perhaps, I will ask the neighbor to bell her animals or keep them on her side of the street; they kill and soil wherever they go.

Several years ago I was criticized for not being solemn and respectful enough on Memorial Day weekend. Now, more than ever, I am aware of death and dying; I think about, remember and memorialize dead comrades and others who have smoothed the road. I have become a memorialist; you are reading my effort. The candidates will, no doubt, spend the weekend in ways that will meet our requirements of them; a combination of solemnity and wholesome celebration of the beginning of summer. Senator Dole watched the big basketball game last night and rooted for the underdog; no surprise there. President Clinton is playing golf this Sunday morning. Won't he go to church? Be careful; very careful.

The United States is small potatoes when it comes to war dead. Russia, with its millions of war deaths, will soon have a presidential election and a prime minister will be elected in Israel; these elections may have considerable impact on our political process; there is uncertainty. The greatest uncertainty, I believe, is whether the potential voters who are undecided are paying attention to what is going on. People seem to move to the right when they are frightened. They circle the wagons and hunker down to protect themselves even when the danger is from within. Both parties seem interested in frightening us about what will happen if the other is in power after the election.

It is a day for staying indoors; unsuitable for the beach, the bay or even an outside barbecue. The forecast for tomorrow is not favorable, but I am anticipating a pleasant time by Bodkin Creek, at Teresa and Steve's place at the Chesapeake Bay. It is a very beautiful setting; excellent for them, family and friends. They have a boat, pier and small beach. I do little more than sit and watch while I'm there. Oh yes, I also eat. Often they have fresh crabs that they caught off their own pier or nearby. Teresa's parents do a lot of work there. Roy is retired, but works harder than most at his own home and at the creek. Betty is a great cook and gracious hostess. Teresa has four married sisters and there is often a big crowd of adults and children, all family, celebrating at the creek. I will bake bread and a chocolate pound cake for tomorrow. Deb is making beef ribs. The event will usher in the new season for me.

The rain and chill will not prevent tonight's annual Memorial Day concert at the Capital. Tomorrow President Clinton will perform at the Tomb of the Unknown Soldier. No matter how sincere he may be, it will be a performance, fully covered and commented on.

It's a washout; no trip to the creek today. Teresa called to say the celebration will be at their house in the suburbs of Ellicott City. My activities will be the same; only the view will be different. Last evening I baked ten loaves of bread, two for today, and this morning I baked a chocolate pound cake in loaf form. I made a chocolate-raspberry icing that will not be applied until the cake is plated.

Wreaths have been laid, speeches delivered, prayers said and songs sung to honor those who have served and those who died serving. Crowds are gathering at the Vietnam War Memorial, near the new Korean War Memorial, for a special program. These memorials are extraordinary artistic creations that elicit strong reactions. So many have suffered greatly and lost so much. How easy my life has been.

The rain persisted all day. Deb did the driving to and from Ellicott City where we joined the crowd and enjoyed a double celebration; there was a birthday cake for one of the children. I shot pool, schmoozed, snoozed and snacked. It was relatively calm despite more than a dozen children.

Roy has recently been diagnosed with a potentially serious condition and will undergo a series of tests soon. It reminds me of my ordeal ten years ago. It is time for me to revise my will; I'll call Murray Kivitz and do it soon.

Every day is a holiday now that I am retired, but I continue my work with patients while I sleep. Last night I met with a woman who died a month before I retired. I don't know whether I'd brought her to life or joined her in an afterlife. She was in her eighties, broke her hip and had been hospitalized. I visited her at the hospital and when I got up to leave she threw me a kiss. I did not recognize it as a goodby kiss but it was; she died that evening. She expected and hoped to die soon. After her death I, too, felt relief. I do not remember the content of last night's dream except that we were talking and she was smiling.

This morning I confirmed my appointment this afternoon with the strabismus expert at Walter Reed Medical Center. So far I have had no improvement from last week's injections of botulism toxin; my neck is about the same and my right shoulder is even more uncomfortable. My symptoms depend a lot on my activities. It was impossible for me to get comfortable yesterday while I rode as a passenger in Deb's car and it's likely that it fatigued me and increased my discomfort. The overactivity of my muscles keeps me from having a sedentary day. The dystonia is complex; it is quite unlikely that strabismus is an important factor in the etiology of my symptoms. Still, I hope the new expert will come up with something helpful; a few new tricks that afford temporary relief would make the trip worthwhile. I have considered codifying the multitude of tricks and devices that are used to ease the dysfunction and discomfort that are a part of neuromuscular disease; writing this down may help coerce me into action.

An afternoon at Walter Reed was interesting, but not very fruitful. As expected, I have a phoria that accounts for the double vision I experience, but there is nothing to suggest that it is a factor in my dystonia. A new pair of reading glasses was prescribed. The eye department was quite large with many resident physicians in training and a big dose of the chauvinism that usually accompanies training centers. I am disappointed but not surprised; no additional relief in sight. Do not miss the pun.

A surge of political and politically related events keep the kettle boiling. The three defendants in the Arkansas Whitewater fraud trial, all associates or former associates of Clinton, were found guilty and face stiff sentences. This tends to encourage continued activity by special prosecutor Starr and congressional committees. It is likely to remain prominent throughout the campaign. It hurts the President. The jury spokesperson, a very articulate woman, stated clearly that the jury did not disbelieve President Clinton's videotaped testimony, but that will not keep the Republicans from using the verdict as further reason to cast doubt on his integrity.

The Hindu Party government in India lasted less than two weeks. A new coalition will be formed by other parties that distrust the Hindu Party. The deadly religious and ethnic strife in India has not been quelled by the democratic form of government. They make us look downright civilized.

Israel is voting for its prime minister today. It is a very close call and the dominant issue, amazingly, is more peace process or less peace process. The candidates sound the same, but everyone understands how they stand on that issue.

I had lunch with Murray, revised my will and saw his new office suite. He continues to work hard with no sign that he will slow down soon. He is my age; too old for me to keep him as executor of my estate. Deb will fill that role; she has had practice settling her mother's estate.

Public television presented a one hour program on America's love affair with ice cream followed by an hour on presidential character. The experts were unanimous that good character is desirable; there was little unanimity beyond that, not even about what constitutes good character. We have been here before. The public appreciates amiability and light-hearted humility in our presidents. We may not reward or approve a leader who, guided by good character, makes the difficult, unpopular decision. We are a tough bunch to please.

The Israeli election will not be decided until the absentee ballots are counted, but it looks like a victory for Likud leader, Netanyahu, by a narrow margin. Most of the uncounted votes are from Israeli soldiers who tend to support Netanyahu. It is a victory for slowing the peace process, denying Palestinian autonomy and refusing to trade land for peace. Fundamentalism rules again.

As the day ends, Israeli Prime Minister Peres has not conceded but Netanyahu has announced his desire for peace and his plan to pursue it. President Clinton reasserted his support for peace in the Middle East and his intention to assist the parties in their efforts to achieve peace. Those who are not for peace have kept quiet.

I am looking at the world with both eyes wide open and I like the way it looks. My preliminary glasses arrived today. There are still difficulties, but it looks very promising.

The mail included a letter from a medical school classmate whom I cannot remember although his name sounds familiar. He enjoyed the class reunion very much and is feeling sentimental and desirous of increased communication and closeness with old classmates. He regrets the distance and lack of interaction that characterized him as he pursued his busy and satisfying career. He sent this letter to all members of the class; he feels ready to communicate.

Are you ready and what are you ready for? The question drives many people into therapy; a pretty satisfactory technique for delaying action. Fortunately, or perhaps not, we just sort of fall into a lot of things without considering readiness. If you require a high degree of readiness or certainty before you act, you are a cautious soul who delays action, but that may not be enough to prevent things from happening.

I have already alluded to the tension that existed as I was growing up, secondary to my mother's cautiousness and Fred's and my desire to experience life. I felt ready when my mother knew I was not properly prepared to proceed. I did things I knew she felt were unwise or premature. Looking back on it, there was less of a disparity between her view and mine than I felt. She had encouraged me to be independent and to think for myself. She admired assertiveness even though it was upsetting to her when that assertiveness was expressed against her. I mocked what I felt were her excessive concerns about safety, but I learned the lesson that safety was to be considered, not ignored. She wanted my behavior to reflect well on her. I too wanted to be good but mostly I wanted to be my own boss and I was far from ready to leave home and be on my own. Some families pressure the adolescent kids severely to knuckle under or get out; I was not subjected to that kind of domination. It was more a matter of my figuring out when I was ready to do what.

I was ready to smoke when I was ten, a regular smoker when twelve and an addicted cigarette smoker by age fifteen. Dad smoked cigars and pipes, not coffin nails. Mother strongly disapproved, but granted official permission when I was sixteen; the whole neighborhood then had permission. There were never any confrontations about my drinking or having sex; I was too vigilant for that; but mother was very vigilant also and it seems unlikely that she was unaware.

Sex in the '40s and '50s was hot stuff and it did not count if penetration did not occur; pretty funny. Penetration might lead to marriage unless it was perpetrated on an ineligible, in which case it could be risked. That is why out-group people had reputations; you could risk it with an ineligible. So many couples ruined their hot stuff sex lives by getting married and doing what they thought they were supposed to do rather than continuing with what they had been enjoying. Some were forbidden by their religious beliefs from doing, after marriage, what seemed acceptable prior to marriage.

When I went to New York University I met a very nice and very eligible young lady who liked me a lot and almost certainly viewed me as an excellent marriage candidate well before I was ready. Penetration, however slight, was avoided and we separated during the very tense time before I was accepted for medical school. I was ready but not ready; ready for penetration but not for marriage. I was rescued by a terrific ineligible who was attracted to me because I looked so vulnerable, needy and weak as I rode on the Hudson Tubes to school each morning. She was very gentle with me and strengthened me before I went off to Cincinnati.

My new friend was a very poor older woman, about twenty-five, who also went to college in New York City; we commuted each school day. She lived in a run down part of Newark that I could reach by bus; I went there often. One evening, while I was waiting for the bus to take me home, a relative came out of a tavern with a woman on his arm; she was drunk and he did a double take, but then walked past me and they crossed the street. He then returned to greet me. He explained that he was assisting the woman who had become ill, but that she was feeling much better and he would now take me home. I think I told him I had been to the downtown library, but I didn't say when. When we were near my house I asked him to please let me off a block from home and please not tell my parents he had seen me. He reluctantly agreed. Whew, what a relief for both of us. Some confrontations are best avoided; some battles best not fought; not until one is ready.

Ready; get set; go. My timing has worked out pretty well. Those baby birds in the front yard left the nest too soon; a fatal error. Timing is everything.

Caution, the desire to keep options open and the attempt to secure the best possible deal can have a paralyzing effect. The person who is searching for the best possible spouse is called single. Those waiting for the best house to buy are renters. A relative of mine is looking for the best job; he has been supported by his wife for quite a while; chronically unemployed. Is being ready different from being really ready or really really ready or really really really ready? If you feel ready and you don't proceed, consider ambivalence. I am in the process of figuring out what I want. Perhaps I have it.

Early this morning I was awakened by leg cramps. Yesterday I asked Deb to come over and help me put a newspaper mulch around the tomato plants. She did almost all of the work, but I did bend a few times and it was enough to cause difficulty; bending is not my forte. I served a great meal that included my new creation, carrot and sweet potato soup, and an old favorite of Deb's, potato blintzes with sour cream. The sour cream was fat free; surely fat free sour cream is an oxymoron.

It is a perfect day; bright sunshine and cool breezes. Some small squash sprouts have appeared and I put in a few more seeds. Seven rhododendron cuttings remain alive; seven out of twenty would be an excellent result; I hope they persist. The fish are clamoring for food; I have become their servant. The lawn needs mowing and the bushes need pruning and clipping; I'll get to it.

Pat's mother, Mrs. Bush, arrived yesterday and called me from the Smith's. I rushed over to deliver a supply of potato pudding. She was very pleased with my response and so was I. Today Brian Smith graduates from high school and tomorrow Deb and I will join them to celebrate the occasion. I will bake a chocolate pie; it is Brian's favorite. Mrs. Bush will have a birthday soon. I think she will be eighty-nine. She looks stronger than when I last saw her and she sounds enthusiastic about visiting her daughter in Canada. We have a routine; I ask her if she has been behaving herself and she responds that she has no choice.

Senator Dole is on the offensive. While vigorously denying that he will engage in personal attacks, he proclaims that he will bring integrity back to the office of the presidency. The same message is appearing in television spots that show Clinton and Dole but do not speak Dole's name and can therefore be designated as issue oriented and not chargeable to the Dole campaign, which has reached its legal spending limit. That is Republican integrity in action. Both sides can complain about the disparity between words and actions.

I will end this day reading a novel, using my new glasses.

Liar, liar, pants on fire; he doesn't deserve your vote. Substantive issues are used peripherally, but the well orchestrated Republican drumbeat attacks the President's integrity. Grinch Frankly Newrich called him a liar and challenged his interviewer to deny it. This assault will be noticed; it is so loud and persistent. The race is likely to tighten up and become quite exciting. Sometimes one gets what one asked for.

Almost two hours of clipping and mowing took care of more than half of the short version of what needs to be done around the house. I intended to do more after a long cool drink, but it did not refresh me and I decided to be cautious and call it quits on the outside work. It is a very full day with multiple conflicts. One cannot be inside and outside at the same time and I have not figured out how to give my full time and attention to two things at once. Two golf tournaments on television and a terrific novel will keep me on my toes as I recline in bed this lovely spring afternoon.

A large, spicy Indian late supper is better than an alarm clock; I am up before the birds. Last night's celebration of Brian Smith's graduation was very enjoyable and high calorie. I knew all of Pat's relatives and their friends who participated. Repeatedly I was asked when I will go to visit Pat. I was home before the late evening news and asleep before it was over, but remember hearing the results of the basketball game. The party was so pleasant that I did not think about turning on the final elimination game; if anyone else did they did not act on it.

Most of the adults at the party were born in India, trained in some medical field in India and are now working at hospitals in the Washington–Baltimore area. Their children were all born in the United States. We are a nation of immigrants. I heard no political talk unless you count the impact that the rise of health maintenance organizations has had on the practice of psychiatry.

I wore one of my Indian shirts to the party. I bought it in New Delhi in 1956. Connie, Pat's sister, turned its collar for me a few years ago and it looks like new. Many of my shirts are older than most of living humanity. Life is fleeting; shirts last.

Five consecutive days of heavy rains and cold air have been followed by five spectacularly fulgent days with delightful breezes and delicious fragrances. I did another two hours of outside work this Tuesday morning and now I will enjoy the weather from indoors except when I feed the fish and drive to and from the evening bridge game.

Prostate cancer strikes again. A friend, not very old, has been diagnosed and is now assessing treatment options. He seems brave; he plans to enjoy the summer while hormone treatments take effect and treatment decisions are finalized. It is a disease with a very variable course and outcome. My father lived almost twenty-five years after his prostate cancer was diagnosed, but some suffer a ravaging form of the disease. Treatment decisions are predicated on prolonging life and quality of life.

My prostate is much older and sicker than I am and it has been reamed out often but always comes back fighting: bloodied but undeterred. When my urine is bloody, I can tell by looking whether it is from the prostate or higher in the urinary tract. Sexual activity often bloodies me: it may be connected with my taking aspirin. It makes me more susceptible to infection but probably has little to do with cancer. Prostate disease can be a wonderful excuse for giving up sex. Naah. Is it love or prostatitis? When the old man presses for more sex after his young wife has bitterly complained she has already had too much, it does not seem like love. The old joke ends, "If she dies, she dies." Ain' t love grand?!

Last night I stayed up later than usual to finish the bestseller list novel that I started a few days ago. It was offered to me with high recommendation and I enjoyed it a lot, but I wish the seemingly mandatory sex scene had been left out; maybe alluded to rather than detailed. An effort was made to make it beautifully erotic. The effort was not entirely unsuccessful but I found it too deliberate. Great sex is wet, preferably not from blood, not beautiful. Kinky sex is sex where somebody moves. Life can be beautiful, write what you know about, know what you are writing about and try to tell the truth without including all the gory details.

Most of the novel takes place on a ranch in Montana, where, in real life, people who call themselves freemen are still holed up while surrounded by a multitude of FBI agents who have recently cut off their outside source of electricity. Negotiations have been quite careful and slow; the standoff is nearly three months old. The novelist was a screenwriter; that might account for the sex scene—a movie without it is too unlikely. I hope a film can be produced that combines the novel and real life. The hero, a strong, gentle and honorable horseman who must look a lot like Gary Cooper, would be played by Grinch Frankly Newrich who has come out of seclusion and is now ubiquitous. The film would have to wait until after the election for it is now clear that Grinch, frankly, is in charge of the Republican drumbeat. I would like to weave in a third Montana based plot, the Unibomber, but that might be excessive.

Suddenly, without my detecting the awaited bud, the first water lily is open, dressing up the pond in the afternoon sunshine. Anticipation makes such a happening more special.

The most disturbed partnerships I have encountered have been at the bridge table, not in the office. Domination, disdain, chronic and unjustified criticism, threatening hostility and ridicule are displayed in these punishing, destructive partnerships, and these people usually go home together after the game. One could not maintain such an arrangement if the relationship was confined to the bridge table; no one would put up with it.

Destructive partnerships give dependency and interdependency an undeserved bad reputation. Some of the best stuff in my life could be characterized as satisfied dependency, although I have tended to think of it as arrangements I have earned and secured. The culture makes it unpalatable for men to think of themselves as needy or dependent and recent developments subject women to similar standards. Too bad. Psychiatry has tended to promote that negative view of dependency. It is difficult to buck the tide; mistakes are made and then they are perpetuated as part of an orthodoxy that punishes effective disagreement.

There is a big difference between grooming oneself and being groomed. No doubt it has a neurophysiologic basis. My dystonic neck and shoulder discomfort is greatly relieved if someone gently places their hand on my upper back. I can reach the area but my own touch is much less effective. It is difficult to understand but there is no doubt that it is the case; it is the way I am wired. My wiring is now defective but it is the defect that dramatizes the way most of us function. I like living alone and enjoy a variety of solitary activities but for me life is a partnership game: so many pursuits are best with a friendly partner.

The bravery of believing Catholics has always impressed me. They believe that the sacrament of marriage will bind them together forever, through eternity, and still they subject themselves to that sacrament. That takes guts.

The nonword "litiginous" first appeared in my life when I was in medical school and it became part of my vocabulary. It recurred several times in lectures about paranoia that I attended. I have tried to track down its origin, so far unsuccessfully. Someone, in a seminal article about paranoia, used that non word or the printer somehow added the letter N and the word litigious became the long perpetuated non word, litiginous. I used the non word during a therapy session with a lawyer. Pretty funny. It can be very difficult to correct mistakes, even petty little mistakes that are inconsequential. It is the important mistakes, those that impact severely on people, that are the most resistant to change. It takes a naïf (the emperor has no clothes) or a hero to effect the important changes.

This morning, for the first time since my cataract surgery six weeks ago, I walked to the game at Andrews. The excellent weather continues, as predicted, and it was my plan to walk but I got out of bed so late that I barely had time to include it. I woke up before dawn and was enjoying the comfort of relaxed muscles when I fell back to sleep and did not reawaken until an hour before game time. I am retired; it is entirely acceptable that a retired person be that relaxed, but it still surprises me.

I forgot my glasses and warned my partner that I did not seem to be firing on all cylinders. Then I went on to play better than usual. We probably won.

There is an atrium with a fish pond at the Andrews Officers' Club; it contains about a dozen large, colorful fish, probably koi. This morning I put in my dibs for a couple of fry if they are forthcoming. My fish show some interesting patterns but none are as variegated and amusing as those at the club. The club manager said they were not expecting but was willing to take my name and telephone number, just in case. I'll keep an eye on those fish. No, I'll keep my eyes on those fish; they now both work.

Patients have been calling. They are surprised by my retirement greeting: "Aloha." I must refrain from being too jolly; they often are having some difficulty when they call and do not make it clear up front. I listen and sometimes recommend someone they might call for evaluation and treatment. Some of us are not very lucky.

This retired person is up before dawn and at the computer on a humid Sunday morning. I feel busy.

Yesterday morning M called and asked how I am doing. I invited her to come over for a food package and a look at the computer. I recommended that she read my latest file to get up to date on what I've been doing lately. Before she left she printed most of what I have written. It is the first time it has been printed; that makes it seem more substantial even though it contains so many old weather reports. M wondered if she would learn additional things about me and we agreed, not much. Perhaps a few details. Her food package included a loaf of bread, ribs, carrot and sweet potato soup, cassoulet and three kinds of cake. I was making baked spaghetti when she arrived and meant to give her some of the previous batch but I forgot.

In the afternoon Wes and I played in the Alcatel Worldwide Bridge Contest. Thousands of people all over the world play the same bridge hands at the same time; there will be worldwide and regional winners. Omar Sharif had played and analyzed all the hands and a booklet with his analysis was distributed after the game. The contest attracts most of the world's best players; that increases the fun. Wes and I had a below average game. We got off to an unlucky start and things never improved.

The French tennis matches preempted regular television programs and I watched, but my favorite show was on early and I caught it, too. Exciting uncertainty does not require interesting content; there is not much going on politically that has not been thoroughly analyzed. There is now only a pretense of dealing with substance. It is pure theater. I suppose the television personalities who ask the questions would lose their jobs if they only asked a question when there was doubt about how it would be answered.

Still more contact with and reminders about patients; it would be more accurate to call them former patients. A long distance call was followed by a check, paying a five-year-old bill; a partnership agreement honored. It is time for me to write a few letters telling people that I am managing well and asking them to pay their bills and let me know how they are doing. Old partners pop up: a book written, a book reviewed, an editorial piece, legal difficulties, an obituary and friendly telephone calls. Yes, retired, but still connected and pleased about it.

The gladiators battled hard yesterday. The results were lopsided in the main events. There was little doubt about the outcome in the golf tournament and the basketball game but the men's finals of the French tennis tournament remained in doubt until it ended. It was like a prizefight with a knockout puncher who might do his stuff and win right up to the last minute, no matter how far behind he is. Something similar to that is going on with Clinton and Dole: Clinton may have a weak chin and Dole may have a knockout punch.

Two medical school classmates called to say hello. We had exchanged greetings before that "let us communicate more" letter that was sent to all of us. All calls carry some ominous overtones; maybe something bad happened to precipitate this call. There was some news of difficulties. One of our most admired classmates, who must be near eighty, has been having a hard time and may be near death. Al, who called me, may go to visit him. Al's father died last month at age ninety-two. Both of his parents were very kind to me when I was a medical student. Mr. Freemond had arranged a department store charge account for Ria and me so we could buy a few sticks of furniture when we were newlyweds. He also had someone help us select good quality things. The solid maple dining table and chairs are still in fine condition and used daily at Deb's house

The other call was from Buddy, Yale Piker, who was a classmate, and we were also in psychiatric residency together. He is having great difficulty with his vision but that did not prevent him and his wife from going on a recent group birding expedition. Once when I called him I heard his wife, Mitzi, in the background, ask if there was bad news. It was just a friendly call.

Punam and Bippi, Pat's friends and former neighbors, invited Mrs. Bush, the Smiths, Deb and me for an Indian dinner and last evening we enjoyed the company and the food and celebrated Mrs. Bush's eighty-ninth birthday. Pat called while we were eating. It was Selena's birthday yesterday. It is likely that Pat is lonely.

It is seven weeks since the surgery and my eye has healed well. Dr. Tran examined me and wrote a prescription for new glasses today. He enjoys telling me that my corrected vision will not be better than normal and I like hearing it; it has not happened yet but it will.

Senator Dole resigned from the senate during the noon news so that most of the panegyrics and his farewell address could be covered live by the networks. I am not criticizing his deliberate tactics, only recognizing that what is happening is well planned and choreographed. Encomiums can be worth a lot even though they too often resemble meconium. There was much high praise and mutual admiration in the senate today.

Former Colorado governor Richard Lamm, a Democrat, has been quite visible and vocal as he indicates his willingness to seek the presidency if he is nominated by the Ross Perot financed Reform Party. He feels his chances of winning the election are quite slim and he regrets that his candidacy would probably benefit the Republicans, but he strongly asserts that the major parties are not properly addressing the deficit or the importance of greatly curtailing entitlements. He said out loud that entitlements must be cut ten times more than is currently being proposed. It was only four years ago that Ross Perot proclaimed that the American people would gladly pay an additional twenty-five cents tax on a gallon of gasoline to bring the deficit under control. I remember hoping that he was correct. Maybe we are reaching the point where we will do it, though not gladly.

The rain and heat have encouraged the garden. I make no effort to eat the apples or cherries; they are for the birds and squirrels. I overplant tomatoes, squash and peppers so there will be plenty for me and for the insects and animals. This year there may not be enough to go around: a mole has undermined many of the tomato plants and there are rabbits, large and small. It is the first time a mole has joined the harvest, but live and let live.

Squash seeds are sprouting. There is room for at least another dozen plants. The habanero pepper seedlings remain very small; it will be lucky if they bear fruit. The seven surviving rhododendron cuttings are fading; maybe one or two will make it through to next year. The lifeline is a slender thread. The fish thrive. I must avoid killing them with manna; bread crumbs from heaven can be fatal.

The Republican ultraconservatives did not prevail yesterday in Virginia. John Warner was renominated and will run to keep his senate seat; his victory was clear-cut. Virginia is probably the home base and political center of the religious right, so Senator Warner's decisive win was unexpected.

Citizen Dole was aggressively attacking today. The drumbeat is the same. He tells us that he is the good guy who will bring back the desirable things he claims have been lost under our Democratic president. He plays the good cop and leaves the direct and explicit excoriation of President Clinton to his bad cop compatriots. He is attracting a great deal of positive interest and coverage.

I called Bob Wilkinson, my civilian primary physician and friend whom I have not seen recently, this afternoon and told him that I almost dropped in on him today when I drove near his office on the way to Bethesda. We briefly exchanged news. I did not say that the trip through town was to complete a new last will and testament. We want to get together for dinner. Soon. His wife has not been well and that makes things difficult for them. His office mate was out of the office in connection with the impending death of a very elderly mother. I am repeatedly referring to death and dying; so much of it is going around.

Steven called to make sure I will be going to the house by Bodkin Creek on Father's Day, this coming Sunday. He is not working next week so we may finally get together for some sightseeing and lunch in our capital city. We will decide about it on Sunday. It has been a very long time since I have eaten Chinese food for lunch. Insufficient Chinese food can cause Jewish people to become disoriented. Washington had a kosher Chinese restaurant to insure the well-being of the local orthodox Jews. An infusion of Singapore noodles could be therapeutic: a treat and a treatment.

This unintentional punster awakened before the birds with the realization that I asserted that insufficient oriental food can cause one to be dis/orient/ate/d. It would have been cuter if I had done it with awareness but the unconscious too can be very creative. A dreamer told me of sitting before a table laden with desserts, just desserts. This morning I combined thoughts from my asleep, doze and awake states. I was to attend a Chinese banquet that would take place in a hall covered with g(u)ilt. The occasion would begin with spicy poontang and end with just desserts. It sounds like a slice of life. I am in charge, maybe, of what I tell about my thoughts and behavior. I am still trying to be authentic but I would like to be amusing, not boring. I would like to please without sleaze.

This week the Washington area bridge clubs have been participating in a tournament in clubs. At several clubs the same bridge hands are played simultaneously. When a session has ended, the scores from the entire area are compared. Each club has a winning pair and there is one pair that wins overall for the area. This afternoon Bill and I won overall. We have had a successful partnership. It takes skill and luck; we had both today.

Protective gear is the phrase I thought when I awakened dreaming this morning. I was jogging, perhaps walking, in the street facing oncoming traffic that almost ran me down. Streetwalking can be dangerous. Protective gear is essential these days to avoid serious difficulty but protective gear is not enough; good judgment is required. For almost twenty-five years I spent a lot of time on the streets of Washington as I commuted to and from my office on my own power; jogging until my dystonia exacerbated and then walking. Except for tripping once or twice, I suffered no serious or dangerous incidents; people were sort of friendly or they ignored me. I knew there was some danger and I hoped that my routine would stay about the same if I were mugged; it never happened.

During the last ten years of my practice I routinely carried an adjustable, metal, medical type cane when I walked the streets. I used it primarily as a swagger stick. It was a part of my street identity. It identified me as someone who probably had a condition but could adequately protect himself; it was a potential weapon. About a year ago I put the cane in the back of my car and stopped using it. Of course there are some dangers out there but for me most of the dangers come from within. I believe that is the case for most of us. What we do to ourselves can be pathetic. We damage and disadvantage ourselves both emotionally and physically. In this wonderful free country of ours we have very many options, including the right to give ourselves a difficult time.

What would be protective gear at a Chinese banquet? A bib or a napkin would be useful but one might still get egg on his face. Now that I have said it I realize that these thoughts were precipitated by a recent event. Someone whom I respect and admire has splattered himself embarrassingly; it is a source of discomfort for him and those who care about him. It is a sequence that occurs thousands of times a day but has little impact on outsiders except perhaps to give them a chuckle. Imperfections make news. If you are caught with your pants down you are em/bare/ass/ed and it becomes a source of entertainment. Maybe I'll keep my pants on; maybe not. So far I have never been mugged. Whatever I do, I hope I will be able to laugh about it with you and that no one suffers greatly.

The FBI has no egg on its face today. After eighty-one days the standoff with the freemen in Montana ended without violence or deceit. It is a victory for all of us. Next we will see how the rest of our system deals with these rogues. There is still plenty of time for things to go wrong.

A new poll indicates that Dole has surged from down twenty to down six. The criticism of the Clinton White House continues with vigor and with the persistent suggestion that President Clinton is not trustworthy. The administration too often has egg on its face and an appearance of amateurism. When we are presented with a Keystone Cops sequence, the Republicans question motives and the legality of the comedy. It doesn't look good.

The National Basketball Association shows a series of advertisements in which a fan says, "I love this game." I love the game, too, but this is the last week of spring and the Bulls and the Sonics are still battling for the championship in a best of seven final. Last night I once again fell asleep before the game had ended; superb athletes doing their thing was not enough to keep me from the sandman. My athletic nose was up and running before the early morning news, so it was a while before I learned that the championship series is not over. If they're not careful the old season will abut upon or overlap the new season. Then it will resemble our system of political campaigning: long, drawn out, never ending and a weird combination of interesting and tedious.

The newspaper reports several stories about religious matters that have considerable political overtones. The Southern Baptists have asserted their strong evangelical mission and their policy of proselytizing Jews to accept Jesus Christ as the messiah. In Africa black Africans are kidnapping still blacker Africans, enslaving them and converting them and their children to Islam. Those Montana freemen are in custody but do not recognize the state or federal government, and they hate and blame those who do not share their fundamentalist Christian beliefs for ruining their America.

God tells the orthodox how to behave and God's word must be followed. Mankind has been subjected to many plagues, none worse than those based on the word of God as heard by zealots. There is no virus more virulent than religious orthodoxy. Amen.

No matter which scheme one adheres to about how it came about, it is a wonderful world, full of amazing and beautiful things. A blue dragonfly hovering above the pond displays both qualities. A butterfly drinks while perched on the edge of the pond. If one counts all, and why not, there are many millions of living creatures with me as I survey the side yard and consider doing a bit of garden work.

Lazybones prevailed; no work done today. Except for that annoying double image when I watch television while reclining, it was a comfortable and relaxing afternoon with golf, bowling, boxing and a smattering of odds and ends.

The Russian people are voting today. A Russian observer stated that he finds little difference between Democrats and Republicans in the United States; we will be about the same no matter who wins our election in November. But he states that the Russian people will probably be choosing a system of government today. I hope he is correct about the United States. I fear totalitarianism and I believe that orthodoxy breeds totalitarianism.

A slow motion secret suicide pact is in process. The Democrats and the Republicans have given up on murdering each other; they are too inept to succeed at that and are putting their ineptitude to use toward self-destruction. It is a shameful performance but it is also funny. I enjoy jokes about President Clinton but it frightens me that he may become a joke. Citizen Dole is coming across as a man desperate to avoid the grave. Their henchmen, I mean associates, can't be as dumb or corrupt as they seem.

Our spectacle was out of the center ring, briefly, as Yeltsin danced his way to a near tie with Zyuganov in an eight man presidential election in Russia. The Russian system requires a runoff election. If it happens it will be a big improvement over bloody coups. Our process is getting bloody but the wounds are self-inflicted.

Father's Day at the creek was very pleasant. I was relaxed in spirit but my body remained uncomfortably dystonic. Although I avoided almost all physical chores and spent the entire weekend sitting or reclining, I felt very tired and ached severely when I reached home last evening before sunset. Moaning helped a lot so I did a lot of it. I slept through most of the game but was aware of the postgame hubbub; the Bulls finally clinched the championship and the basketball season (there must be gods) is ended.

My Father's Day loot came from each of the kids but it is clear that the choices were made in accordance with Deb's perception of what I needed or wanted. She is watching after me. A couple of items are for use in the shower. I guess I'd better start washing more often. It has not felt necessary in retirement; maybe it smells necessary.

Kelly and David were cheerful and friendly yesterday. Kelly had the world's sweetest disposition until she developed severe, recurring middle ear infections during her second year. Now she is comfortable and sociable again. David avoided direct eye contact with people outside the nuclear family during his first year. Steven characterized him as shy. Dave is very verbal and aware of things that are potentially threatening to him and his. A few weeks ago he was quite interested in my rheumy right eye and yesterday he called my attention to a small spot of dried blood on my cheek. The world is a threatening place where we strive to protect ourselves.

We ate no blue crab yesterday. There was some talk about the recently imposed restrictions on both commercial and recreational crabbers. The Chesapeake has been polluted and overfished until nearly depleted and yet it is sweet smelling and seems to be swarming with life both above and below the water. I am already looking forward to my next visit to Bodkin Creek.

Washington is such a special place; so interesting, important and simultaneously a cosmopolitan city and a small town. It is one of the few places where you can be run over and killed by a car driven by a foreign diplomat while you are standing on the sidewalk. It is a place where the rules are for other people and yet strong, sophisticated powerhouses are chewed up, spit out and forgotten. Nowhere do people work harder. Nowhere is the agenda more important. We have impressive monuments to the past; people and events. History is written here; some of it sticks to the facts. This is the power center of the world. Try to believe me, I am telling the truth.

One false move and you are dead. Well, not always, even though it so often feels that way. The big boys know that the opposition is out there gunning for them and yet they proceed as if invulnerable. They are the major players in the big game and they keep right on trucking. It is a great show.

So often the men and women behind the scenes are very admirable, dedicated and extremely hard working ideologues. They are patriotic citizens and they often sacrifice a lot as they try to do their job. They are the people I have had the pleasure of working with in our capital city, a very superior bunch. I am trying to remind myself that behind the spectacle, behind the three-ring circus, serious work goes on. Whether it is addressed or not, it does go on.

One false move in the garden and you are dead. There is rabbit fur on the lawn. A deluge soaked the area last night and has invigorated the lawn. I have watered the tomato plants regularly and they had a recent growth spurt and have flowered. That will very likely lead to tomato salad in the last week of July. The tomato mavens are about two weeks ahead of me. Rain is predicted for the next few days. The area will be lush.

Man does not live by bread alone, but add a bit of peanut butter, a cup of tea and a friendly partner, then life can be beautiful. Yeast bread is my speciality; I bake it regularly, eat it daily and give it to grateful recipients often.

Every step in the breadmaking process makes a significant difference in the final product, so it is likely that each batch will be different. It is important to remember that no matter how a loaf turns out, that is the way it is supposed to be. Let no one intimidate you! If you forget the salt the loaf will be tasteless; don't let other people eat it. Grind it up and feed it to the fish or use it to thicken soups and gravies. Start an earthworm farm; the worms will love it. Do not forget the salt.

The quantity of bread will depend on the amount of water you use. I like to make a big batch that results in eight to ten loaves. You might prefer to make much smaller amounts and bake more often. There are many recipes available and infinite small variations. My preference is a mixed grain loaf. I will take you through the process and identify some of the variations you might try.

Start the dough two days before you plan to bake it. Get a large stainless steel soup pot, twelve- or sixteen-quart size; it will accommodate a lot of dough. I keep the pot covered most of the time but it is not necessary and the end product will vary more if you leave it uncovered, for yeast that lives in your house will float into the pot, grow and alter the taste. Put the salt on the counter near the pot so you won't forget it. You will use one tablespoon of salt for each quart of water. Put three quarts of room temperature water in the pot and add one package of yeast and a handful of sugar. Get a wooden spoon with a handle that just barely fits in the pot and stir; you want the sugar and yeast to dissolve. Add one cup of whole wheat flour and three cups of rye flour and stir. You can use more or less of these flours but I recommend at least a half cup of whole wheat and at least one cup of rye. Cover the pot, or not, and go away for a while. You can stir as often as suits you but it is not necessary.

Have fifteen pounds of bread flour available. Unbleached flour or any wheat flour can be used but bread flour is best. Return to the pot after four or five hours and add flour and stir until you have a thin gruel. Add a bit more flour and another handful of sugar, stir again and go away.

While you are gone the yeast is growing rapidly; that is why the salt has not yet been added for it would inhibit the growth of the yeast. Stir it every few hours if you enjoy fiddling around. Return to the pot on day two, give it a stir and make some critical decisions. If you want the bread to be pareve or if you want to feed someone with lactose intolerance, do not add milk. Powdered milk will add protein and change the texture of the loaf. A cup of barely dissolved powdered milk could be added now and probably all of the lactose would be converted and gone by baking time, but the loaf would not be pareve. Now it is time to add flavorings, spices, herbs, coloring, nuts, raisins or whatever. You might like the effect of molasses, cocoa or coffee. I prefer to add a finely chopped onion and a teaspoon of ground fennel. Caraway seeds or fennel seeds are very nice too. Add what you decide to add, stir and add flour until you have a thick pea soup consistency. Go away.

During the afternoon or evening of day two dissolve four tablespoons of salt in a quart of warm water, add it to the pot and stir well. Add a cup or more of flavorless liquid oil and stir well again. Now add flour while stirring until you have a thick porridge consistency. Remove the wooden spoon and scrape it clean into the pot; no waste, please. Let the spongy dough rest for a while and you are ready to get the dough into final consistency.

Put two large stainless steel mixing bowls on the counter next to the pot and put a couple of pounds of flour in the bowl closest to the pot. Late in the evening before baking day or early on the morning of baking, stir the pot with a large ladle and put several ladlefuls from the pot onto the flour in the mixing bowl. Add enough from the pot to make a very thick, sticky mass and then mix it by hand and add flour until the mass is not wet and you can pick it up without its falling apart or sticking to your hands. Clean your hands by flouring them. Flour the mass of dough lightly, transfer it to the adjacent bowl and cover it with plastic; a plastic shopping bag is suitable. Now repeat the process: flour into the bowl, ladle the mixture onto the flour, mix it and flour it until it holds together and does not stick to your hands, transfer it to the previous batch in the second bowl and cover it with plastic. Keep repeating the process until the soup pot is empty and clean; no waste, please.

Let the dough rise for an hour or two. It will be more moist than when you left it. Press it down and add small amounts of flour until it is not very sticky. Cover it and let it rise for another thirty minutes. Now the dough is ready to be formed into loaves.

This single batch of dough can result in a variety of finished breads depending on many factors. The size of the piece is important; rolls will be different from small loaves and loaf size will make for differences. The container the dough is baked in is important and the absence of a container is also significant. The length of time the dough rises after it is shaped and the oven temperature will affect the finished product. It is not too late to include fillings or toppings as each piece is formed. If you decide that you like baking and you do it repeatedly, I hope you will become innovative.

Gather four non-stick loaf pans, an air-cushion cookie sheet and a container half the size of the loaf pan. Use a dough cutter or a knife to cut off a piece of dough about the size of the half-a-loaf container and knead it with floured hands until it is smooth and elastic. Put that piece into a loaf pan and mash it down with your knuckles. Cover the pan with plastic and put it aside at room temperature. Repeat the process until all four loaf pans are full. See how much dough you have left. If it is less than will fill two loaf pans, shape it into one oblong loaf and put it in the middle of the cookie sheet. If it is more than that, divide it in half, shape two oblong loaves and place them on the sheet so they are not likely to meet when they rise. Cover the sheet with plastic.

You do not know how long you want the dough to rise, nor do I. It will make a difference. This dough contains a lot of yeast and could be baked right away. I prefer to let it rise for at least thirty minutes.

If you have a standard two rack oven, put one rack at the lowest level and the other at the middle level and preheat to 375 degrees. Uncover the loaves and put several diagonal slashes in each loaf using a serrated knife. Place the cookie sheet on the lowest level and the loaf pans above. Bake the bread until it is golden brown; it will be done in an hour or less. When they are adequately baked, each loaf will sound hollow when you strike it with your knuckles; careful, they are hot. Unpan (a perfectly fine word even though it is not in the dictionary) the loaves and let them cool on racks. Do not, under the penalty of a severe reprimand, eat any of this bread until it is almost at room temperature. Enjoy the process and enjoy the product.

I am relieved that I have at last revealed my love affair with bread.

Last evening my bridge partner did not show up; a missed communication. I returned home and was dozing and then asleep long before the bridge game was over. It still surprises me that I fatigue so easily and so quickly and yet I am refreshed by a few hours' sleep. Now I am up early, hours before Steven's expected arrival. It has been a very long time since just the two of us have been together for any purpose. The rain should not deter us from our planned trip into the city to see a bit of the Smithsonian and have a meal in Chinatown.

Flash floods are all around the area and a drowning has occurred. Steve drove through heavy rains coming here but we did not get wet as we enjoyed our excursion into town. The National Museum of American History, a very interesting part of the Smithsonian Institution, kept us busy for two hours and incited our appetite for Chinese food. A late lunch was spicy, delicious and ethnically correct for our needs.

Steve read what I have written in the past week and we sat and talked. We could not remember when we last were together without others. Perhaps this was the first time; it's possible. We talked about medical work, his professional future, my retirement and the role reversal that is occurring. We talked about women: his, mine and ours. He asked if I had a title for what I am writing and I told him it would include something about partnerships.

The body tends to remember. Our immune system will react to foreign substances and we may experience a strong and sometimes dangerous response to subsequent exposure. The nervous system reacts and adjusts to substances that reach it and then goes through a readjustment when those substances are gone. Citizen Dole took a lot of flack this week for telling us that not everyone who smokes becomes addicted. He did not say that nicotine is highly addictive; our country was founded on the tobacco trade and he has personally benefited greatly from the largess of the tobacco lobby. While most of us are addicted to nicotine, citizen Dole seems to be habituated to the tobacco lobby.

As usual, there is room for disagreement about facts and thoughtful people come to different conclusions about reality. It seems likely that the world was round a few hundred years ago when those who thought about it concluded it was flat. The consensus can change rapidly or not. Individuals may feel stuck with old beliefs and behavior or might conclude that they are adhering to their personal preference. The concerned other will say that you are hooked, addicted, habituated; you respond that you are doing what you do because you prefer it and you will stop when you no longer want to continue.

I try to stay aware of my arrogance, catch myself and behave as if humble; sometimes I succeed. My arrogance is so great that I do not believe I am arrogant, yet I know that I am. These grand feelings of power, ability and control can cause a lot of trouble. If it were not for the trouble, there would be no reason to rein them in. We do not characterize behavior or substances as addictive unless we recognize a downside, trouble, associated with them.

What I am calling arrogance someone else might call hopefulness. One is hopeful that no accident will occur while safety devices are not used; hopeful that one's genetic heritage will keep one from developing cancer secondary to smoking; hopeful that this time one can drink alcohol without going on a prolonged drunk; hopeful that one's unfaithfulness will go undetected; hopeful that one's amazing body will manage well if the prescribed medication is skipped; hopeful that one will score well without practicing or studying; hopeful that the clever system will beat the odds this time and forever more. Believing and hoping are not quite the same. If you believe you are going to win the lottery you are delusional. If you believe you will go to heaven if you pray and follow the rules, you are just another arrogant human being.

Every time I decided I had finally beaten my cigarette smoking habit, I started smoking again. It was funny and sad: funny because I had warned others about this phenomenon a hundred times and sad because it impinged on my grandiosity. It has been very difficult for me to put aside my arrogance and surrender. The twelve step people know all about surrender; I have worked with them often through the years. My personal program has only one step: surrender. It is unlikely that I will ever complete step one; too arrogant.

The conventional wisdom tells us that people lack self-esteem; they must learn that they are wonderful and take control of their lives. That view is the other side of what I have been addressing. There is every reason for us to experience fear and trembling; we have so little control and are often buffeted about by circumstances. Much of the structure we create is an attempt to keep us from disorganizing anxiety. At the same time we are so smart and creative and we are not helpless. There are small but often very important things we can do to influence what happens to us as we take our trip. A lot of what happens in psychotherapy has to do with coming to terms with our limitations while identifying the small but important things we can do to make our life more the way we say we want our life to be. Small changes can make for large differences.

Maybe I will become a preacher; too late, I am already preaching.

There is a coterie of women who play regularly in the Thursday and Friday bridge games I attend and who smoke in the back room or off to the side when there is no back room. They are a clique primarily because they smoke between rounds during a bridge session and smoking is prohibited in the main playing area. That combination brings them together frequently. They stink the place up only a little since the air flow at both games is quite adequate. A couple of them are aware of my strong feelings about their persistent addictive behavior; I have tried with some success to avoid being a nag, condemnatory or obnoxious, but it is likely that I have been unjustifiably intrusive. They are not interested in my view or my experience and it is probable that people who care a lot about them are on their case just as I was chronically on Ria's case. I occasionally feel angry about it but in an ongoing way I find it sad. The result is so often pitiable. Smart, effective people spoil the last part of their lives. These women offer each other a lot of support to continue their smoking. I doubt that they intend to encourage each other to continue smoking, but they do, and that is saddest of all. One of these days I may join them for a fix; I hope it does not happen. Not all friendly partnerships are constructive.

No one is perfect but some aspire. Give it up.

Bridge and cooking have kept me busy. My efforts to work in the yard are feeble and unsuccessful; the lawn needs my attention. The heavy rains have filled the pond, soaked the ground and caused damage and deaths. Since yesterday I have cooked large quantities of sweet potatoes, baked beans, nectarine cake and fish cakes. The freezer is nearly full again. If the storms knock out the electricity I will be in trouble.

This morning I was startled when I realized I was reading without glasses. It is easier and better with glasses but the new lens works very well for reading, without assistance. I have stopped bringing glasses to bridge and can see the cards and keep score easily. With glasses both eyes seem the same and without glasses one eye can see what the other cannot. That is a very big improvement.

The bridge hands were quite interesting today. My partner, Tully, and I played well; it is very likely that we won. His table presence reminds me greatly of myself thirty years ago, very slow and deliberate. He is my regular Friday partner. I have been looking around for another man with whom I might establish a weekly bridge partnership. Three of the five sessions I play most weeks are with a steady partner.

Each year around the Independence Day holiday, the Northern Virginia and Washington Area bridge leagues hold a joint tournament in Virginia. It is the only time that I play in Virginia. I boycotted their games because they continued to allow smoking in the playing areas for far too long. Even now the arrangements they make concerning smoking are barely acceptable. On the first evening of the tournament, July 1, I will play in a team event with three people who live near me. We agreed to drive to the game in one car and it is Rava who decided to be the driver. After the decision I remembered that it might be a problem since she is a smoker and I do not want to ride with her if she will smoke while I am in the car. I mentioned it to Tully and suggested we might drive separately. Today I brought it up with Rava, essentially asking her to decide if it was too much of an imposition to have her desist from smoking while I am in the car. I brought it up in what I intended to be a conciliatory manner and explained that it would be very easy for us to use two cars. She seemed displeased that I brought it up and I don't believe she made a decision about it.

It would have been much better if I had anticipated this problem. I initiated the idea that we all drive in one car; it was not a good idea. Rava is a very smart and alert person who is quite aware of my reaction to the smoking clique. It is not appropriate for me to try to influence her or impose upon her for her own sake and it would have been much better if I had protected myself up front and avoided this unnecessary confrontation. Now I am suspicious about my motives. I like and admire her; she is a generous person, an excellent cook and a fine bridge player. Why was I not more aware that I would create this unnecessary tension? I am a troublemaker.

My mailbox is by the street, at the end of the front walk. Its stand is not firmly secured; I periodically straighten it and readjust its height. It's an old problem. This morning I dreamed that an Indian man was where the mailbox is but it was not there. He tried to sell me an elaborate, black mailbox that was shaped like a birdhouse. It was large and had a sturdy base but was very low to the ground. It had a tag saying it cost $177 but the man said I could have it for $117. I thought that was too expensive; I declined without bargaining. Now that is a very sexy dream. When you understand it, please explain it to me.

The goldfish seem to be on automatic; what they do has an uncomplicated, reflex quality, not at all convoluted. I have all the same basic drives that those fish have but I get so fussy and complicated as I express or inhibit the expression of those drives. My standards intrude and I go through a cost analysis before I proceed. Both the standards and the intricacies of the cost analysis are largely unknown to me and yet I am significantly ruled by them.

A man went to the doctor because his penis had turned green. The doctor recommended amputation but the man sought a second opinion. He received the same advice but felt a third opinion was worth seeking. The third doctor examined him carefully and told him there was no need for surgery; it would fall off by itself.

So far I have not changed the subject. Whether it is firmly rooted and straight or not, do I want or need a new box for my mail? If I want it, what price am I willing to pay and why am I unwilling to negotiate a fair price? Would I be more inclined to consider it if, no matter what color, it was guaranteed to be free of gilt? There are so many questions and so few answers. I do not mind the questions but I want some dreams with more answers. Lazybones.

My spelling has always been defective. Dream scenes make creative use of misspelling, words that sound alike, slang and idiom. I am very pleased with today's dream. It helps me to confront my concerns, ambivalence and uncertainty about what I want and how much it is worth to me. My maleness is more than sexual but sex has been a very important part of it and I am reluctant to give it up. Perhaps it is too costly.

Frankly, really, honestly, you know that no matter what verbal tricks I use to reinforce the verity of what I tell you, I might be lying. Frankly, Really, Honestly and You Know were the guests interviewed on this Sunday morning's news/entertainment shows. The questions asked and the opinions of the questioners were much more telling than the responses given by the guests. The Clinton White House is now suspected of being not only amateurish and sleazy but also dangerously mean spirited and guilty of a serious breech of security and illegal invasion of privacy. The Special Counsel has been authorized to investigate charges that FBI files were illegally obtained by White House staff for nefarious purposes. It is enough to make this Democrat cry even if it does not reverse the strong tide in favor of Clinton over Dole. It reeks.

Yesterday I mowed the grass until I was ready to collapse; not exactly good judgment but better than continuing until I collapsed. Today I went out to finish the job and it was done, almost certainly by my neighbor; I will check on that later. This house has given me great pleasure and, as with sex, I am reluctant to give it up. My position has been that when I am no longer able to maintain the place, including mowing the lawn, I will move out and sell. It is a stance that does not make much sense. I am moving away from it; the stance, not the house. It made sense for me to retire because of the nature of my work and the isolation and lack of supervision that went with it. There is no need for me to give up this place while I continue to enjoy it so much. One of these days I will decide to hire someone to mow the grass. There are many chores connected with the house that I have never done and it has pleased me that I have avoided them. Evolving standards and compromise make sense.

Enjoyment comes easily for me; I have been accused of being too easily pleased. No member of my nuclear family has perceived me as a marshmallow; I sometimes hold to severe standards. Tough standards can be inhibiting. It is rare for people to give up an activity because they fail to meet their own high standard of enjoyment. Enjoyment is not usually perceived as performance and it is performance that characteristically concerns people; performance anxiety is rampant. I worked with a sexually inexperienced thirty-year-old man who was taken on by a woman eager to train him. He was concerned about how he would perform. In the course of his training he had a grand insight. He reported to me that being good at sex was similar to being good at going to the opera; you are good at it if you enjoy it a lot. That goes for a lot of things. It is worth remembering.

A fellow named Peter Mingent
Was of urine quite incontinent
After psychotherapy he still wets the floor
But it bothers him no more
You can tell where he's been by the scent

I awakened with that limerick version of an old joke. Our culture remains so ambivalent about psychiatry and psychiatrists. Psychotherapy is often seen as an unnecessary self-indulgence with great destructive potential; it might erode one's standards or free one from important constraints. Insurance coverage for the treatment of mental and emotional illness is almost always less adequate than for all other categories of illness. The health maintenance organizations often deny treatment for emotional difficulties, and when treatment is authorized, psychotherapy is not provided by psychiatrists or physicians. They want to spend as little as possible and would use the clerical staff as therapists if they could get away with it.

Once again I have come back to the medical care problem. All sides agree that the cost of medical care must be dealt with and that it is desirable that high quality care be available. Beyond that, the talk is mostly political rhetoric. The focus now is determined by the Republican drum beat: character, character, character. It is likely to remain that way since it is their best chance for success. Maybe substantive matters will be put aside until after the election. I was pleased to read that several large physician groups, the American Psychiatric Association included, have registered their preference for a single-payer system.

A fierce storm with strong winds reached here right after Deb called to say she was on her way for Monday dinner. I anticipated that there would be a power failure and managed to have everything cooked and hot. We ate by flashlight. Power was restored before dessert. We spoke to my brother and his wife and made plans for them to stay with me over the first weekend in August. The school year has ended but Fred is finishing up odds and ends and will be working through this week. Their summer weekend visit has become a regular event that I enjoy and appreciate. I use my condition as an excuse to avoid travel. Phyllis and Fred are more energetic and generous.

It is too wet and dark to assess the storm damage; it can wait until tomorrow.

My good luck continues. The destructive storm included two tornadoes, one of which passed a couple of miles from my house. Houses were destroyed and thousands of homes are still without electricity. My damage is limited to a few broken tomato plants. The electricity was off for about an hour. I did nothing special to protect myself from the storm. Yes, I stayed indoors but that was it; no hiding in the cellar or an interior room as was advised. Arrogance, not ignorance or stupidity.

I remember reading a newspaper account some years ago, perhaps true, about a southern town that was struck by a tornado and suffered extensive destruction limited to an all-white part of the community. Soon thereafter a second tornado struck and again the damage was limited to the all-white part of the town. A community leader was enraged and was reputed to have said that if God did not even things up soon he would form a vigilante party and see to it himself. It stuck in his craw that his God had not demonstrated that He was on his side. True or not, that is a beautiful story of religious faith as practiced throughout the world. If your gods do not perform in a timely fashion, help them along.

The faithful may feel obligated to act for their deity. Today in Saudi Arabia a five-thousand-pound bomb was detonated on the perimeter of an American military housing enclave. Preliminary reports indicate that several hundred American troops were injured and twenty were killed. No doubt this dastardly deed, this obscene act of terrorism, was perpetrated by devout religious fundamentalists who did their duty as it had been revealed to them. Eventually the devout killers or someone like them will be arrested, tried and beheaded by the devout Saudi Arabian authorities and we in America will say little or nothing about the way the arrest and trial were conducted or about cruel and unusual punishment. If the American Civil Liberties Union says anything, Dole will blame Clinton's character.

Weather report: It is a glorious day, warm and sunny with low humidity. The tomato plants, some broken by the storm, have had another stupendous growth spurt and have escaped from their stakes. The storm would not have damaged them at all if they had not been tied to those stakes. If there is a direct correlation between tomato production and the size and vigor of the plants, there will be a very successful harvest. The squash plants are doing well also and show several blossoms. I am hopeful that the puny habanero pepper plants will survive and produce but I was optimistic about those rhododendron cuttings and they have faded.

The robins are queuing up around the black cherry tree waiting for the myriad morsels to ripen. Lots can still go wrong but it looks as if all species will soon be eating off the land around here. Someone should speak to the squirrels and try to get them to stop sampling things before they are ripe. The cats, I fear, have already had rabbit stew and bluebird pie.

I went all around the house, covering the entire yard, with the long-handled pruning shears that Deb loaned me. It turned into more of an observation tour than a work project. After about ten minutes of actual work my arms felt weak, my hands trembled and my back got quirky. I accomplished less than a quarter of what I had intended. It was the dead miniature leaf Japanese maple that did me in; too heavy for the shears. I will saw it down eventually and replace it if any of the seeds I planted germinate and survive. The secluded bed of Japanese maple seeds probably contains over one hundred seeds and one, only one, has sprouted so far. Last year there were many sprouts but no survivors.

President Clinton did not look like he was smirking; he was appropriately grim as he spoke of mourning and condolences to be followed by pursuit and punishment. Nineteen Americans are dead from the bombing and our vulnerability to further deadly terrorist assault is acknowledged.

Today's *Washington Post* reports that the Republicans have been soft-pedaling their criticism of Clinton's patriotism because they have learned that he worked as a secret operative for our government while he was a student overseas. Things get stranger and stranger.

Last evening I watched a rerun program about the 1960s quiz show scandal and its aftermath. The congressional hearings revealed with certainty the extent to which the viewing public had been defrauded. It is estimated that over one hundred people had perjured themselves when they testified under oath before the New York grand jury. None of them went to jail but many offenders were severely affected by the undeniable revelations and the public was confronted with its naiveté. Perhaps it prepared us a bit for other important instances of lying and disingenuousness by respected authority.

Sometimes it just seems too dangerous to tell the truth, the whole truth and nothing but. The truth will often have an unwanted effect far beyond one's self and in ways that seem unfair, disloyal and potentially quite disruptive. Today there is still a strong tendency to lie to preserve the illusion that the authority is not corrupt. After the truth is told and the corruption revealed, we are usually reminded that only God is perfect.

I am trying to record my truth. Several times I have felt blocked by the need to avoid revealing someone else's truth. In telling about myself I have told important private things about others, but I have been selective and careful about how I involve the living and all who might expect me to keep their confidences.

When working with people I would often ask, "What is the matter with the truth?" Most of the time there is nothing the matter with the truth. It is as if the evil spirits will get you if they can find you. The sooner the truth is told the greater the likelihood that it will be built upon constructively. Why doesn't it feel that way? Maybe it is connected with an awareness that the authority or the important other may be corrupt and untrustworthy. When that is the case the truth is likely to reveal it sooner rather than later; surely that is desirable.

When I was interviewing for acceptance into the psychiatric residency program at Cincinnati General Hospital, I said something that led an interviewer to say, "Do you mean that if we knew all about you we would reject you?" He was correct; I felt vulnerable, was showing my best face and did not feel that I was being authentic. I missed the opportunity of being accepted into the program while trusting them with the authentic me. Cautiousness with a very important partner is a put-down of your partner and yourself.

So, I have not revealed the dream I had last night after watching the program about the quiz show scandal. Why am I not more trusting? It feels too risky; it reveals too much about too many.

A PR firm is gearing up to begin a postconvention blitz for candidate Dole; he has nearly disappeared during this past week and when seen he was not at all convincing or inspiring. President and Mrs. Clinton, in contrast, are prominently seen and are the focus of books, articles, investigations and commentaries; almost all are disparaging. The reaction to the President's words following the terrorist bombing has been muted. Events have kept him highly visible every day; he looks and behaves properly presidential. The polls suggest that the voters believe he is a liar and they will vote for him. A lot can happen in four months.

When I returned home this afternoon from bridging and feasting at the Friday morning game, there was a message from Bill W; not the original Bill W who founded Alcoholics Anonymous but someone I worked with for many years. He and his wife, with the help of haircut money, put all of my family through school; I have told them that and thanked them for it many times. He called to check up on me and he left questions about my progress in bridge, cooking, reading and writing. I have finished the strawberry and the peach preserves they gave to me when I retired but I have not yet completed the two philosophy books. I hope to see them around the Christmas holidays; for several years I have gone to their home, sat by their Christmas tree, acknowledged their cat and chatted while eating cookies and drinking tea. We are closely related by life. I saw them every month or so during the last few years of my practice; Mrs. W was the primary patient but they both attended our sessions and they both took a daily Antabuse tablet to help them avoid consuming alcohol. Mrs. W took additional medications that helped control troubling symptoms that ended her work career and disrupted her life.

Our meetings during the last decade were held primarily so that I could eyeball them; actually see them, watch them interact and assess the need for further intervention. Both of them wanted our meetings and I felt they were indicated and helped avert serious relapse. They knew that I was readily available and that they could reach me by telephone when in need; it happened many times. A videotape of one of our meetings might seem strange. They often brought me a bag of fresh greens and Mrs. W usually ate frozen yogurt and had a large drink. We laughed a lot and she would ask if I was testing her sense of humor. We talked a great deal about cooking and food. Mr. W, now a retired bureaucrat, should have been a Jesuit or a philosophy professor. He often brought articles for me to read, things he found interesting or provocative. Several times I cautioned them to avoid letting anyone know how much fun we had; Blue Cross would not understand.

What we had—the continuity of care, the ready availability of service and the freedom to use the format that best suits the patient's needs and leads to a trusting therapeutic relationship—will soon be available only to those who will pay for it without medical insurance. For better or for worse, it has been decided that the system can not afford such care and the voices, mine included, that advocate such care and claim it is the most economical now and in the long run are derided. People won't even know what they are missing. Blue Cross and many others just do not understand. They will do things on the cheap and it will lead to very costly complications. Live and learn.

This evening I spoke to Mr. and Mrs. W and told them that their call incited me to write about us. Mrs. W has developed some new symptoms from her new medications and she complained that her visits with the psychiatrist are very brief. They are managing well. I hope the new treatment program will be adequate to keep them stabilized and avoid the need for a hospitalization; a hospitalization of even one or two days would be more costly than a year of properly managed outpatient treatment, and the cost to the patient and family is much more than monetary.

Mother took me to downtown Newark on a shopping trip when I was a young boy. Fred was not with us; I was about six. We went by bus and I think we went to Bamberger's department store and to Woolworth. Mother purchased a couple of small house plants and it was my job to hold one of those plants as we rode home on the bus. That is one of my earliest memories; it may have happened. The plant I carried was a common tropical corn plant, *Dracaena fragrans messangeana*, still a popular indoor plant. I see them everywhere, large and small, but I have never seen one in bloom. That small specimen from Woolworth lived and it grew at about the same rate that I grew but it finally outstripped me and brushed the ceiling. The plant was then given to Uncle Jack; he had a Hudson dealership and the plant was placed in the showroom where it continued to grow and where it bloomed. The newspaper found that newsworthy and included a picture of the blooming plant. It was claimed that such plants flower only once in a century.

My corn plant must be at least twenty years old. It was kept in the living room for some time; there is a water stain on the hardwood floor to prove it. Since Ria left I have kept it in the kitchen, except in summer and early fall when I leave it on the back porch. It has been a slow grower and is barely three feet tall after all these years. Perhaps it is stunted because of the care I provide. When it is indoors I water it every week or two or if it looks very dry. When it is on the back porch I water it much more often, every three or four days. When I watered it yesterday I noticed a foot-long stem covered with multiple clusters of small buds was growing from the top of the plant. It droops into the plant rather than standing upright atop the plant but I had previously noticed no sign at all of this long extrusion so I suspect it grew very rapidly. My corn plant is about to flower. Shall I call the newspapers?

Instead of playing bridge I got a lot done in the garden this afternoon with a big boost from Deb. All the squash is planted and most of the mulching is done. Most of the pruning and sawing for this season is accomplished. This is the best week to start rhododendron cuttings; that is still before me. Soon I' ll be picking tomatoes.

Tomorrow Deb and Darrel will come for dinner. Darrel was once Deb' s boss and they have become close friends. I like him and have not seen him for over a year so I suggested he join us here for dinner. I plan to show off by presenting seven courses. Everything is ready except the potato salad; it will be done before I go to bed.

The attention to the White House in connection with its security procedures, staffing and main occupants has me worried. Although some of the reports are not at all credible, some serious charges are quite believable and will, no doubt, be investigated extensively. The tide can turn. I suspect that the public will figure out before the candidates do that getting elected is not what is most important; it will not happen until after the election.

The handling of the FBI files by White House staff is most bothersome to me. It smacks of the breaking into a psychiatrist' s files some years ago but this time no breaking in was required, they just ordered up the dirt they wanted. I hope I am wrong about it but it seems likely that is what happened and unlikely that it will go unpunished. Even if it was done out of immaturity or ignorance, I hope that any illegality will be punished.

When I was doing reserve duty in the 1960s, I became aware of a deplorable incident. A young physician went to the commissary while in uniform and was reprimanded by another officer for looking unmilitary and disreputable. He was quite untidy and he needed a haircut by any ordinary military standard. He was reported and did not like it. He proceeded to obtain the medical records of the complainant without having any medical need for those records. He made no use of any information in those records but obtaining the records was improper, threatening and offensive. His action became known and he was in trouble again, and for a much more serious offense. What is to be done when an individual behaves in an immature manner and then compounds his distressing act with something much worse, an act of professional malpractice? I believe it would be excessive to end the medical career of a young physician for such behavior but surely he deserves punishment that will impress him and he requires a period of supervision and oversight. That guy was not working at the White House. Despite history, we want and expect fairness and competence at high levels.

It was my intention to serve many small courses for dinner to permit me to show off without overfeeding; I failed. Eliminating the soup helped a little but we ate until stuffed. There were no new creations, just old standbys. It was good to see Darrel again. We talked a bit and I sent them off. I' m ready for sleep.

Bob and Elizabeth Dole appeared on both the Today Show and the Regis and Cathy Lee Show this morning. They looked good and were well received. Some votes were gained and none were lost. All those little bits and pieces add up. The Republicans have effected a change in momentum that keeps their hopes alive and they will try hard to build on it. They are trying to represent that the undecided voter has a choice between Eagle Scout and Huck Finn.

In the 1930s my parents belonged to the Republican Club in Newark. I remember it as a social club that produced a musical show periodically. Mother sang in some of those shows and I think she made some effort to obtain work singing on the radio early in the Depression when money was very scarce. When I was three or four Mother took me with her when she went to New York City for an audition. I remember, or perhaps I remember hearing, that afterwards we went to Dinty Moore's famous restaurant for lunch. I was an immaculate, very well behaved and mannerly child; so much so that Dinty Moore was impressed and treated us to dessert. It probably happened; appearances were very important to Mother and I got the message.

The members of the Republican Club sometimes worked for the Republican Party and they voted Republican on the city and state level but all the people I knew voted for and felt a strong allegiance to

President Roosevelt. He was a heroic figure who transcended party affiliation for the people in my parish. I had no awareness of how vulnerable people felt or the extent to which they viewed President Roosevelt as their savior. I suspect that some of them worked at the polling places as Republicans and then voted for that Democrat. I learned that we were Democrats when I was very small and membership in the Republican Club was irrelevant. The reasoning then, clichéd or not, was that the Democratic Party represented the have-nots and the Republican Party was the party of those who have and who want to keep down and exclude outsiders. Things have not changed very much. I do not know why we did not belong to the Democratic Club. Maybe it did not produce periodic musicals.

This evening the Mid-Atlantic 4th of July Regional Bridge Tournament begins and the first event is a KO team event. Our team will go in two cars; I hope that division does not keep us from playing well as a team.

Feelings of vulnerability are so very prevalent and justified. When children and young adults behave as if invulnerable, attempts are made to educate them, persuade them or even physically restrain them. It's a balancing act for each of us to figure out what behavior makes sense, what is too dangerous and when something is so important that it is worth doing even though it puts one at great risk. Safe and dangerous are often correlated with good and evil. Intergenerational conflicts often pivot around these matters and most often it is the parents who are on the side of safety; they think they are doing their duty. They teach good and evil and safe and dangerous and then they try to enforce what they have taught. It is difficult to get it right; too much or too little is usual and leaves the parents open to criticism and the kids at risk. Nobody is perfect.

Magic, religion and superstition can help us to proceed with a little less trepidation as we take our parlous trip. I reported early on that I thank God and knock on wood that I am not religious or superstitious. I repeat it in case it was not offensive enough the first time. There is so little we can do to protect ourselves and those we care about; we do not want to miss a trick.

There is a Christian notion that I like a lot, but it leads me to think of most people as unchristian; the idea that all people are God's children. Parents somehow fail to teach it in word or in deed. It is a wonderful notion; so civilized and generous. In practice we behave as if we are not at all special but just another animal species with a small pack mentality. Those family values are, in practice, exclusionary and competitive; you are part of the family or you are an outsider to be dealt with as a threat. Remember, the family that preys together eats together.

The archbishop of Milwaukee has written that the Wisconsin Welfare reform proposal that has attracted so much praise and support is not in keeping with Catholic social teaching; it abandons children and is more Welfare repeal than it is Welfare reform. He is asserting the disparity between doctrine and practice; another example of Christian behavior being found too expensive.

Montana does not have an exclusive on the dangerous, alienated militia groups. Twelve people have been arrested in Arizona for a variety of offenses that center around violence against the government, against us. They have family values and they do not include us in their family.

The bridge tournament is in progress; it has occupied me and exhausted me for the past four days. I will play today and tomorrow but rest on Sunday. We were eliminated in the first round of the KO event but I have fared better in the seniors competitions. Tully and I were fourth overall in a ninety-one pairs competition and yesterday Rose and I had a fine first session section top but I fizzled in the afternoon. My usual hotel air bronchitis began on the second day and persists; it is my version of Legionnaires' disease. The seniors events suit me very well: they start early, have a brief break between sessions and are ended before 7 o'clock. Last night I was in bed reading before sundown and watched the fireworks and news before falling asleep.

Rose has asked me to play with her more often. She is a good player and an excellent artist. I indicated that I am looking for some new regular partnerships with men, not women. She felt that was not fair; I felt no need to explain or defend my decision. If I don't succeed at establishing a new partnership with a man, I suppose I will relent and seek out a woman.

Everyone is an outspoken patriot, especially the candidates. All photo opportunities are accepted; children, hats and animals make excellent props. The silliness of it all is ignored; both word and gesture are so staged and yet required. First, be visible.

It can be very stressful to be under constant surveillance unless you are certain it is a benevolent watchfulness. My mother used to keep a close eye on me and I know I am still often in the thoughts of others who wish me well; that is far different from being watched constantly by people and devices and not knowing why it is happening. I have worked with people who are occupied with and greatly influenced by the focus on their activities. If the FBI has aerial cameras and other sophisticated electronic equipment trained on you, it can dramatically affect your life. If aliens are studying you it is likely their observations will feel intrusive and influence your decisions. It is difficult enough if you know that God or Santa Claus is watching you while you sit on the toilet, and you are pretty sure they wish you well.

Some of us are raised to follow special standards and values; we feel best about ourselves when we adhere to the party line. Others are taught to follow the rules to avoid punishment. Probably a combination of the two are at work in all of us. What would I do if I thought I could get away with it? Not much, I hope. How would I spend the rest of my life if I thought the world was coming to an end soon? I know the answer to that question. I am one of the now generation; for me it is now or never. There is very little time left for me and, come to think of it, for you also. My plan is to keep doing approximately what I am doing. I am under surveillance by people whom I care about and that influences my behavior.

What would I do if I believed the government had me under constant observation? Would I conclude it was benign or would I find it threatening or offensive? It would be difficult to ignore no matter why it was being done. I suspect it would keep me occupied and would alter the course of my life. It might even affect my bridge game; heaven forbid. Wait a minute, it might improve my game. Maybe they could tell me where I put the garden gloves and my door key. Last evening after the game my car battery was dead. After a jump start I got home and left the car at a nearby gas station where I did not leave my house key; it has disappeared and it is likely that it and the gloves are hiding together.

Your FBI file might make interesting reading.

The tournament ends tomorrow but it is over for me; fatigue and bronchitis have done me in. It was a lot of work and a lot of fun. When I arrived home this evening I spotted the lost key by the breezeway door. Why didn't they also return the gloves?

It is the wee hours of Sunday morning and I am wide awake after about four hours of sleep. Coughing and congestion kept me from resting comfortably in bed. The tournament was great fun but I am confronted again with my reduced endurance. Today I hope to recuperate, follow my regular routine and do a bit of yard work. Maybe I'll finish reading the philosophy of Plato; I'm nearly through it and find it tedious. I keep trying to read the classics but it has been tough going. It is the same for me with poetry: I much prefer to hear it. Then it makes more sense; I feel and understand it better. Shakespeare challenged and defeated me, yet my favorite play is *A Midsummer Night's Dream*. I have seen it performed six or seven times; it seemed very different on each occasion but always captured the magical craziness of love and lust.

When people tell me they are in love, I feel their pain and hope it doesn't happen to me. It seems to thrive on uncertainty and lack of fulfillment; it has such an urgent quality and feeds on doubt. It does not survive secure capture although it can evolve into a lasting caring that I find more desirable. Pity those who repeatedly seek the thrill of being in love; they do a lot of chasing around and find their lasting relationships lack the thrill they desire. It is the chase and the capture that is thrilling, not the having. How inconvenient. So many people are fiercely inclined to behave in ways they themselves feel are unworthy and deserving of punishment; how unlucky for them.

The traditional rules often recognize our biological tendencies and guide us in ways that are in the best interest of our species—not always, or at least with disagreement about what is best. Those traditional rules have great value for so many; it is threatening when new rules are proposed. Too many choices. When I was in the Philippines, Catholics were permitted to eat meat on all days, Fridays included, but many American Catholics felt uncomfortable about it and would not indulge themselves even after their priest assured them there was no rule against it. I felt disappointed when a colleague I admired told me that Filipinos were not "real Catholics." He required firm, unchanging rules. This is the stuff that is driving our politics and will determine which lever we pull in November.

It has been a relaxing, warm and sunny day. I mowed most of the lawn but put off all other physical work; there is more that needs doing. There is still time for some reading.

Knowledge: what the philosopher seeks and what is revealed to the religious. I did not intend to write a religious screed but I have had little positive to say about religion. I am aware that many religious are thoughtful seekers of knowledge and truth. I am admiring of and grateful for the humanitarian work done through religious organizations. I am pleased that people find comfort and hope through their religious activities and beliefs. I deplore sacrifice, crusades and wars performed in the name of God. I am appalled when believers are required to impose their religion on others. I am amused when attempts are made to logically prove and support religious tenets.

Last night I finished reading the Modern Library edition of *The Philosophy of Plato*. Once again it was tough going for me and I did not read every word; the Socratic method is interesting yet tedious. This morning I will start *Introduction to Aristotle*; it won't be the first time. In my freshman year at New York University, I was required to write a paper disputing Saint Thomas Aquinas's proof, including Aristotle's unmoved mover, that God exists. When I'm given a book, I try to read it.

It is a page turner; I've been turning the pages very rapidly. My good intentions flew out the window and I've found excuses to avoid a meaningful read. This afternoon I went shopping for bedroom curtains; I was reaching deep with that one. There is work to be done in the garden but it is too hot and humid for that. I will do some more speed reading until it's time to leave for the bridge game at Andrews.

Hurricane warnings to the south, drought in the west and a spectacular, low humidity day in Maryland; perfect weather for starting new rhododendron cuttings. There are three survivors from last year. Now there are twenty new cuttings in place. If we live long enough I'll replace some of the dead oriental hollies with those rhododendrons; it's part of my master plan.

The tropical corn plant is in full blossom and very fragrant. There is a striking similarity between the tiny racemes of the black cherry tree and the single large flowering stem of the corn plant. Instead of thousands of one-inch racemes, the corn plant has one two-foot-long structure that shares shape, color and fragrance with the racemes. I wonder if it will fruit; the million black cherries will soon be ripe.

Citizen Dole could not attend the week-long meeting of the NAACP; he had a prior commitment to attend the All Star Game last night, a flagrant snub. President Clinton held meetings with Israel's prime minister and let the American people know that he would like to be reelected. Governor Lamm has been on the talk shows where he asks us to think of the major parties as corrupted and morally bankrupt. He wants us to give up our entitlements and indicates he will help us to do that if we elect him. Fat chance. The stock market has been gyrating. The pundits predict that all important stuff will soon be put aside and our focus will be on the Olympics. More circus.

An asteroid crashed into the Gulf of Mexico and caused dramatic weather changes and the extinction of many species of plants and animals. Yesterday there was a huge volcanic explosion in New Zealand but I saw no mention of it in today's newspaper.

Late yesterday afternoon I was invited to the Behres' for bridge and dinner. Their middle son, Mike, a family practitioner, visits with them every second or third Wednesday; they often golf together. Herb's back acted up so they canceled the golf and I became a fourth for bridge. It was the first time in about twenty years that Mike and I conversed; it confirmed how very much we and this area have changed. When he was finishing his family practice residency at the University of Maryland Hospital in Baltimore, a small community north of Washington and west of Baltimore, Middletown, recruited him and some colleagues to start a rural practice in their underserved area. A medical building was constructed as part of the community's effort to entice these young physicians and they were won over. Mike has practiced there since then and his practice is very different now because the area and the medical resources have developed so rapidly.

Beautiful Maryland still has many country areas but the population has increased greatly, the road system has become excellent and the Washington–Baltimore area is now part of an East Coast megalopolis that contains very few isolated or difficult to reach enclaves. Mike no longer has a small-town rural practice. Now it is very similar to a big city practice: specialists are readily available and most hospital care is provided by others. Much has been lost and much has been gained. So many dramatic changes have occurred in one generation. On those rare occasions when I pine for the past, I remind myself that, on balance, things are better than ever before. Even with all its mumbo jumbo and ethnic strife, the world is more rational and safer. I like clean water and indoor toilets; may they spread throughout the world for all who want them. I read that more people have died of malaria than from all wars. Only one hundred years ago people fled the Washington area during the summer to avoid malaria, yellow fever and dysentery. Let's not yearn too much for the past.

The era of effective antibiotics began shortly before I started medical school. Diagnostics and therapeutics have changed dramatically for the better in the last fifty years; those changes have been accompanied by skyrocketing costs. Physicians are compensated for performing diagnostic and therapeutic work; that is how they earn money. The system hardly recognizes preventive medicine; it pays for procedures.

This past week there has been a furor in the District of Columbia about contaminated water. Additional chlorine has been added to the water in an effort to clean up the corroded old water pipes. Modernizing the system will be very expensive and little of the money spent will go to physicians. I believe that the most important improvements in health and quality of life have resulted not from treatment but from preventive measures. Effective sewage treatment, clean water and vaccination have benefited us more than all the treatment procedures combined.

Yesterday the Surgeon General issued a report on exercise and health. It reviewed many studies and it recommends that some regular exercise be a part of one's routine because it has so many health benefits. Last year the Surgeon General issued a report on nutrition and health. It provided nutritional guidelines that would, if followed, prevent disease. Three decades ago the Surgeon General issued a report on smoking and health. There is so little we can do to protect ourselves but that little can be extremely important in influencing the course of life. Go for it.

Ross Perot insists his Reform Party is not about him but he will accept the will of the people if they choose him to represent the party. He did not promote the candidacy of Richard Lamm, who recently reiterated that he would like to be selected as the Reform Party presidential candidate. It has a humorous quality; he supports the will of the people who will select him. He is a determined man who is used to getting his way but he has an eccentric, clownish quality that makes him more a spoiler than a serious contender. His message has been successfully communicated: important change is necessary. The devil is in the details.

Hurricane Bertha is rushing north and will soon be over Adam's house. Steve and his family have been somewhere in the islands all week and are not yet home. It is a big, dangerous storm and it is headed here. Whose side will the gods be on? If I am on the wrong side, there may be serious injury and damage to me and those I care about. If I am lucky it might cure my bronchitis; the cough is wearing me out.

In Northern Ireland Protestants marched in a parade through Catholic neighborhoods as they do each year to assert their hatred and dominance and to insure that they will continue to be despised and resented. I think all of them claim to worship Jesus Christ. Ain't religion grand? Whose side are you on?

Hurricane Bertha has brushed Maryland, lost power and gone up the East Coast. The heavy rains filled my pond and things were blown around; there was little serious damage. This morning, while I was out,

Steve called to say their trip home took twenty-two hours but all are well. Lucky. Why do people vacation in the tropics during the summer?

Wes and I had our regular Saturday afternoon game at the Washington Bridge Center. Near the end of the session we played against Charleen who was close friends with Ria until they had a falling out that I believe was connected with their conflicting views about my motives when Ria and I separated. Charleen has a light-hearted air and a good sense of humor. I'll have to ask her about what happened between her and Ria.

The midget married the tall lady. Somebody put him up to it. Some partnerships seem strange and unlikely but most of them make a lot of sense; we settle for what seems equitable after failing to secure a great bargain. We are our own marriage brokers and we are almost as good at it as a professional. Congress is trying to pass a law that would limit marriage to a union between one woman and one man. There was a lot of speechifying about avoiding things that would undermine this conception of traditional marriage. It was a repeat of the sanctity of marriage debates and it reinforced, from my prejudiced point of view, that when the Republicans proclaim the importance of personal responsibility, they lie; their interest is the promotion of fundamentalist notions. Personal responsibility is acceptable to them only in their narrow framework of good and evil. Of course, they do not mean any of it; they are just after the votes.

There is a resurgence of fundamentalism throughout the world. The proof is in the bombings.

Citizen Dole has been diagnosed as suffering from a severe case of foot in mouth disease. It is of unknown etiology and is not related to mad cow disease, although both conditions are usually fatal. There is no specific treatment but quarantine has been imposed by Dr. Republican Handlers and all spontaneous productions will be prohibited. A strict regime of carefully scripted encyclicals has been prescribed for its palliative effect. This observer believes we are seeing the latest development in the Clinton–Dole mutual suicide pact.

Who has the moral high ground? Everyone claims it; me, too. My feelings of righteousness do not inhibit my tendency to proscribe orthodoxy and vilify its coercive practitioners. I'm afraid of them and it is unlikely that they are afraid of me. I would like it if others did things my way but I feel no urgency to impose my standards on others. I do things my way while they do things as their gods require. Heaven protect me from those religious storm troopers.

President Clinton expressed his expectation that the American people will judge him on his actions as president and not on accusations and innuendo. He keeps telling us that he is doing a good job and he wants us to reelect him. No matter what he says, that is what I hear.

Ross Perot is getting a lot of coverage again. He frustrates seasoned interviewers by sticking to his script and declining interruptions. He is driven by his love of the American people. If we hear his words and respond, we will be saved. The savior has a Texas twang and speaks the truth. Our fate is in our own hands, free will; he will not coerce us.

Fred and Phyllis will be here two weeks from Friday. My plan is to make dinner for them Friday night, take them and others to the Officers' Club Saturday night and make brunch for a few on Sunday morning. Very little work is required but it was very hot so I put on the air conditioner and the stove and did a lot of cooking. The freezer is already full but I was running short on some of my best products. I intended to make a noodle pudding and a potato pudding but wound up also making a beef brisket, a boneless leg of lamb and bean soup. It took most of yesterday and all of this morning, a lot of work. All will be fine because I will use the "that is the way it is supposed to be" method; I had too much going on at once, however, and made some unintended deviations. I forgot the sugar in the noodle pudding and will correct for that by applying apricot jam when it is served. The lamb was nearly done when it was time for me to leave for the evening bridge game, so I shut off the stove and left the lamb in the oven. It did not burn but it came close; most prefer well done. The brisket in onion gravy is just right and the bean soup, made from a conglomeration of things, including brisket gravy, is excellent and entirely unreproducible.

It took seven weeks for the reading glasses prescribed at Walter Reed Medical Center to arrive but arrive they did yesterday afternoon. I tried them at once by starting to read a magazine while lying in bed. I did not like them and after a few minutes I started to feel ill. I hope it was due to the glasses; I will take them with me when I see Dr. Tran on Friday. My head tremor became worse and I felt seasick. I was back to my usual abnormal state in about twenty minutes. I have suffered several bouts of true vertigo through the years but I have never been seasick. Two years ago Adam and his family took me on my first cruise. We hit such rough seas that free medication was made available. I was knocked about and had a couple of bruises and abrasions but I took no medication and suffered no seasickness. Those are powerfully unsatisfactory glasses, if it was the glasses.

Richard Lamm continues to contend to be the Reform Party's nominee for the presidency of our country. He insists he is not being capricious; he believes that many in Ross Perot's party are ready to accept new leadership and that Perot is not the best candidate. Perot furthered our assessment of his credibility by declaring he thinks Lamm's candidacy is just wonderful.

Charleen had no recollection of the two exchanges I asked her about; no big surprise since they occurred over a dozen years ago.

Recently, for perhaps the tenth time, the huge natural earthen dam that separated the Mediterranean Sea from the Atlantic Ocean buckled and ruptured from extraordinary water pressure and millions of tons of water rushed into the Atlantic. Things finally settled down to the presently existing equilibrium. Last night Mark Russell had two half-hour political comedy specials on television. They began at 9 o'clock and I watched for at least a minute before I fell asleep. It was not until this morning that I learned that a Trans World Airlines plane on its way to Paris exploded last evening just off Long Island with the resulting death of two hundred and thirty people. The latter catastrophe has dominated the news. We receive frequent updates and are told many details about those who died and about their surviving loved ones.

A Pennsylvania town of about five thousand was severely disrupted by the plane crash: sixteen teenagers and five of their chaperons were killed. They were all wonderful, talented and much loved. All of the dead people who have been identified on television were good people; if there were any unworthy or less than admirable people on board, we are not being told about them. President Clinton reported that every effort will be made to determine the cause of the crash. He asked that we not jump to conclusions and he requested that we include the deceased and their survivors in our prayers. I will think about them and about the pain and disruption experienced by the survivors.

The media bombardment concerning the plane crash has been extensive, persistent and mostly inane. Surely we are given what they think we want; that is even sadder than the crash itself. In so many areas we are given what will sell and we keep on getting it until we stop buying it. The best salesperson wins the prize. The line between professionalism and self-serving pandering can be unclear and debatable.

Our political process may be readying us to make needed changes soon and without great upheaval. The debate has changed in important ways. We don't want to be like Canada where patients are put on a list and wait for a magnetic resonance imaging examination, but there is something abhorrent about our system that includes television advertisements encouraging people to come in for an anxiety-free MRI on their whim and without inconvenience—and almost always paid for by medical insurance.

The opening ceremony of the Olympics is in process. There is much discussion about security measures at the Olympics, in air travel and for federal officials and buildings. Recent bombings have exacerbated our awareness of our vulnerability and we focus on a narrow aspect of what endangers us. It is a great opportunity for security systems salespeople. It diverts us from the recommendations made in the reports from the Surgeon General. We go for the quick and easy. Nobody is perfect.

It is natural phenomena that will get most of us in the end, not fruitcake bombers. I went to the ophthalmologist this morning and reported that I was very pleased with my vision. The new reading glasses from Walter Reed will be put aside and Dr. Tran will see me in three months to make sure there is no negative reaction to the artificial lens. The cataract, a natural phenomenon, is removed and does not endanger me. Next I went to Dr. Zottl, my dentist, and complained that the right upper molar discomfort I reported last December persists. He accommodatingly found a cavity there and another elsewhere. I will see him again next week to have those natural phenomena repaired; they won't do me in. I'm being deceptive; I believe that all things are natural: fruitcake bombers, bombs, what we do to ourselves, Styrofoam cups and tutti-frutti ice cream are included. Even unnatural acts. Artifacts are as natural as dinosaur tracks.

Severe thunderstorms and a tornado swept through the area early this evening. Homes were damaged and three people were hospitalized. In China flooding displaced over a million people and almost one thousand people have been killed. Once again I did not take security measures; I stayed upstairs rather than repairing to the basement. I wonder how many of those killed in China had sufficient warning to move to high ground.

The dangerous weather has passed. It is calm over the East Coast. The massive search and investigation continues off Long Island. The accumulating evidence is not yet conclusive but the experts suspect an explosive device caused the plane crash. A parade of relatives, friends and associates of the deceased has appeared on television and many hours have been devoted to discussions about our vulnerability and how we will deal with it. We are fascinated with close to home tragedies and we hardly notice massive disruptions and death in China or Bangladesh. What a bunch we are. We have family values.

This is a most spectacular July weekend with cool temperatures, low humidity and pleasant breezes, perfect for spending some time at Bodkin Creek. That is where I'm headed this lovely Sunday afternoon but not until I've watched the political shows; they began early this morning.

Several conservative columnists have started a cannibalistic feeding frenzy; they are throwing a seventy-third birthday dinner for Bob Dole and he is their intended main course. Those bloody Republicans may eat him alive.

It was delightful at Bodkin Creek, almost perfect, but whoever painted the sky did not do such a great job for it had an artificial look. While I lounged in the shade, schmoozed and snoozed, others swam, played ball, boated into the bay, fed the ducks, scrambled around on the jungle gym, built sand castles, sunbathed and did odds and ends of work around the grounds. I helped a bit in the preparation of the picnic dinner and I contributed a large loaf of bread, a chocolate pound cake and a hearty appetite. After dinner Kelly took off her bathing suit and paraded around naked. I told her to put on a hat.

Deb did the driving from her house to the creek and back to her house so, except for about thirty minutes of mowing the grass, my day was restful and sedentary. Nevertheless, after unsuccessfully trying to reach Pat, I fell asleep a few minutes after eight and awoke, groggy, before ten. I reached Pat; she had returned from a three day visit with relatives in Fort Lauderdale. Soon after the call I was asleep again. My nose was up this morning well before dawn so I got up too, made some seasoned rice for tonight's dinner and resumed this reportage.

Today the Earth is being ravaged by floods; many homes were destroyed in Canada and there is despair in China. Ten thousand Japanese, mostly schoolchildren, are ill with food poisoning and some have died. The source of the infection remains unknown. People are massacring each other in Africa to keep in practice and to make sure they retain their tribal hatreds. All of this is happening today. We remain focused on the efforts to recover the TWA crash victims and on resolving the uncertainties about the cause of the crash. It is likely that more people died this past week than in any other week; there are so many more of us lately.

Here in beautiful Maryland the birds, mostly robins, are feasting on black cherries; they swarm about my backyard tree and create a minor tumult as they tear the cherries loose from their stems. I am enjoying it almost as much as they are. My own harvest is not far behind. So far I have eaten one small squash from the garden. The crape myrtle is now in full bloom and that is a sure sign that the local tomatoes will soon be ready. I'm ready for them. It's summertime and the living is easy; easier for some of us than for others. What a lucky guy I am.

Grinch Frankly Newrich tells us that he smoked marijuana while in college but that he is sorry about it and knows it was wrong. He deplores the cavalier way that some White House staff dismiss their history of drug use. It's nice to have him back in the thick of the political battle again; I missed him. He is the cornerstone in the foundation of the Republican revolution; a brick if ever there was one.

We enjoy another idyllic summer afternoon. I am the least active of the fauna that live here. The pond area is very beautiful and gives me great satisfaction. The goldfish rush to me as I approach with the manna they now expect. Small, intensely blue dragonflies hover above the water and occasionally alight on the reeds and lily pads; they are probably depositing their eggs in the water but I have not observed it happening. There were no butterflies as I watched; too bad, I enjoy seeing them drink from the edge of the pond and find it as amazing as anything I have encountered. Away from the pond, in the back of the house by the vegetable patch, the bees pollinate the squash blossoms, a rabbit nibbles dandelion leaves and the birds continue their assault on the black cherry tree.

In addition to observing the local activity, I have read the newspaper, bought groceries, started a batch of bread, watched the Olympics and successfully swatted a mosquito. Yesterday I started reading Honoré De Balzac's *Old Goriot* and I intend to read more of it today. It is not so safe and peaceful everywhere on our planet. Torrential rains continue to flood large areas around the Yangtze River in China where millions of people have been displaced and are in great danger. In East Timor the Indonesian invaders continue to kill off the indigenous population; they have religious differences. In Burundi and Rwanda the slaughter continues and there is little reason to expect that the Tutsis and the Hutus will end their cycles of mass murder. Here the focus remains on the TWA crash, its victims and its cause. What happens in faraway places interests us only to the extent that it threatens us; I'm included. Natural phenomena abound.

Everything gets incorporated into the political process. President Clinton appeared at the main events where he performed his duties in effective fashion. The number one main event for the past nine days has been the TWA crash; it dominates the news and has led to a serious reappraisal of air travel security. It was predicted that politics would take a back seat to the Olympics but not even the Olympic medal count and the TWA body count can stop the clamor of the political parties for our attention and our support. They are willing to fool us if we insist.

All the current congressional activity has been identified as part of the wooing of the electorate. Both the Welfare reform bill and the medical insurance reform bill are much more efforts to court us than efforts to improve our lives or correct important defects in current programs. We have established a strange, neurotic partnership that no longer serves us well but we make little effort to break out of the arrangement and we do not trust the alternatives that have been presented. There is an eerie sense of stability and predictability that accompanies these disturbed arrangements and tends to perpetuate them; so much like a bad marriage or any other neurotic partnership. Efforts to establish constructive dialogue to improve the arrangement are viewed as potentially too disruptive, so we stick with the devil we know.

A pipe bomb exploded early this Saturday morning at the Olympic Centennial Park. It was discovered before it exploded but still killed two and injured over one hundred who were attending a rock concert. A warning call was received just prior to the explosion and the authorities have classified the explosion as an act of terrorism. That sounds right to me. Yesterday in Iraq a powerful bomb exploded in a building just after Saddam Hussein left; he was not hurt. It is pretty difficult to prevent such incidents if the perpetrators are sufficiently motivated.

Terrorism is deplorable but it is a drop in the bucket in that it makes the world only a little bit more dangerous. One person's terrorism is another's important political statement made out of weakness. If freedom fighters view themselves as terrorists, they are probably proud of it and eager to gain sufficient strength to support different, more effective modes of gaining their ends.

Please remember that I feel optimistic about our near future. The world is less dangerous and people are more rational; it's a combination that warrants hopefulness. We will eventually be another extinct species but the next ten thousand years look pretty good to me.

There is a frog in the pond, at least one; I saw it this morning when I fed the fish. My pond is at least half a mile from the closest standing water. It is a difficult trip from there to here for a frog, but here it is and it is a frog with some bright green skin and a narrow snout, not a toad. If it were a polliwog or a very small specimen, I might propose a Lamarckian explanation but it is a full-grown frog. It is much too small to be the old grandfather who deserted more than a year ago when I emptied, cleaned and repaired the pond. Well, I am pleased to have the new occupant no matter how it got here. The more the merrier.

Georgia dominates; the games go on. The authorities believe that yesterday's pipe bomb explosion was the work of indigenous dissidents, probably paramilitary white supremacists. The recent explosive incidents have resulted in a temporary truce between the Democrats and the Republicans; they are afraid to criticize each other for it might backfire and create still another explosion.

Grinch Frankly Newrich was interviewed on television. He spoke rapidly, as I would expect from a salesman, and, as usual, he peppered his speech with his middle name. It is so good to have him back. I assume that when he does not say frankly he is not being frank, and when he does say frankly it is just a bad habit that he will overcome when he is no longer in elective office.

All the time and money that is being expended strongly suggests that those whose resources are spent believe that there are many people who will vote but have not yet decided for whom they will vote. It's possible.

Cherry pits litter the yard. Small Granny Smith apples, each partly eaten, are scattered about; those impatient squirrels destroy the crop. There was one nearly ripe tomato; I picked it to protect it from my voracious competitors. It will ripen on a window sill. One yellow squash was harvested for tomorrow's dinner. *Old Goriot* and the Olympics have helped me enjoy a relaxing weekend.

Candidate Dole has shown his mettle by declaring that America must not submit to terrorism. His statement so inspired me that I am now seriously considering throwing my hat in the ring to be selected as his running mate; the job still seems to be open. I would lend balance to the ticket. The Republican big tent philosophy would be much more credible if I were included. President Clinton also declared that

America must not submit to terrorism. It's a popular theme this week. Dole did some singing at a rally yesterday. This may be an opportunity for bipartisan activity: Clinton on the saxophone, Grinch on the drum (character, character, character) and Dole vocalizing.

Dinner with Deborah was very tasty this evening. The main course was ribs with mashed potatoes and a mixture of onion, corn and yellow squash in butter sauce. We had citrus flavored pound cake and stewed rhubarb for dessert. Deb has been working hard on a computer malfunction and she left early to continue that work. We had a lot to eat even though I served no soup. Soon after she left I ate my penultimate Snickers ice cream bar, not because I was hungry but because I enjoy them so much. My supply is depleted only because I could not find them when I grocery shopped. I could live without ice cream but I hope it never comes to that.

The Virginia Billets are well; I just called them and spoke first to Adam and then Saria. Adam's feet hurt a lot and make things difficult for him. He said he called me yesterday but pushed the wrong button and spoke to Steven. I suggested he question his motivation. He wants to buy some computer software for me so that I can play computer games. I told him, again, that I already spend sufficient time at the computer and that I want to avoid an addiction-like pattern. I steer clear of science fiction, mysteries and puzzles other than bridge hands because there is too much risk that I would get hooked. He told me that Saria is annoyed with him. He did not tell me why and I did not ask but I advised him to limit himself to ten minutes at the computer each day and to make himself obviously available to his family during the time he would have been at the computer. It was a lighthearted exchange with serious undertones of mutual criticism. Saria and I talked about their garden, the children and their August plans. She did not tell me why she is peeved with Adam but she thought it was a great idea that he limit his time at the computer and make himself more obviously available to the family.

When I feel insulted or unfairly criticized by Adam, I usually retaliate; not too much, I hope. If I wanted to talk to Adam and I pushed the wrong button I would question my motivation, and only if I decided I did not want to call him would I avoid pushing the correct button. I think Adam wants a kind of credit for thinking about calling me. I don't find it creditable.

The short list for candidate Dole's running mate includes three governors and two senators; I was not included. The campaign process is having a corrosive effect on Bob Dole and, although I want him to fail in his bid for the presidency, I hope that the admirably hard, patriotic fighter can avoid becoming a brittle, shattered and pathetic old hypocrite; it could happen.

The progression of events around here this year is probably very similar to what has happened here in the past fourteen years; that is how long I have been living alone in this house. It is unlikely that my observing and recording things has had any impact other than making me much more aware of the details. Earlier I claimed that something happened recently but on checking the geologic time divisions, recent includes only the past ten thousand years: the period of modern humans. The claim is that the first life forms appeared about five billion years ago. Creationists aside, each life is just a flicker, our species will not be around very long and Bob Dole is not so very old after all. Living, no matter how brief and insignificant, is the only game in town. It is up to each individual to make something of it.

It's the connections that give the game of life meaning. I keep coming back to my uncertainty about how I want to be connected. I think that the way it is ought to suit me just fine but I feel a bit of discontent and uneasiness that suggests some action is indicated. If there is a change that would result in a clear-cut improvement, I have not found it.

Today's big news stories are shocking examples of corrupt authority. In the District of Columbia a father has been charged with repeatedly having sex with his daughter. The evidence against him includes videotapes that he took while abusing his child. In Atlanta there is strong suspicion that the pipe bomb was detonated by a security guard assigned to protect the area of the explosion. The fox guards the hen house.

On the Op-Ed page of *The Washington Post*, Elizabeth Hardwick, a novelist and essayist, suggested that for the sake of equity the antiabortion zealots propose a constitutional amendment that requires celibacy until one marries. The piece does not have a tongue-in-cheek quality but it holds little hope that the Republican convention will concern itself with fairness and balance.

Definitions are so important. I have heard no voice raised in favor of irresponsibility but there is no unanimity about what constitutes responsible behavior or moral behavior. Is there a difference between responsible and moral? Are there instances of acts that are moral but irresponsible? How about responsible but immoral? Let me hear from you.

A Welfare reform bill that does not reform Welfare is about to be passed and then signed by the President. Politics, not morality or responsibility, rules. I would find it more tolerable if our legislators called change what it is, change, not reform. Some are more deserving, us, and some are less deserving, them. We want them to be moral and responsible; we know that we are moral and responsible. What a wonderful bunch we are; they are not so hot.

July was quite cool; too cool for the tomatoes to ripen. August will be very hot, it always is, and there will be many delicious tomatoes but little more. The birds and mammals have done their damage and the insects are destroying the squash. Maybe those hot pepper plants will survive and fruit but it is not likely. I was overly optimistic about last year's rhododendron cuttings; they have all died. Phyllis and Fred arrive tomorrow and if we are lucky a large tomato will be ripe enough to eat this weekend.

Our elected federal officials are rushing to get a few things done before adjournment so they can go home and tell the voters that they got a few things done and they deserve to be reelected. They won't say much about term limits or campaign finance reform. They will take credit and they will place blame; that is what we require of them. It is difficult for me to blame them for doing what we demand of them but I'm trying. It's our fault, not theirs; if they are authentic we probably won't elect them, and if they are authentic we certainly won't reelect them. We get what we invite but all of us deserve better.

A quiet orgy of talking and eating is over. I remained in bed until 7:30 this Tuesday morning and now, despite many aches and pains, I feel recovered from a very pleasant but tiring weekend. Phyllis and Fred arrived late Friday afternoon. Fred's back was stiff and painful after the five-hour drive. Our conditions and disabilities did not interfere with the talk or the eating; it began at once. Deb joined us for dinner. We ate, recalled, rehashed, remembered, reminisced and surprised each other with our personal versions of what transpired; we sometimes have very different recollections of places and events. Fred remembers clearly that the sweet potato man had his oven on a pushcart and put the hot potatoes in brown paper bags. I remember that the man who came around with a horse-drawn wagon and collected newspapers would appear in the fall with his wood-burning stove on that same horse-drawn wagon and sell the baked, hot sweet potatoes wrapped in the newspapers he had collected earlier. Of course, the man might have switched his modus operandi and we both recollect what actually happened.

Saturday morning I proposed that my suggestion that we go to Bodkin Creek be put aside for a future visit; we did not have enough time or energy for that trip. The alternative plan, a visit to the Hirshhorn Museum, was canceled when Fred indicated his back hurt too much to risk it. We stayed home, ate and talked. Phyllis expressed great interest in reading my writing and she did that after I modestly and cautiously described it as mostly drivel and weather reports. I was pleased when she reacted enthusiastically to what she read. Fred's discomfort eased as the afternoon progressed. We had snacks and drinks as the group gathered before going to the Andrews Officers' Club for dinner. Herb Behre arrived first; Alice is in Boston. Teresa and Steven arrived with T's parents, Betty and Roy. Deb was next and last were Diane and Lloyd Eisenberg who have been my friends since the late 1950s when Lloyd and I were stationed at Andrews. (I was at the hospital the night their first child was born.) I enjoyed the evening a lot.

We had a large brunch Sunday morning. Deb came early to help and Steve, T, Dave and Kelly arrived on time at 10:30. We proceeded without Elliott and Jenny, who showed up a little before noon. I shoveled in a lot more food and it was a happy and noisy time. The kids fed the goldfish and all of us saw at least one frog. Five water lily blossoms were open in all their glory, special for me to show. Deb weeded around the pond to help it look its best and it did. Phyllis and Fred packed up and left before 2 o'clock and Steve and his family followed. Deb, the Schiffmanns and I snacked and talked for another two hours. It is not clear why doing so little tired me out so much; perhaps it was because I stayed in an upright position so much of the time.

During the morning Dave asked me if I believe in God. I told him I do not and added that I hoped that did not worry him. He claimed that he is not worried and added that he also believes in angels. I hope that he is not worried but I believe that his asking the question is an indication that he is concerned. When Adam and Steven were kids, they told me that the mother of their good friend, Kermit, was crying because she loved them so much and she believed they were going to hell because they did not believe in Jesus Christ. I suspect that David is concerned about how such religious truths will affect his father and other nonbelievers. Later in the morning Deb gave David a Snickers ice cream bar. He ate it quickly and wanted another but the consensus seemed to be that one was sufficient. I proclaimed in a loud and authoritative voice that one Snickers ice cream bar was not enough. It worked. Soon I will call Dave, remind him that I was influential in his getting the second ice cream and ask him if I can be one of his angels.

Phyllis said she would like to visit again in the fall. I would like that a lot.

The tomatoes must be picked soon after they show the first blush of pink; if they are left on the vine any longer they are ravaged. The crop looks good and so far I have harvested over one hundred intact fruit, eaten four, given away eight and made three quarts of salsa. The salsa includes a couple of homegrown squash and one habanero pepper from last year's crop; it's a little too hot but it was not hot enough without the habanero. The next batch will be just right.

Traces of the Olympics remain and our most occupying bombings remain unsolved but we are back to politics, hot and heavy. The Republicans are fighting hard with each other but they seem determined to keep control of the legislature and elect Bob Dole. The abortion issue underlies most of their internecine battles; the antiabortion forces are winning and defeated a Dole attempt to have the

Republicans take a more moderate position for the election. No compromise is tolerable when God has issued instructions.

Apparently no commandment has been issued about taxes or about giving away the store to get elected. Both parties have the same motto: DO WHAT IS REQUIRED TO GET ELECTED. It makes an unattractive bumper sticker. Take a blatantly political stance and then bring in the experts to affirm it as best for the voters. Lower taxes, stimulate the economy and pay later, much later.

A long article in *The Washington Post* raises serious questions about Bob Dole's character. I did not know that Dole pressured his first wife to initiate their divorce. She had nurtured him through the early days following his war injuries and she and their seventeen-year-old daughter were unsuspecting victims of his family values. There is a strong suggestion that he used spurious grounds for obtaining an emergency quick divorce and that he used political influence and cronyism both in the divorce procedure and to secure a job for his daughter's mother. Oh well, nobody is perfect.

The experts say that to win Dole must pick as his running mate someone who is well known throughout our country. His choice might bring some new excitement to the campaign. Maybe a natural phenomenon will shake things up or perhaps a deus ex machina will turn the tide or save the day or resolve the plot. Both Perot and Buchanan would gladly take the deus role, but I suspect they would not be playing.

San Diego awaits Dole, his short list, his final selection and any other surprises he may have in store for the Republican convention. All the speculation is fun and the different reactions to the tactical moves are both interesting and amusing. Since Dole is known for his tenacity and grit, I think I will be surprised only if he quits.

The National Aeronautics and Space Administration announced today that its scientists have strong evidence supporting the likelihood that there was primitive bacterial life on Mars millions of years ago. They have concluded this after two years of studying a meteorite that probably came from Mars ten million years ago and landed in the Antarctic thirteen thousand years ago. The evidence and the numbers were described and explained. How amazing. So what? So perhaps we are not alone. It is also further evidence that Bob Dole is not so old. The creationists only have to deal with six thousand years while the rest of us try to comprehend millions and even billions.

President Clinton reacted in firm presidential manner to the NASA announcement; he told us that a conference will be held next year to discuss what to do next. There is a story, perhaps apocryphal, that during the Eisenhower administration a scientific speculation about intelligent life on other planets was suppressed because it was felt the people were not ready to deal with such a notion and might run amuck if they lost faith in their traditional beliefs. If there is life, especially intelligent life, on other planets, perhaps we are not so special. Almost anything might be possible.

A Jewish guy was walking along the beach, tripped on a shell and released a genie who granted him one wish. He asked that all the oil in Arabian lands be moved to Israel. The genie consulted a map, said it was impossible and asked the guy to make another wish. He wished for exciting sex with his wife. The genie said he would take another look at the map. Nevertheless, almost anything is possible.

My bridge playing was terrible today; I played like a novice. Not even that well. All the excitement about life on other planets and unlimited possibilities must have distracted me. My preoccupation with sex, politics and the wonders of our planet and the universe has created an overload that might disrupt my partnership with Bill. He did not say much about my poor play but he didn't like it. A gift of tomatoes goes only so far.

The afternoon heat and humidity is excellent for ripening tomatoes but incompatible with mowing the lawn. I will stay in the shade, read and think about natural phenomena such as television waves, spy planes, hummingbirds and diet Pepsi. I am amazed and distracted by these wonders. It's a good time to finish *Old Goriot* and start *The Odyssey* for the umpteenth time.

The Republicans are keeping busy in San Diego while they await their candidate's arrival. They voted to support a constitutional amendment to prohibit abortion and for legislation that would deny automatic citizenship to children born here but parented by illegal immigrants. Predictions from early this week are being supported by rumors. The consensus is that Bob Dole and Jack Kemp do not like each other. The rumor is that Dole has contacted Kemp and the big surprise at the convention will be that Dole has chosen Ronald Reagan to be his running mate. That way we will realize that on the geological time scale Bob Dole is not so very old after all. I guess that I am out of the running.

Adam called late last evening; he and Saria will arrive tonight in time for dinner. The meal will be very similar to what I served last Friday. Allison and Michael are vacationing in southern Maryland and will be picked up tomorrow afternoon when they will all proceed with Saria's folks to West Virginia.

My bridge playing was better this morning and my appetite was excellent but I feel uncomfortable. My neck and my thorax are often painful and the thoracic pain is different from what I've previously noted. It feels superficial and is probably still another manifestation of my dystonia.

At this very moment I am making salsa. I gave about twenty tomatoes to bridge players this morning and another twenty will go into today's salsa. We will eat some of it this evening. Another twenty or more are ready for picking but a steady rain has kept me out of the garden.

The Kemp rumors dominate the political news. The Republican convention may remain quite contentious even after Bob Dole arrives. It does not seem to me that the Republicans have given up, but so much of the tumult has a suicidal quality. I was up much later than usual last night and was struck by the disdain that the late night funnymen express about the Dole candidacy. I repeatedly say that Dole is not so old but most people seem to think he is too old for their vote. I hope that is correct and that he and other Republican candidates will be soundly defeated. Nevertheless, I am less disturbed when slurs and ridicule are heaped on the President than when Dole is subjected to similar treatment. I suspect it is a generational issue for me and perhaps that is what underlies the ultimate decision for most voters. Young Bill Clinton is the butt of many jokes while old Bob Dole has become a joke. I hope no sympathy backlash develops.

I have been thinking about immaculate conceptions. The personal responsibility devotees, who want the father of each newborn identified and held responsible, are very often people who believe in immaculate conception. If one believes in immaculate conception, every birth might be a double miracle and every child may be doubly holy. Who is to be held responsible for the holy child? Surely all of us.

It is unofficially official that Kemp will be Dole's running mate. The announcement will be made today. The newspaper is full of information about Kemp and about how Dole and Kemp have related; they have not liked each other. The Republicans remain tenacious fighters who will campaign to the finish and do what they feel is necessary to win the battle.

Last evening Deb and I waited until nearly 9 o'clock before we ate, Saria and Adam arrived before we started dessert, they ate, all of us had dessert together and then we spent several hours talking and reading. Adam eagerly showed a ten-inch telescope he has borrowed; it is likely he will buy a similar instrument. He nearly became an astronomer; his decision to become a physician was not made until his senior year in college.

Adam is very interested in what I have written, especially what I have written about him. He and Saria read for several hours and this morning they reported that they were enjoying the way I have said what I say. They also found some misspellings undetectable by computer; alley, not ally, surely, not surly and wedding, not wadding. I am experiencing some of the obnoxious pride of authorship that I have read about and seen but it does not include having my spelling corrected. I am not a very macho guy but I have taken a strange masculine pride in my poor spelling and awful handwriting.

Allison and Michael were picked up and all were back here a little before noon. I left for my bridge game at 12:30 and when I got back there was no sign of their whirlwind visit: no people, no dog, no guinea pig and everything neat as a pin. Some of my most important connections were on the way to West Virginia for a week of vacation. I hope to see them again on their way back. They invited me to join them on a planned cruise to Alaska. I declined without giving it much consideration. They get credit for inviting me and won't have to put up with my being there.

I have followed my usual Sunday routine: the newspaper, political shows and sports shows. Several times I thought about mowing the lawn but did some kitchen work instead. I realize now that I have been afraid to mow because of my chest discomfort; I am more aware of it and find it worrisome. It still feels musculoskeletal but it might be pleural. That infectious bronchitis I had persisted for four weeks and I still cough a bit although I think the infection is over. If I don't feel a lot better in a few days I'll seek an examination.

The Republicans are expressing new optimism as they gather in San Diego. Kemp brings life to Dole's prospects. It is not over yet. They arrived this afternoon with a big splash, by boat. It was reported that Kemp spoke briefly and the crowd responded enthusiastically but when Dole spoke the crowd started to disperse; how surprising.

This weekend the Smithsonian Institution celebrated its 150th birthday. Bob Dole isn't so old. I am going to stop making references to his age.

There are two political conventions in California today and no mystery about their outcome. Still, the process is of interest for there are lots of opportunities for infighting that might influence the November election and the future of the major parties. Crusaders, fruitcakes and fruitcake crusaders can change the course of history; sometimes dramatically.

Richard Lamm has not gone away. His complaints about how Perot is unfairly controlling Perot's party have a peevish quality. His expectation that Perot would be fair may be feigned but, authentic or not, he has confronted all of us with the grandiosity and deception we suspected was there alongside Perot's money and vision.

Patrick Buchanan has been in the wings while his sister appears as his representative and declares victory. So far he has refused to endorse Dole. How will he participate in the convention? He is doing God's work and I suspect that he works for himself.

This evening Colin Powell, who seems to think that he is Black and Republican, will deliver the main address after George Bush, Gerald Ford and Nancy Reagan have had a say. A lot of people will be watching and some will be swayed.

Double-talk prevails: the people who claim they want the government to downsize and stay out of their business are the same people who know how all of us should behave and they are ready to impose their standards on us. Worse yet, many of us are flirting with the notion that the predictability and regularity of totalitarianism is desirable. No one gets mugged in Singapore, except by the authorities, and the streets are so clean. Democracy is quite messy.

The convention is in progress and Republican excitement and hopefulness is evident. What is happening on the podium is entirely theater but the audience reaction and participation is partly authentic. All of this is directed at the undecided voter—undecided about whether to vote and undecided about which lever to pull.

The big tent Republican Party put on a good show last evening. The star acts began at 10 o'clock so I missed the grand finale. I watched and listened to President Ford who delivered a very humorous, snappy speech. I listened to President Bush who spoke stirringly of patriotism, courage, family and honor. I saw and heard the well-prepared encomium for President Reagan and Nancy Reagan's remarks of appreciation. Then I fell asleep and missed the top enchilada, General Colin Powell.

A thirty-second film clip of General Powell on this morning's news told the whole story. All who preceded him declared that the Republican Party is the party of inclusion and it was clear that their remarks were directed at us. General Powell was talking to them and told them that they must become the party of inclusion. Did they hear what I heard and did they cheer him for telling them that they are not yet what they claim to be? I hope to read about it as soon as the morning paper arrives.

Excellent coverage of the convention in the newspaper included the full text of Mrs. Reagan's and of General Powell's deliveries. The entertainment critics gave the convention high ratings while pointing out how highly controlled and choreographed a production it was. Several people did not appear because they refused to deliver the script that they received from the producers. The networks were criticized for interrupting or failing to cover speeches and instead following peripheral matters such as Buchanan's arrival. I watched PBS which got the highest marks for both coverage and commentary. The Republicans must be very pleased with the smoothness of their opening night, its extensive coverage and its positive reception. I thought it was a good show; good enough to keep me up until the last act.

There were a few boos but General Powell was quite well received by the convention delegates. Most of the ideas and feelings he expressed were entirely consistent with what I think of as the underlying principles and values of the Democratic Party. I would like to live long enough to see a person who identifies himself as a black man get elected to the presidency of The United States of America. That's not right; I would like to see a person, who the electorate believes is black, elected to the presidency and I don't want to live to be one hundred.

It is a bleak November day this August 13: wet and quite chilly, unsuitable for sightseeing or mowing, just right for baking a cake. Done. This evening I will miss day two of the convention coverage rather than miss my bridge game. It's a matter of priorities.

I dreamed (no I didn't) that Perot and Buchanan had a stigmata face-off and it ended in a tie.

I slept with blankets and a quilt. A front passed through last night bringing a delightful, breezy summer day. I mowed for an hour, rested and mowed for another hour but there is more to be done and I will get to it another day. Adam called; they are enjoying themselves and plan to be here on Friday. I'll be pleased to have them for dinner and perhaps they will stay the night.

The convention coverage was just ending when I got home last night. Either I saw the last minute of Susan Molinari's keynote address or it was a replay. President Clinton was attacked and criticized by several speakers who are pro choice, the Christian right remained far in the background, no one would admit to having read the party platform and there is a great openness about how all of it is designed to impress women and narrow the gender gap. The newspaper reports suggest that day two was much less impressive than day one and I have concluded that I did not miss much. Today's script has been released. It includes the second Mrs. Dole and Bob Dole's daughter by his first wife. Everyone will say good things about him. I'll watch until I fall asleep.

The high degree of scripting and managing of the convention robs it of a feeling of authenticity and there is little or no spontaneity. The producers are probably skilled professionals who sincerely believe that their efforts will sway the targeted audience, the undecided voter. What does that say about their assessment of the people they are trying to influence? It suggests to me that they do not have much respect for the intelligence of the undecided voter. James Baker, former Secretary of State, doesn't agree with me. He feels the Republicans are effectively and accurately portraying themselves as a big tent party and he came close to predicting a Dole victory.

Buchanan has taken a pragmatic stance and endorsed Dole to help defeat Clinton; first things first.

This sleeping beauty was awakened by the kiss of "The Star Spangled Banner" as PBS ceased broadcasting for the day. I had listened to a panel of experts that began as the convention resumed but I saw nothing and heard nothing after that so I relied on this morning's newspaper for reports on day three. It followed the script precisely: it eulogized Bob Dole. Please remember that one can eulogize the living as well as the dead. The Republicans have been criticizing the media and the media have responded by repeatedly referring to the heavy scripting of the convention and the absence of news. It is all circus.

Enthusiasm at the convention is a lot like a laugh track on a sitcom but several prominent Republicans have been trying to whip up optimism and enthusiasm beyond the convention by claiming that the triad of selecting Kemp, a successful convention and $74,000,000 in matching funds will drive Bob Dole to the White House. Maybe it's so; it has me worried. This evening I will try hard to stay awake and watch and listen until the convention ends. A nap this afternoon may be required.

Rather than nap I finished mowing the lawn, gave myself a haircut and made potato salad. I remain faithful to Ria in ways that mattered to both of us; no one else has cut my hair since she last did it. My new potato salad recipe is better than any other that I have encountered; it contains chopped spiced green tomatoes made by my neighbor's sister. My lawn mowing is below average; nobody is perfect.

The mail includes a book review sent by Bill W. The message he sends is clear: if there was a beginning, there is God. He takes me back to the unmoved mover and he wants me to think about it. I doubt that he is trying to save the soul he believes I have, but maybe.

The Republican convention has ended. I remained wide awake, listened and watched all of the final session and then heard the PBS commentators followed by Ted Koppel. It was worth it.

Jack Kemp is an ebullient optimist who presented an uplifting view of our country with great emphasis on helping all citizens achieve the American dream. His hand movements are distracting and intriguing; he went on too long, but he was authentic and presidential. He wants what I want for our country. He showed no trace of the divisiveness and exclusiveness that the Republicans have been so arduously denying throughout their convention. He rings true while the others have not.

Bob Dole claimed an old man's wisdom and emphasized his probity, tenacity and respectfulness. He began with artful rhetoric but went on to take some cheap shots, pander to the convention audience and present a distorted and negative view of where our country is at this time. Not only did I not agree with him, I felt he was lying to keep his core Republican constituency that has been so carefully hidden during the last four days. He insists he is a truth teller but his speech suggests to me that he lies. Whether he was telling the truth or not when he said that things are not as good now as they used to be, I disagree with him.

The Republican big tent convention was a disguised revival meeting and its theme song was "Give Me That Old Time Religion." Elmer Gantry rides again.

The Chesapeake Billets have not yet arrived; I'm ready for them. I continue to experience non-exertional thoracic discomfort that has not interfered with my sleep or my activities but continues to concern me. I have no fever and very little cough but I still wonder if something other than my dystonia underlies this symptom. It feels like it might be pleural or diaphragmatic in origin. It did not keep me from eating too much at bridge or preparing dinner. I experience occasional small gasping breaths that are sort of like an incomplete hiccup; that is a lot like some of my other involuntary, jerky movements.

An unsolicited copy of *The Washington Times* was delivered to my door this morning. I suspect it was part of an effort to garner votes for Bob Dole without having his campaign charged for the effort. He was given very favorable coverage. A small column addressed the concerns of the Christian right about the failure of the convention to adequately portray the differences between the parties. Nothing that happened at the convention was left to accident and the perpetrators bragged about it.

Summer has just begun, it is half over and almost ended. My nose was up before dawn and it was almost 6 A.M. this Sunday morning, so the days are getting shorter.

I enjoyed another whirlwind visit by the Chesapeake Billets. All six, including one dog and one guinea pig, arrived Friday afternoon and they were gone before noon yesterday. The kids are a pleasure to watch. They had enjoyed a week of exploring West Virginia and Virginia. It could not have been a restful week for them, especially not for Saria, but all seemed relaxed, content and happy.

Wes canceled our Saturday game. Rose was available and soon after my visitors were gone I went to the bridge game. Rose seems uncomfortable playing with me, too aware that I might be displeased with her performance. We had a poor beginning but our opponents were most generous toward the end and we finished third out of thirteen. On the last hand, non-vulnerable against vulnerable, I opened 4 hearts. Rose raised me to 6 hearts. Best defense would have held me to ten tricks but our generous opponents let me make the contract. Bridge, life, is a skill game but there still is a big luck factor in how things turn out.

Mrs. Bush and Connie arrived from Canada on Friday and Deb and I had a nice visit and a delicious Indian dinner at the Smiths' last evening. Mrs. Bush will be back in Florida with Pat this afternoon. I wore suspenders and was able to unbutton my trousers and eat more. I must be getting thinner because my weight remains about the same while my belly gets larger. I felt well last night but my chest still has twinges of pain.

Politics galore: interviews and discussions on television, newspaper reports and columnists and book reviews. How pleased I am to find expert support for my reaction to Bob Dole's speech. Reliably objective David Broder noted that Dole's speech undercut the usual assessment of Dole as a person of integrity. More of the same came from more partisan reporters.

Only fifty thousand votes were cast by Reform Party members, Perot winning over Lamm by a two to one margin. Richard Lamm was interviewed this morning. He was very supportive of the need for a reform party but would not support Perot. A biography of Perot was reviewed in today's newspaper; no surprises but much that seemed worrisome. Enjoyed is not quite the right word but we get so much more information than previous generations enjoyed. Sometimes it may help us to make sound decisions.

I use a flexible scale concerning the human life span: life is just a flicker, thirty is the one-third mark, fifty is the halfway mark and after sixty I speak of the remainder. Bill Clinton is having a big birthday bash this evening in celebration of his fiftieth birthday tomorrow. It is too important a political event to be canceled because of a fatal crash this morning of one of the airplanes that followed the Clintons as their Colorado vacation ended. No matter what he does or does not do, it has important political impact. A picture in the newspaper shows him with a large but unlit cigar in his mouth. Will that gain votes for him? I would rather have seen a picture of Dole smoking a cigarette and looking louche; it won't happen. Please, Mr. President, be careful and do not smirk.

My arrogance has kept me from going to the hospital about my chest discomfort just as it delayed my going to the neurologist concerning my dystonia; I want to make the correct diagnosis myself. Now I think it is likely that I am experiencing a spontaneous pneumothorax. Since my discomfort is increasing, maybe I'll go to the hospital.

The Malcolm Grow Medical Center emergency room personnel worked quickly and efficiently. No cause was found for my discomfort; that is the good news and I am reassured. My electrocardiogram and chest x-rays were essentially normal. The discomfort persists but I am used to aches and pains as you no doubt know by now. I have also experienced a few of those unusual, short, hiccup-like respirations this morning. It is unlikely that anything life-threatening is causing the symptoms so I will grin and bear it.

President Clinton spoke briefly yesterday afternoon before leaving for his multimillion-dollar fund-raising birthday party. He paid respect to the support people who died in the morning airplane crash. His voice was appropriately serious but I thought his mien was not; he looked as if he were smirking.

The Reform Party met in Valley Forge, Pennsylvania; Ross Perot was nominated as its presidential candidate, Richard Lamm spoke without endorsing Perot and Perot proclaimed that he will fight hard to get the truth to the voters. After all these months of election year politics, we are finally getting down to inter-party battling. Intra-party conflicts remain large but the Republicans demonstrated that such conflicts can be put aside to win the big battle.

The big birthday party raised ten million dollars for the Democrats. President Clinton smiled appropriately. People paid as much as ten thousand dollars to attend a birthday banquet with President and Mrs. Clinton. It was a celebrity extravaganza.

Steven called to say hello and let me know that they have returned safely from an enjoyable vacation and a worthwhile medical conference. I told him about my visit to the emergency room. He was critical about some of the things they failed to do as part of their diagnostic evaluation of me. I' m satisfied with the effort that was made.

My enjoyment of food is greater than ever. Last evening I served one of my most favorite meals and Deb and I stuffed ourselves. We started with baked apples; the main course was turkey club sandwiches dunked in pea and tomato soup with side dishes of potato salad and baked spaghetti; dessert was grapes and peach cobbler with ice cream. It was a spectacular culinary achievement by this retired shrink and, yes, I do say so myself. Fancy it was not, messy it was and not only was it delicious but, for me, it had great sentimental appeal. My mother often served a very similar meal but she allowed no bacon on the sandwich and she made peach pie; she was deservedly famous for her Crisco pie crusts.

The ice cream was served later, dairy not permitted in a meal that included turkey. The soup Mother served was made by combining one can of pea soup with one can of tomato soup and Mother called it purée mongole. My soup was made from scratch. Deb had never heard the pea and tomato soup called purée mongole but she reminded me that Ria often served a similar meal using canned soups.

Man does not live by turkey club sandwiches alone. I worked with a fellow who spent his adolescence in a concentration camp. He recalled that his intense sexual drive faded fast and that he and many others were occupied with securing food and shelter while avoiding physical punishment and torture. Personal circumstances are so important in determining our focus but it is hard to remember that truth when things are going well. It isn't so easy to remain philosophical or to dwell on the qualities that we think distinguish us from other species when we are very frightened or tired or starved or in great pain. From my advantaged perspective it is one's connections ... alliances ... partnerships that are most important in securing a satisfying quality life. How lucky I am to have the sandwich, the soup to dunk it in and people who are important to me and available to share my good fortune.

M called and asked me to look up something about footnotes in the WordPerfect manual. Apparently she gave me her copy. I was able to find what she sought. Last week she called in a confused state, suffering from severe hypoglycemia. I called 911 and she was promptly rescued. I identified myself to the 911 operator as a retired physician. Several times recently I have so identified myself; it can be a convenient designation that carries only a little responsibility and a bit of authority.

Yesterday I asked my bridge partner about a mutual friend who has been ill. Neither of us has been in touch with him but we are both aware that his illnesses have taken a toll and that his overall functioning and his bridge playing have suffered. The duplicate bridge crowd is an aging bunch that is dying off much faster than it is being replenished. About fifty local members have died in the last decade. Many of us play right to the end and play well; some continue to play when their skills are sadly diminished. Poor play is of no great consequences but it is sometimes sad to see such deterioration.

Also at the game yesterday was a professional player who was a teenaged enfant terrible when I returned to bridge around 1966. He was a tall, skinny kid back then. Now he is around Bill Clinton's age and even beefier than the President. His life has revolved around bridge and he has lived up to his early notices; he is one of the top players in the world. It gives the game an extra dimension of excitement and pleasure when one gets to compete against such talent. I'm ready to play again this evening and I will walk to the game to see how or if it affects my thoracic discomfort. After the game Alice and Herb will drive me home and get some homegrown tomatoes.

The nearest gate to Andrews Air Force Base closes promptly at 6 o'clock. I was the final one through it last evening as I took my mile and a half slow walk to the bridge game; it went well. I sat in the lobby and watched the television news until the game began. Tully and I had an uneven, mediocre game but it included some interesting problems that will be helpful to our play in the future.

This morning I'm sneezing and coughing a lot but, so far, no chest pain. It surprises me each time it recurs. It is a lovely day; a record will be set if the temperature does not reach 90 degrees today. A cool summer. Maybe I'll go into town and see the new movie about the cosmos at the Air and Space Museum.

Last night I fell asleep watching a former close associate of Bob Dole who had a lot of very critical things to say about Mr. Integrity. He portrayed the candidate as still another influence-peddling sleazeball who has always focused primarily on perpetuating his career. The truth is so very difficult to discern. Perhaps with President Clinton, more than with all of the others, what you see is what you get; it is not always pretty but it is clear. I am only beginning to see the mean Bob Dole whom I have heard about.

Deb called to say hello, I told her my plan and she decided to join me for the afternoon. We had a quick lunch and headed for the Smithsonian where we went through the new Sackler Museum and the Museum of African Art before seeing "Cosmic Journey" at the Air and Space Museum. It was an interesting and enjoyable few hours but also tiring. It was hot and humid, my thorax hurt intermittently and my throat felt irritated. I may be asleep before dark.

That delectable, quiet body state lasted for nearly an hour this morning before my nervous system switched gears. My mouth moistened and my nose began to run; my right shoulder started to move on its own and I heard a loud crack in my neck and a belly rumble. Not until I got out of bed did I experience one of those shallow hiccup-like respirations and an accompanying twinge of pain; no cough yet. Before the action began I was revisiting a bridge hand that appeared Tuesday evening.

A 8

K Q J 6 5   10 9

7 4 3 2

The king was led and must be taken by the ace to keep the suit from running. The defenders will be on lead only once more. If they continue with the queen and jack, the 7 becomes a winner; if they continue with the 10, the jack must overtake or that side will get no more tricks. Sometimes the lowly become very powerful and important.

President Clinton made a big deal of it when he signed the new health insurance legislation yesterday. Simultaneously the Republicans derided his role and took credit. The very important deficiencies in the legislation were hardly acknowledged; it does not provide for the uninsured poor and it will not keep the insurance companies from selectively raising premiums.

Every action and every inaction is campaign fodder. The minimum wage was raised amid controversy, a Welfare reform bill will be signed today despite great turmoil and disappointment within Democratic ranks and President Clinton is pressing to put cigarette sales under Food and Drug Administration supervision.

All agree that the future belongs to the children but there is great dispute about the implications of that reality. Our species has always cannibalized children—treating them as chattel, disposable and easily replaceable. Now there are powerful voices protesting when we revert to old neglectful and punitive ways, but politics rules. My guess is that currently most of the slaves in our world are children and the vast majority of slaves are not men; women and children are most powerless. Women and children first, to suffer from the spurious budget balancing act that appeases potential voters.

The holiday sounds begin today when the Air Force Band and the Singing Sergeants perform their annual "Christmas in August" concert near the Washington Monument. Summer has not ended but the year is nearly over; my first full year in retirement has one hundred and twenty-four shopping days until Christmas.

President Clinton has made himself prominent in the news each day this week in preparation for the Democratic convention and the inter-party shenanigans that will follow. All the jockeying around for an advantage disgraces the candidates. They attack each other ineffectively: any effective wounds will be self-inflicted. Three United States military aircraft have crashed in the past twenty-four hours; enemy participation was not required. Watch out for friendly fire; it's what we do to ourselves that hurts the most.

Last week there was evidence suggesting that primitive life forms existed on Mars millions of years ago. This week we are presented with proof of the existence of a unique, primitive, single-cell organism that could represent the progenitor of all life that exists on Earth. This sucker is alive today at the periphery of the boiling turmoil in the bowels of the sea where vents release gases and magma. This organism requires the immense pressures and heat of that environment and it thrives without oxygen. It produces methane. The next time you are bothered by gas, remind yourself that it is a problem that goes back to the beginnings of life; we are all related by gas.

Time marches on, moment by moment and eon by eon. My kids are back at work while I rest, ruminate and recreate. Deb has solved and fixed several small programmatic problems while still struggling with what she suspects is a hardware deficiency. I find it interesting even though I understand only a bit of it. Adam and family and Steven and family are done with their summer perambulations and are working and preparing for school. Teresa's dad will undergo major surgery next week. There is optimism that Roy will make a full recovery but there is also the tension that goes with a sophisticated awareness of all that can go wrong.

One person's moral imperative is another's ethical dilemma. I formerly felt that it was easier for those ruled by moral imperative but now I believe it is not easier, only more clear-cut. Today I plan to do a good deed and to do it gracefully, not spoiling it by revealing it for what it is. I would like to be a more generous person but it would require more generous behavior and I am so lazy and self-indulgent. Maybe I'm kidding myself: I want to do things for others that will be perceived as generous but that are easy for me and not very costly. Dr. Generosity manqué.

The gathering in Chicago has begun. Mayor Daley claims that the city is ready and will showcase the Democrats and itself. Last time in Chicago things did not go well and it was very costly for the Democrats. We are being treated to previews of the convention. Perhaps it will be as scripted and choreographed as the show the Republicans produced. Bob Dole remains on the attack claiming that only he can be trusted and he is bringing that message to Chicago this weekend. I don't trust those Republicans; they are mean.

Two weeks ago I baked a big batch of white bread, rather than the usual mixed grain loaves, because a gallon of fresh milk was not drunk by my grandchildren and milk makes a rich, fine-textured white bread. Yesterday I made a large batch of a newly invented bread based on the waste not, want not adage; call it coffee and coriander mixed grain bread. The coffee was left over from my brother's visit and I noted a tear in an envelope of ground coriander. I have already begun distribution of the eleven loaves and eighteen rolls of this delicious and aromatic winner.

When I was a psychotherapist, people would complain that I never gave advice. Of course I gave advice; most often they did not like it, did not hear it and did not follow it. Now here is some good advice that will greatly improve the quality of your life; listen to it, follow it and you will like it and benefit greatly. Never put tomatoes in the refrigerator and always suck up to the cook. Now don't complain that this retired person never gives advice.

This old fatso was a skinny kid quondam with an appearance that provoked nurturing instincts. No amount of feeding would fatten me up; people tried but failed. Even I failed. During my second year in medical school, when my job provided unlimited food, I decided it was time for me to gain a little weight. I was just short of seventy-six inches tall and I had never weighed more than one hundred and sixty-seven pounds. I increased my portion size and ate even more desserts than usual. It worked; twice I was able to pass the one hundred and seventy pound mark but both times I caught a cold and reverted to one hundred and sixty-seven. All of that changed when, two years later, Ria became pregnant.

Those were very stressful times filled with hard work, long hours and an amazing lack of awareness. I am not sure about Ria but I was definitely cephalo-caudal; I had my head up my ass and it kept me from seeing things clearly. Ria and I gained about the same amount of weight during "our" pregnancy and, no, I did not practice couvade at the time of delivery nor did I experience the immediate weight loss. During the several months that Ria nursed Deborah, I developed a craving for chocolate milk and I wanted Ria to bring it to me. When the boys were born, just fourteen months later, I weighed about two hundred pounds and I remained overweight until I became aerobically fit through jogging almost twenty years later. Amazingly my weight was one hundred and seventy pounds when I could no longer jog; now it hovers around and rises a bit above one hundred and ninety. When I was lean and fit I could eat unlimited quantities of food without gaining weight; no longer. Nevertheless things are better now than ever before, no matter what Bob Dole remembers.

The journalists and pundits are paying a great deal of attention to the impending convention while they assure us that there is little reason to pay any attention to the impending convention. President Clinton is meandering toward Chicago on a campaign train and will not arrive until shortly before it is his turn to speak. His newly published book, released "fortuitously" this month, was reviewed; panned as banal.

Every move he makes is examined for Machiavellianism and those who raise questions about his motives have a twinkle in their eye and a smile on their face that suggests the questions are rhetorical; answers are not required and will be ignored except for their amusement value. It is circus that we want and it is circus that we will get. It is not possible to detect sincerity when it is so important that the performers project themselves as authentic and believable.

Last night I watched an excellent movie, "My Left Foot": man with severe cerebral palsy overcomes adversity and becomes a talented painter and writer. What a terrific species we are. Christy Brown's mother gave birth to twenty-two children; thirteen survived to adulthood. That is wonderful—better than fifty percent. I heard that salmon manage to have only one in a thousand fry reach maturity. Our species is ever so much more successful and superior. Salmon have been around for a very long time but there is some likelihood that our species will outlast them unless we are determined to keep them around.

Let us convene.

It isn't that conventions are soporific, it's that they fail to keep me from falling asleep. When the morning newspaper arrives I will read all about it. Richard Gephardt said some very nice things about the character and courage of President Clinton and the Democrats in Congress, Ron Brown was remembered and praised and then I slept. Was it an auspicious start? I hope so.

The big show in Chicago got mixed reviews and extensive coverage. Christopher Reeve spoke about family values and Sarah and James Brady continued their crusade for the control of handguns. They were obviously sincere, authentic and entirely credible; just what we want in our elected officials. The most amazing act is the show of unity; all bitterness and most conflict is squelched and does not appear on camera. We are advised by the media that a little dissent will appear but that it will be a deliberate performance designed to convince the undecided that Bill Clinton is a centrist. It is not only a circus, it is a magic act where each trick is described and explained before it is performed. Now that we are naked, exposed and revealed, there is no mystery or romance left to sustain a passionate love affair.

The second act has begun and will end with a presentation by Hillary Rodham Clinton. I will play bridge this evening and read the reviews tomorrow.

I saw the droning, postclimactic finish to the second night of the big show last night; it was unimpressive. Today the newspaper and television reports and reviews of what happened while I played bridge are interesting but, again, the show was not very impressive. The old-time liberals, Jesse Jackson and Mario Cuomo, said what they say the way they say it; it was well received. Hillary Clinton was the centerpiece of the show; she received a grand reception and proceeded to stand her ground while avoiding anything controversial or threatening.

President Clinton stopped his train to listen to his supportive wife's address and he cheerfully told us how very proud he is of her. His traveling show is, by far, better than the event in Chicago. Each day he gives something to the American people, but not too much to scare them. George Will, in his newspaper column today, called the President a political Elmer Gantry; George almost always gets things wrong when he gets off baseball. There are several Elmer Gantrys out there and they are all part of the Religious Right: corrupt, phony and manipulative. My Democratic president is fair, flexible and strategical. Those pigheaded Republican zealots—we tenacious Democrats will persevere. The two-party system works; those stingy, mean Republicans have helped us to be more frugal.

Labor Day weekend marks the end of summer. My vegetable garden is on the wane but with thirty-six plants I hope to have at least one homegrown tomato for breakfast each day until the middle of October; until Election Day if I am very lucky. All the ingredients for the world's most perfect breakfast are available to me during August and September; I religiously celebrate each day with a ritual morning meal that I consume while standing over the kitchen sink. The meal consists of two courses: the first course is one slice of toasted homemade bread slathered with cream cheese, sprinkled with garlic salt and covered with thick slices of homegrown tomato that are liberally (not conservatively) coated with mayonnaise and topped with a large leaf of iceberg lettuce.

The second course is a repeat of the first course. Now if that ain't heaven there is none.

If I conclude that there was a beginning and therefore, by definition, there is GOD, I hope I will choose the homegrown tomato as the supreme representation of GOD on earth. There is an old Yiddish story, I think it was written by Shalom Aleichem, about a poor beadle who died without ever having done an evil deed. When the angels noted it they decided to reward him, and when he arrived in heaven they gathered around him and told him that in recognition of his feat they would grant him anything he wished. He thought about it briefly and asked for a slice of bread and butter. I'll bet he did not know about homegrown tomatoes.

These unscheduled Wednesdays just slip by. It is convention time. Nighty-night.

Roy's surgery went well and he was resting uncomfortably when I called last evening and spoke to Betty. The first couple of days after major surgery can be pretty miserable. Soon after making that call I shut off the light and propped myself up in bed in a way that would inhibit my turning over. This effort to avoid falling asleep almost worked. I remained awake enough to remember hearing both Al Gore and Bill Clinton but I cannot remember much of what they said. The commentators predicted that the President's arrival in Chicago would be shown and that he would speak. I can remember that Gore sounded forceful and that he was not wooden; he was probably given flexibility coaching. Once again I will read about it in the newspaper.

The weatherman has predicted a pleasant Labor Day weekend; the big weekend that marks the end of summer and getting back to school and business. I can remember crying as we left the New Jersey seashore after our last day there for that year. The Hebrew calendar is lunar and the new year can occur soon after Labor Day or several weeks later but it always made sense to me that the new cycle was celebrated when trips to the seashore ended and school resumed. I liked school but I never cried when the school year ended and trips to the seashore began.

This year Rosh Hashanah, the Hebrew New Year, begins at sundown on September thirteenth. Deb and I are invited to join the Kivitz family for the traditional family dinner that welcomes in the year. The end of summer is a time for reflection, repentance, forgiveness and renewal. I think the religious are asking, praying, for still another cycle.

The past few years I have contributed a large bread and potato pudding and/or potato blintzes to the holiday dinner; I plan to do that this time too. All of these foods are part of my effort to recreate things my mother cooked and I come close enough to feel that I am succeeding. Last year I brought an extra large bread. Since they were not confident that I would bring it, they bought a challah. When I saw it I asked Murray where he got the roll. That got a laugh.

The senator from Connecticut and the Vice President gave rousing remarks last night in praise of William Jefferson Clinton and the Democratic Party. We expected it and we got it. Candidate Dole's Senate voting record was reviewed and presented as mean and shameful. Stick with us, we are terrific; watch out for them, they are trying to deprive you.

Foul! Republican dirty tricks appear with precise timing. This afternoon Dick Morris, notorious political strategist to all parties and most recently an adviser to President Clinton, resigned from the Clinton campaign after a newspaper report that he had sex with a prostitute in a Washington hotel. The report was delayed a few weeks; not a usual practice for a reputable newspaper. Well, the convention needed a little excitement. If this is hard news, it is hard because it is stale, several weeks old. No one will ever get me to believe that these intelligent, educated, successful, busy people actually find time to have sex with anyone or even by themselves; they are fully occupied with important matters.

The final evening of the convention begins soon. I think I have figured out how to stay awake; instead of watching while in bed, I will stay in the kitchen and make blintzes. Never have I fallen asleep while cooking.

I wonder if the parties have decided that their contest is sort of like Olympic boxing. The object in the boxing match is to score the most points without getting knocked out. Points are scored in Olympic boxing by having the judges see you deliver clean blows; they use electronic counters. In politics there are no clean blows so the decision is made by counting references to God. Keep your electronic counter handy because they come hot and heavy. Remember that a knockout ends the contest.

Let us convene.

The manufacture of potato blintzes is highly labor-intensive and low technology. The use of instant mashed potatoes cuts the process to about five minutes per blintze. I produced thirty units, put them in the freezer and washed the pots and pans before the Bill Clinton movie and acceptance speech began. Then it was time for high technology measures. Before getting into bed I set my Buck Rogers laser sting-gun to zap me every two minutes and to go into rapid fire if it detected sleep pattern brain waves. I was nearly fried but I heard and saw almost all of it.

I'm glad that I gave President Clinton equal time, after all I did stay up for all of Bob Dole's acceptance speech, but I was not very impressed and I was not inspired. Several times during the movie I thought he was smirking while telling about serious matters and his acceptance speech was overly long and repeatedly triggered the laser sting-gun. Also I started getting trainsick as we traveled forward on the right track to the twenty-first century. He gave a long list of accomplishments and initiatives that made his speech sound a lot like a state of the union address. He was very well received and he did not stumble. Today at bridge I happened to mention that I am a bleeding-heart, Jewish, communist, liberal Democrat; it triggered an excited outburst from a very nice lady who can't understand how anyone can stick with such a sleazy guy. I started it.

Two hours until dawn and the decibel level is high. I can't tell if it is the roar of traffic on the Beltway or jet engine noise from Andrews; perhaps both. Atmospheric conditions influence the way the noise reaches me and only rarely would I describe it as a roar. The big hurricane sweeping up the east coast is still far off shore. It has created dangerous surf and modified the weekend vacation plans of millions but it's not likely that it's involved in the cacophony I hear. Maybe the noise is a weekend phenomenon connected with Air Force reserve unit flying. The pilots want to take off before dawn to meet their night flying requirements.

Pat called last evening. She had several disturbing dreams. She has met some very nice people through church and work but she and her mother still feel lonely and a holiday weekend increases their awareness of separation from family and old friends. I can be a tough old bird; this is the first time since she moved to Florida last November that I have felt a tenderness and a desire to be with her in Florida rather than thinking that she knew what she was doing when she left and she will have both the bitter and the sweet of it. I think that if all goes well I will visit her and her mother in January. She is a very sweet lady.

The mavens are still picking over the bones of the convention and will probably continue to do so through this long weekend even after those bones are sparkling clean; unless something quite unexpected comes along. Political mavens can' t feed on hurricanes. These expert observers are remarkably divided about the desirability, impact and effectiveness of the revelative and emotional personal appeals that were used repeatedly at the Democratic convention. It seems that the purpose of political conventions has changed considerably and that itself has become grist for the mill. There remains a unanimity among the experts, not at all reassuring to me, that only a miracle will bring victory to Dole. The Republicans better check on the constitutionality of consulting Scalia and Scalia should recuse himself.

My thorax still hurts, but not often. Almost always the pain occurs in the left lateral area and it appears after I have been lying on my right side. Strange; I do not understand it. The timing of it makes me wonder if it was still another anniversary reaction since it began around the first week in August, that very emotionally charged time when, in 1958, I stopped smoking. It seems quite unlikely. At this moment I realize that August 24 passed without my having had any realization that it was on August 24, 1950, that Ria and I married. Time sure does fly by when you are having lots of fun.

Writing this stuff is a lot of fun for me; never before have I enjoyed my own language so much. In school foreign languages were my bane; they took far too much of my time and didn' t seem worth it. Most of my foreign language teachers were very nice people who liked teaching and wanted the students to enjoy learning; I failed them but I fondly remember them. It is as if I never studied Latin, French or German. One teacher who had learned English as his second language told us that when he first came to the United States his favorite new word was "lotsof" and he would seek opportunities to use it. He told us lots of stories but that is the only one of the lot that I remember.

The rehash of the convention was extensive last night and no doubt it will continue this Sunday morning. Here is my aperçu.

Bill Clinton took a choo-choo train ride.
Hillary grimly told her side.
Al Gore has his Tipper,
Dick Morris a slippery zipper
And the Republicans have not yet died.

The Republicans have not died and they are not playing possum; Dole and Kemp are out there campaigning hard. It is up for grabs until Election Day. Both sides are capable of committing unassisted suicide and that alone keeps it exciting and uncertain.

Wes was not feeling well yesterday and canceled our game. I played with Rose, for the last time. It was a disaster of missed communications. The reality is that I'm having trouble establishing another bridge partnership that feels right and is successful. That says considerable about me. I'm thinking about it.

Three football games, tennis and golf; if the gods wanted man to watch one channel they would not have provided the remote control. The new season is welcome even though the Redskins lost their opening game. The professional athletes are so very talented; it is a pleasure to watch them.

Deb will be coming over for dinner tonight; we will be at Steve and Teresa's tomorrow for dinner. Several times this afternoon I thought about mowing but I stayed close to the television. The lawn can wait until midweek.

The Monday night football game began at 9 P.M.; I missed it. I wanted to see it but, even more, I craved relief from the neck discomfort and accompanying fatigue I was experiencing after a very pleasant Labor Day. The television was still on when I awakened and at 2 A.M. my nose started up, so I was fully awake when the ABC station issued a special report: The United States has fired one or more missiles at Iraq in retaliation for Saddam Hussein's attacks on the Kurds in northern Iraq. Are we at war? Surely the people of Iraq must believe we are at war with them. President Clinton had announced that we would retaliate for the prohibited actions taken by Saddam Hussein.

Yesterday was glorious for those of us who were not struck by missiles or subjected to other man-made or natural disasters. I baked a peach and cherry cobbler, watched some excellent tennis until noon and then drove to Deb's, intending to drive us to Steve and his family. As we left her house my brakes didn't sound right so Deb did the driving using her luxurious vehicle. I took my Obusforme back support but it helps only a little.

Kelly and David were not eager to go swimming so we hung around the house, talked a bit, watched cartoons and sports, shot a little pool, helped Teresa cook and ate. Steve was on call but did not have to leave while we visited. The sun was just setting and the sky was still bright and colorful when I pulled into my garage around 7:30; a lovely end to the summer season.

Of course the President was partly politically motivated; everything a president does or doesn't do is partly politically motivated. I don't know how to assess the wisdom or appropriateness of his decision to fire missiles at Iraq. The conventional wisdom is that the American electorate likes it when we flex our big muscles; we don't want a president who is a pantywaist and we want to be the best and most important country in the history of the world. We are, aren't we? I deliberately avoided mentioning the gods in heaven in that sentence.

Adam leaves for Colombia, South America, today. This is his fourth or fifth trip there with Operation Smile, the most excellent project that provides free reconstructive surgery to people in underserved parts of the world. Surgical teams with full equipment go all over the world and do their amazing work. The before and after pictures show what an immense impact this work has on the lives of those who undergo such surgery. How deservedly proud and satisfied he and his associates must be. Why would anyone who does such wonderful stuff doubt that he is admirable or need confirmation from his father about his worthwhileness? That is not a rhetorical question but I don't expect a quick answer.

President Clinton spoke to the nation this morning. He told us that after issuing considerable warning our forces have retaliated by destroying Iraqi air defense installations and that we have enlarged the no fly zone that has been imposed on Iraq. He emphasized that our actions would be predicated on what Saddam Hussein does, not what he says. There are strong overtones that further forceful action on our part will be required. The newspaper and television expert commentators seem unanimous in their support of our use of air power and a few voices have been critical of President Clinton's refusal to act sooner. Apparently only Great Britain, of all our major allies, has strongly supported President Clinton's decision.

The President made his remarks this morning from The White House. He left the campaign trail, put on his presidential costume and had a serious mien; no trace of what I have called the appearance of a smirk. How presidential.

I drove the short mile to the service station and walked home well before President Clinton addressed us this morning. Next I converted five pounds of potatoes, three pounds of onions, six eggs and seasonings and oil into potato pudding for the holiday dinner. As soon as it was out of the oven I walked back to the service station, drove home and mowed the lawn; almost all of it. How reassuring it is to be able to do all that without feeling I overdid it. I experienced only a few of those abnormal breaths and no pain.

My first serious difficulty with the computer in months occurred this morning. I started a new file and misnamed it 12 when I intended to name it 13. I was quickly punished; it tricked me into commanding it to erase all of file 12. The trickster called it replacing, not erasing, but I know a disappearing act when I see it. When I consulted computer wonder woman Deborah she assured me that file 12 was safely on the floppy disk.

This is a computer with sentience
It does all my work with great competence.
I take care what I blurt
For its feelings can be hurt
Though you may think that is just plain nonsense.

Hurricanes and missile attacks dominate the news. The twenty-seven missiles fired on Iraqi installations early yesterday morning have been followed this morning by seventeen more designed to eliminate Iraqi air defense. There is no evidence that Saddam Hussein has been influenced by these measures and Republican critics ask why no action has been taken in northern Iraq where Iraqi troops have intruded on the Kurds. More military activity on our part seems likely since so many seem to desire and encourage it. We must show the world that we are determined and capable, not a bunch of sissies. Also, Bill Clinton is not lily-livered.

Heavy rains, flood warnings and thunderstorms are all around the area and they will be followed in a day or two by a powerful hurricane that will probably reach land at North Carolina. It is a big one but it is very unlikely that it will reach this far inland with much force. I exercised my window of opportunity when I mowed the lawn yesterday. My concerns are so often quite narrow and self-centered.

The Wednesday food section of the newspaper has a big article on baking bread. It includes a recipe for making soft pretzels that I will not follow but it has inspired me to proceed; perfect activity for a wet and gloomy afternoon. This may be the first time in the history of our solar system that there have been coriander soft pretzels.

I have recaptured a fragment from a dream dreamed two or three nights ago. Two old bricks were side by side, probably where I have the rhododendron cuttings right outside of where I am now sitting at the computer. I tried to pick up one of them and it crumbled into a thousand pieces. Around 1959 my across the street neighbor and I bought a large truckload of used bricks and I wound up with nearly two thousand relatively intact old bricks that probably came from the southwest area of Washington that had been recently demolished to make way for a much heralded redevelopment. Every one of those bricks has been used around this house in one or another project and some of them have been used repeatedly. I have made a patio, a barbecue, three ponds, front and back walkways, back steps and plant borders. Most of them are currently in use or usable but some have broken and some have shattered the way the brick in my dream shattered.

The freshman physiology course at the Cincinnati College of Medicine was taught in 1948 by a wonderful group of eccentrics, philosophers and creative artists. One laboratory session was devoted to measuring the activity of the isolated (dissected from the body) turtle heart. I think there was one turtle heart for two students and the experiment went on for quite a while. Some of those hearts faded fast and some of them kept right on beating until it was time for us to leave the lab. I was too dumb to figure out that the purpose of that session was to impress us with how not all hearts are alike. Not until the professor put it into words did I get the point of it.

So why did I dream the dream when I dreamed it? Was it because a friend had been hospitalized for cardiac decompensation, Roy had undergone surgery, Wes was not feeling well and many of my friends and associates are old bricks who have survived a very long time (or has it been just a flicker?) and may crumble at any moment?

Soft pretzels can be found everywhere these days. I'll bet the astronauts take them along in space. Once upon a time soft pretzels were associated with special stuff: carnivals, the seashore and that street in Manhattan just past the Holland Tunnel on the way to Brooklyn and Sheepshead Bay. Things are so much better than ever before.

It is illusory that world events have intruded on the campaign. The candidates knew that stuff would happen between the conventions and the election and that all events might be useful. Bob Dole quit his job so he could devote himself to de vote and that is what he is doing. Bill Clinton and the rest of us know that when Bill Clinton is appropriately presidential he is doing what benefits his candidacy the most.

Candidate Dole has become a harping and opportunistic critic of the administration. He is the testosterone kid and the meaner and more aggressive he gets, the more he smiles. If I were on his team I would recommend that he divert some of that energy to sex. An announcement that he and Libby are expecting would bring in de votes. Proof that he still has his moisture would encourage all of us. He claims that he is wiser, not smarter; strong and firm, not slippery; more patriotic, not elitist and, if they were expecting, it would be an indication of family values, not horniness.

A recent report indicates a very great increase in drug use among those who are not old enough to vote. What an opportunity for Bob Dole to declare his determination to use the federal government to quell our fears. His criticism of the administration's anti-drug activities and attitudes has led to much debate and analysis. I do not trust Dole's motives; he wants fear and uncertainty, not debate and analysis.

Drug and substance abuse, habituation and addiction have been very important in my life. Much of my work dealt with these matters. I supported my family on other people's drinking. The use and abuse of legal drugs causes great difficulties, much more than illegal drug use. The use of illegal drugs can be even more disruptive and dangerous but it occurs much less frequently and almost always follows the recreational use of legal drugs. Prescription drugs, alcohol and tobacco probably make up more than ninety-five percent of the dangerous drug use in the United States. We are duplicitous and hypocritical concerning drugs. We like to solve problems with drugs, they are so often curative or very helpful, and we often look for a drug solution when other measures are clearly indicated. Drugs can make some things so much easier in the short run.

A fellow was sitting at a bar when a woman walked in wearing a pair of very tight jeans. He asked, "Miss, how do you ever get into those jeans?" She replied, "You can start by buying me a drink." It's funny because it is so open about the truth of what is going on. Many people go to bars to establish a liaison; it is a part of our culture. It is not so funny when we do things that we would not allow ourselves if we were not using whatever we are using. It is not funny at all when someone uses drugs to control or influence others, with or without their agreement. It is creepy when someone tells you that he took his drug to permit himself to beat his wife or have sex with his child.

I am not an advocate of legalizing illegal drugs; I advocate dealing with all dangerous drugs, legal and illegal, as a very big problem that requires rational policy that is not controlled by special interests. It is a tall order. The legal drugs are the gateway drugs; most of the government-sponsored scientific studies about drug use are political, not scientific.

My interest in drug abuse is more personal than professional. Several people, friends and family, have been severely affected medically, socially and occupationally by their drug use. I have watched dozens of my acquaintances spoil the last years of their lives or die prematurely because of their drug use. It is a disheartening and sometimes pitiable spectacle. My own love affair with nicotine is ingrained in my nervous system. It takes strong magic to keep me from succumbing again to the nicotine succubus. Incantations and talismans are not covered under Medicare.

A new day and a new entry but it is only a few hours ago that I was here, trying to be somewhat amusing while writing about very strong feelings. I think I awakened a deep seam of uneasiness, perhaps dread, in myself; or is my present uneasiness unrelated to the thoughts and feelings I experienced before going to bed? I will try to reconstruct the events preceding the anxiety dream but first the brief dream and my feelings on awakening.

A tall man, considerably my junior and perhaps a minor celebrity, actor and writer, was about to enter a deep crypt or dungeon. He was carrying a pocket book, not large, and he was accompanied by a woman. It was his idea that he would remain in this coffin-like place for eight years while the woman would remain with him only briefly. He would occupy himself all of the eight years with reading the book. As he started to enter this self-imposed situation, someone shouted, "Don't let him do it." I awakened with a claustrophobic feeling. It was a feeling of dread but not accompanied by palpitations or rapid breathing. My uneasiness was so great that I decided to get out of bed, get some fresh air and have a diet soda.

I repeatedly refer to the dreadful things people do to themselves. What do I fear I will impose upon myself? Will I isolate and limit myself, give up sex, read a small book and follow it with eight years of omphaloscepsis? I am not aware of any such plans. Will I start on a course of action and find that I am unable to extricate myself? It's possible. I am not now afraid of death but I still have fears about the dying process. Perhaps the dream is about that process. Ria must have experienced that suffocating feeling many times during the last years of her life; how awful for her.

Wes called last evening as I was getting ready to shut off the computer; it was almost 9 P.M. He is still having a lot of difficulty following oral surgery and the Dr. Big Oral Surgeon will reoperate tomorrow. He told me some bridge gossip about me and spoke some about himself and his family. He asked me about Pat and I told him it was likely I would visit her in Florida in the new year.

The end of that telephone call is the dividing line between what happened before I went to bed and what transpired after I went to bed. It is likely that my dream was precipitated by a confluence of before bedtime and after bedtime thoughts and feelings. I wanted to watch a 10 o'clock program about the kids who will be graduating from high school in the year 2000 and while waiting for it I watched an old program about earthquake studies in California and Japan. It was quite interesting even though I remembered much of it. It included several scenes of rescue workers searching for victims entombed in collapsed buildings. That seems pertinent to my dream. At 10 o'clock I turned to the proper channel and set the sleep timer so the set would go off at 11:30, right after the news.

You know me: I was asleep in a flash. I awakened with my discomforting dream two and a half hours later.

So, I have made a great to-do about a disquieting dream that awakened me. It helped me to think a bit more about my peculiar nature. I feel relieved and refreshed. It is almost time to get up. I'm going back to bed.

It feels like another day, mid-afternoon after playing bridge and eating excessively at the Friday food game. The game went well; there was no flooding in the below ground-level recreation room at the Masonic Lodge. There is considerable flooding less than a hundred miles to the west and we are experiencing high winds and bands of heavy rain while remaining under a tornado watch and a flood watch. My trees and bushes are being whipped about but, except for some broken branches,

I have seen no damage. All of the weather associated with the hurricane will be past here in another few hours. It looks like another lucky miss.

November 5 is less than nine weeks away. There are still some undecided voters but not enough to matter. Now what is needed is a knockout punch that will require those who have firmly decided they will vote for Clinton to vote for Dole. It can be done; whether it is accomplished or not, it won't be pretty. Dole will keep on jabbing but his cornermen must have told him that he can only win with a knockout. Hit him with a Morris, a Whitewater and a Flowers. Jab at his substance but give him a roundhouse to his character; that is his vulnerability. I may be wrong about it but I sure have stuck to my original position. That nice lady at bridge said it when she angrily asked how Democrats could support such a sleazy guy. She did not say a word about substantive matters; those little jabs will not get the job done.

First light, a cloudless sky, birds chirping, planes flying and the only signs of the storm are knocked over tomato plants and a few broken tree branches. The pond is not full so we probably had less than two inches of rain. Not far from here some areas had over a foot of rain and creeks and rivers have flooded and caused severe damage and death. A local weatherman declared that the storm came through with the force of four hundred atomic bombs. I think I'll start watching another station.

President Clinton declared North Carolina a disaster area and then went to Florida to campaign. He did not participate in the christening of a new battleship because his lawyers advised him that his attendance would be considered a campaign activity. They were just doing their job but everyone understands that all of his activities are campaign activities.

Candidate Dole did not fire his two chief media consultants; they quit as he prepared to replace them. Jack Kemp has not fallen off the end of the Earth; the elitist liberal media has colluded to ignore him.

We claim that we promote democracy around the world. Our activities suggest that we want stability that does not threaten us much more than we want the peoples of the world to be free and safe. I am not against self-interest but I don't like it when we are self-aggrandizing or hypocritical. Votes are garnered by telling the electorate how wonderful and worthy it is, not by pointing out that our self-interest can be excessive and can exacerbate severe hardship and terrible oppression around the world. When the Republicans stress morality they criticize others, not themselves. No candidate ends an appeal for votes with "God bless the world." Almost no one wants to hear about our alliances with regimes that regularly subject their citizens to torture and unnecessary deprivation. We want confirmation that we are wonderful; it's not enough that we are among the best.

Events at the Naval Academy are usually covered under local news; we have had too much of it recently: car theft rings, cheating, drug use and honor code violations. Yesterday a woman plebe was arrested and charged with murder and, flash, the chaplain was allegedly videotaped flashing young girls in a department store. Remember, nobody is perfect. The chaplain is a lieutenant commander, which suggests he has been in the military for a while. Has he been engaging in such behavior for a long time or is it a new development? Chances are that the murder was a once in a lifetime event. A member of the Academy faculty, who wrote critically about its ethos, resigned last month. He broke a code of silence when he was openly critical.

It can be very difficult to buck the tide and refuse to close ranks to protect the honor of a group or institution that has done much that is deserving of honor. Honorable institutions are beginning to recognize that it is better in the long run to have an ethos that eschews the denial of defects and encourages the uncovering of wrongs.

Suppose the chaplain did expose his genitals to some young girls in a public place; what will happen to him? What would be an appropriate response? I hope you would like to know more about it before you decide. What about the plebe who is accused of murder; if she did it, what is an appropriate societal response? I'd like to know a lot more about it before I decide and even then I doubt that a decision would be clear-cut for me. I am vigorously in favor of rooting out and punishing corrupt authority, but at the same time I'm a bleeding-heart liberal who looks for mitigation and the possibility of rehabilitation. Those who impose punishment are fallible and often wrong in their conclusions about guilt. I think I will again read *The Ox-Bow Incident*.

It is easy for me to identify myself with the chaplain and the plebe and to think of them as a lot less lucky than I. Last week a woman told me that her husband's cardiologist murdered him. I sought no details but assumed she meant that the doctor was less than fully competent and it resulted in her husband's avoidable death. I wonder if I have ever been called a murderer. I thought about committing murder once almost thirty years ago. I thought my kids were getting drugs from a schoolmate and I wanted to protect them. It was a very stressful time for me. I wonder if I would have done it if I had concluded that it would have benefited my family. Given my traditional paternalistic view, I might have. I was almost a murderer. Those feelings disrupted me. I have never exposed myself where my genitals would be seen by someone who would be offended or upset but I have felt some pressure on occasion to present myself sexually in a way that would be inappropriate and potentially dangerous. I'm very lucky that such thoughts and impulses have been slight and have not pushed me around. I don't have to know much about him to know that the Naval Academy chaplain is a lot less lucky.

Jack Kemp has been sighted in Harlem, rumors that Saddam Hussein is on retainer with the Democratic Party have been denied, rumors that Bob and Libby are preggers have not yet been confirmed and the nation is occupied with football, tennis and baseball. Almost no one noticed that Mike Tyson knocked out whomever that was he fought in the first round and that Mike is again the reigning heavyweight champion. The new television season is getting more attention than the presidential campaign. It is a very quiet Sunday; unexciting even though all local rivers are overflowing their banks and will not crest until tomorrow. Boring.

The U.S. Open tennis finals were not boring. The Washington Redskins' football games are always too suspenseful to be boring; uncertainty is the mother of excitement.

What has happened to those pretty young women who looked like members of the Junior League as they stood on downtown street corners and distributed free sample packages of cigarettes? If proposed restrictions are put in place, those women will need a new modus operandi. A long newspaper article gives me hope that the Justice Department investigation of the cigarette companies will lead to successful prosecution and result in major changes in tobacco distribution and use. The whole liability picture might be changed if it can be proved that tobacco company researchers developed a designer drug that was safer than nicotine and company officials decided to conceal it and not use it. Big bucks are at stake. Maybe it hasn't been such a boring day after all.

My grandson is being picked on by neighbor kids. Steve is riled up about it and has not figured out a satisfactory way to deal with it. He and Teresa have considered moving, but they understand that no matter where they go they are likely to have neighbors. They live in a very pleasant looking suburban area with large but not imposing single family homes. The neighborhood people tend to get together for social occasions (I have met some of them) and they seem pleasant and interestingly diverse. They are not without troubles. I'm pretty sure that one young woman, a mother, was drunk or stoned when I met her one afternoon. In their diversity they have different notions about many aspects of what is currently called family values. There are many versions of being responsible and lots of different notions about how to raise children. It's difficult enough to get agreement about such matters within one family.

My kids remember very little about the Philippine Islands. They remember growing up in one house with no moving about. I also grew up in one house and my parents did not leave it until after I left home. I think each of my kids still has a door key to this place. That is a kind of stability, growing up in one place, but it is not necessarily an advantage; so much depends on the place, including the neighbors. This neighborhood worked out a lot better for some than for others. Some suffered a bad patch but recovered, while others, heavily involved in drug use, have had disrupted lives and have failed by any ordinary standard. It is easy and tempting to assume that you did something right when things work out well. Maybe, but there is a big luck factor.

The last time I saw Abe Kraft was over twenty years ago and it was a brief meeting that I recall only vaguely. He was a thin man, wearing a tweed jacket and a bow tie. He was pleasant and I think he had a gift shop or a flower store. When we were growing up he lived four houses from me and I was afraid of him. He was one of about ten kids who were two or three years my senior and he was the only one of that group who picked on me. I remember him chasing me home and then trying to break into my house to get me. I thought he would kill me or hurt me severely, he was so angry. I don't remember what it was about but I remember being frightened. That memory is not typical; most of my recollections about the neighborhood are pleasant. There were a lot of kids and lots of games in the neighborhood before I was permitted to walk to the school playground three blocks away. We played alley ball, stick ball, touch football and marbles. Mothers were abundantly available and kept an eye on things. My mother was opposed to my fighting and made her position very clear but I remember little need to fight; it was a pretty friendly and supportive environment during my prepubertal years and even afterwards.

I have worked with people who suffered the difficulties of growing up in an unfriendly neighborhood. One man was beaten up with some regularity. His father reacted by telling him it would have to stop and if it didn't he should expect a worse whipping when he arrived home. He felt desperate and finally solved the problem by hitting several kids on the head with a brick. His brick work led to a sobriquet, Crazy, and no one picked on him again. Desperate times call for desperate measures.

David will be seven years old in a couple of weeks. That is very young to be a worrier. I'll bake a chocolate pie for him.

We have a muddy mess wherever the rivers flow and a lot of damage upstream where record flood levels were reached. It is a great week to be retired or at least stay out of Washington. Traffic was snarled for hours yesterday. Apparently most people went to work even though they had a wonderful excuse to stay out of the city. A new hurricane is doing damage in the Caribbean so there may soon be more to come.

Elizabeth Dole is making the morning talk show rounds. I'm happy to perceive her as too scripted and hard-edged but what else would you expect from me? The Republicans, to their credit, are jabbing away at substantive matters. They are asking religious school advocates and city dwellers to give further consideration to the desirability of school vouchers. Dole's attack on the teachers' unions has backfired so far, but they have not given up on it and are trying to turn things around. Tenacity is not their short suit.

Even Republicans want a compassionate federal government during and following natural disasters. It is President Clinton, however, who is dispensing emergency federal funds to the hard hit areas of North Carolina, Virginia and Maryland. Circumstances seem to favor his reelection. Hard hit people keep showing up on television saying that they don't know how they could survive without federal help. It is not a propitious time to promote devolving power away from government. Bob Dole tells us that Democrats trust government and Republicans trust the people. I like honest representative government.

Many summer beach homes were destroyed along the North Carolina coast by the hurricane. I wonder if anyone will cry, "Welfare queen," when the owners of those homes accept federal money and subsidized loans. Who is deserving? Who are the elitists? If your compassion is reserved only for your own, I will not characterize you as compassionate. The Republican big tent is a three dollar bill.

Puerto Rico had sixteen inches of rain yesterday and most of the island is without electricity or potable water. It was a lovely day here. I walked to the evening bridge game and enjoyed playing some interesting hands. I thought Tully and I had surely won but we were only second. My fault. Today it's a lot like Puerto Rico: we are experiencing flooding rains that strangle the area, but no power outage so far.

Ross Perot treated the nation to an infomercial last night. He announced that he has selected an economics soul mate, Pat Choate, to be his running mate. Perot and Choate claim that they will participate in the campaign by better defining the issues for the electorate. I am surprised to find myself thinking that they may successfully accomplish that constructive role. They have nothing to lose by honestly presenting their views about very important matters. That might help to draw out both Clinton and Dole about important, controversial issues that they would rather put off until after the election. It is to be expected that the less chance you have of winning, the more eager you are to shake things up.

I have been pressing too hard to maintain my interest in the political process. I do not like feeling bored and I think I require uncertainty to maintain my excitement. The possibility of a knockout blow is remote, but I keep it in the forefront because it is all I have had. Now I may make too much of Perot in an effort to keep myself interested. Of course I can always fall back on the reality that anything can happen; remember Harry Truman.

President Clinton presented our nation's highest award to private citizens, the Presidential Medal of Freedom, to eleven honorees; a very impressive group. In a separate ceremony Dick Morris was presented with the chutzpah award for the twentieth century. It is not true that Grinch Frankly Newrich cried when Morris told the audience to kiss his big book advance and royalties. It is probably an indication of our national immaturity that we remain attracted to big stick men and we are turned off by spadones.

Rainy Wednesday afternoons are cooking times for me; again today. It is a bit of a problem since the freezers are full until Friday when I take some things to the holiday dinner. When I last saw David he expressed disappointment that I did not bring a chocolate pie. This afternoon I baked two chocolate pies with a secret ingredient: pineapple. It is my birthday present to Dave. There are probably a number of things he wants in addition to chocolate pie. His parents can provide what they find appropriate.

The pie is better than any chocolate pie I have tasted. It is a testimony to my devotion to my grandson that I will give him one of these pies rather than eat it myself. You can make such a pie and add your own secret ingredient; I described my method when I made the chocolate pecan pie several months ago. Add your own secret ingredient; try raspberry syrup or your favorite flavoring. Warning: Do not overcook.

Iraq shot a missile at one of our aircraft today. Reports suggest they did it in a way that ensured they would miss. Saddam is telling someone that he is not cowed by the United States. He seems to be firmly in control in Iraq. I thought an insider would kill him.

There is turmoil in Colombia where their vice president resigned in protest over evidence that their president is closely linked to drug syndicates. Adam is still there. It sounds scary.

My instructions were unambiguous; I did not experience the uncertainty that Deborah felt about what was expected. If I got it wrong I was quickly notified. I was supposed to be admirable but cautious and when the two came in conflict I was supposed to work it out in an admirable but cautious fashion. Mother made the rulings but I incorporated her system and have been engaged in that balancing act all of my life. It is a pretty good system and only rarely has it felt burdensome. The big trick for me has been to figure out what I think is admirable and to behave in ways that I, myself, admire, rather than looking to Mother or others for their approval. I still seek their approval but it is worth little if I don't concur.

We think the French are arrogant. Most of the world thinks that we are arrogant, immature, unsophisticated, bullying and wonderful. Saddam Hussein is tweaking us and playing on our character weaknesses. The little guys—that includes almost everyone—admire him for his bravado so his behavior becomes self-aggrandizing. We seem to be mobilizing for some heavy action. If we act, I hope our actions will be worthy of our self-respect.

There is much commentary about U.S. policy and action in Iraq. No one confirms President Clinton's contention that our missile barrage led to a success. Everyone knows that we are not involved to prevent genocide; we are there out of a self-interest that is petroleum based. Most of the world is willing to watch and wait when neighboring tribes with a long history of mutual hatred try to kill each other off; it is too difficult and expensive to try to stop them. Tribal warfare finds no innocent civilians, only hated enemy. Tribal victors have not caused a holocaust, they have protected their people by destroying a very dangerous enemy. We tend to think of those tribal people as primitive and hardly civilized, but our history shows that we are barely half a step ahead of them. It is a big half step.

New developments by the hour: An aircraft carrier, stealth bombers and B-52 bombers are being moved into place. The Republicans are criticizing President Clinton, claiming he has not been forceful enough and that Saddam Hussein only understands a very vigorous display of force. We are having a pre-election war. Candidate Dole's minions are doing the dirty work of criticizing our Commander-in-Chief and pressuring him to change course. Dole devotes himself to de vote by declaring his full support for our fighting men and women under all circumstances. He proclaimed that he is the most optimistic man in America and that he expects to win the election. Puffery is permitted while campaigning.

Preparations continue in a way that I fear precludes our backing away from the very aggressive use of air power. There is bipartisan agreement that we must impress Saddam Hussein sufficiently to keep him from asserting himself beyond Baghdad. He is not easily impressed. The Iraqi people are said to be largely unaware of what is about to happen. I see them as relatively powerless victims of a dictatorial regime. I wonder if the people in Iraq view themselves as the Iraqi people. The West created most of the countries in the Middle East and Africa and did it with little regard for tribal boundaries. I think we are seeing family values in action. Saddam's family has the power and imposes on all the other families of the area with high regard only for his own.

It is Friday the 13th and Rosh Hashanah begins at sundown. The sky has cleared and the refreshing cool breeze is most welcome. I will pick Deb up and we will join the Kivitz family before sundown.

The celebration was very pleasant and the food was delicious. There were a couple of new faces. Murray had several siblings when his widowed father married a widow with several kids. They did not stop there; it is a large family with many children and grandchildren and lots of complex relationships. Alex, Murray's older brother, has diabetes and has had his legs amputated. He complained that his wife, Dotty, is pushing him around a lot. Dot recently bought a new car, and when Alex was asked how he liked it, he said that it had plenty of leg room. You get the idea; we are a bunch of alta cockas who have learned to live with and laugh at adversity while we enjoy the antics of the younger generations. The holidays are a time for sentimentality and overeating in addition to cleansing and renewal. Fundamentalist Christians and orthodox Jews believe that God completed the creation of the Earth 5,757 years ago. Happy New Year. You do not have to be a believer to enjoy a grand anniversary celebration. If you don't like the gefilte fish with red horseradish, you can have quenelles with savory sauce.

Fancy Nancy prefers quenelles to gefilte fish;
Ethnic food is not her dish.
Her good taste and Anglophile leanings
Give her a classy sheen;
She is discriminating but not mean.
She's Yiddish but she seems so British.

We put on no highfalutin' airs as we welcomed a new year.

Bob Dole spoke to the Christian Coalition meeting in Washington, D.C., today. Before Dole arrived Pat Robertson declared that only a miracle from God could bring victory to the Republican candidate. Was Robertson implying that there is some source of miracles other than God? Dole and Robertson clasped hands and raised their arms in the spirit of unity. Could it have been in the spirit of victory brought about by a miracle? It was a chilling union for me; those zealots do terrible things to promote their cause. If religious zealots come to power I fear a modern day Dark Ages with a Malleus Maleficarum and Inquisition. I hope you have gotten the idea that those guys frighten me.

Our troops and military machinery are poised for action.

Stand-up comedians who made the transition to television were shown doing some of their best stuff last night. Political humor was prominent. It was not a courageous show; most of the material shown was relatively gentle, but it reminded me of how the thin-skinned need not apply for political office in America. No elected official is sacrosanct. It is the comedians who try to confront us with important issues and ask us to reconsider our acceptance of the conventional wisdom. We need these court fools to raise important questions and to expose self-deception. We are now royalty holding court in our home and we can call for the jester whenever we want to be prodded and coaxed to think more about important matters. We are so lucky.

I live with luxuries that were not available to royalty a few moments ago. Clean comestibles and a full array of spices are always at hand. My mattress is a bit lumpy but quite adequate and the bed is conveniently located near the toilet. Then there are the conveniences that run on electricity; I would be considerably inconvenienced if some bad guy destroyed the Potomac Electric Power Company. Several Republicans, peculiar people but not comedians, are pressing President Clinton to initiate air strikes on the power plants that supply Baghdad. No doubt that would make life more difficult for a lot of people, but our side does not want to hurt those people; we just want to protect our supply of relatively inexpensive oil.

Maybe oil is inexpensive in the same way that cigarettes were inexpensive. A lot of undesirable things are happening now and there is a huge bill that will come due soon. Entrenched interests and laziness keep us from serious efforts to start needed changes. There must be a humorous way to address these important issues. We tend not to include all costs when we estimate the price.

I planned to go to Cohen's famous resort in the mountains for two weeks last year. It is the food there that makes it famous and expensive. When I learned that a hotel near them had equally excellent food and was half the price, I went to the less costly resort. My first day there I went to play tennis and bought a can of tennis balls; they were very expensive. I told the pro that at those prices I could have gone to Cohen's. He explained that at Cohen's they get you by the meals.

The breaking news this Sunday morning is that things have simmered down a bit; all skirmishes so far today are verbal battles between Democrats and Republicans. Is it possible that we have gotten all suited up for the big game in Iraq but we will not, after all, play? I hope so.

We need an honorable and humane way to proceed in Iraq that will not upset the American electorate. It may be possible to avoid a shoot-out without feeling sissified. The news today is an admixture of weather and death; they surround us and the networks believe that is what we want to hear about. They give us a commercial followed by a murder, a murder investigation, a murder trial or a report of some disaster. All weather reports are preceded by commercials. Individuals killing each other excite our interest while we wait for weather and traffic reports. It annoys me but I am so pleased that we, as a nation, are not doing any killing today. If we were it would have been on the evening news.

Snow in the Rockies last night, gusty winds and squirrels squirreling nuts here and I'm still hopeful that the tomatoes will keep on coming for another month. The meditations of Marcus Aurelius are interesting and easier for me to read than *The Iliad* or *The Odyssey*. There are no reports of big weapons being fired in the Middle East; it has been a nice quiet day. The Commission on Presidential Debates ruled that Perot would not be included in the debates because he has no chance of being elected. Perot did not accept that decision. Gore is a heartbeat from being President, Kemp hopes to become a heartbeat from being President and Perot is trying to make Choate a fruitcake from being President. The polls suggest that Dole is gaining ground on Clinton; anything can happen.

Bright sunshine, cool breezes and low humidity: it's the kind of day when mother would feel chilly and insist that I wear a sweater to school. I would take a sweater with the understanding that I would wear it if I felt chilly. I put sweaters in the same category as hard-boiled eggs and liver: things that were imposed on me that I still avoid even though I know I am being neurotic and foolishly depriving myself. I have never purchased a sweater for myself but I have at least eight of them and I wear one when I will be with the people who gave it to me. They are very attractive and expensive garments that a person without a sweater complex would wear out. This catharsis is helping a lot; I can feel my sweater inhibition lifting as I express myself. It's wonderful but one of these days there will be a drug that will be a specific cure for sweater neurosis and there will be no need to go through the inefficient process of thinking about these complex matters.

Last evening I walked to the bridge game and got a ride home. My body is so stiff that I had difficulty getting in and out of the car. This morning, after a refreshing sleep, I felt terrific. After my favorite breakfast I went out into the glorious day and mowed the grass for two hours; that is my limit. A cold soda, a hot shower and a large dish of praline and caramel ice cream prepared me for these ruminations. It has been a delightful day so far, an excellent instance of how things are better than ever before in the history of the world.

Our military buildup in the Middle East continues but with a much reduced sense of urgency or tension. Clinton continues to address a laundry list of important but small issues while Dole attempts to mobilize enthusiasm by trying to frighten us while telling us that it is Clinton who is trying to frighten us. Perot is whining. The election is seven weeks away and things are so very quiet.

Spiro Agnew has died but his picturesque speech and the people who wrote his words are still with us. I voted for Spiro Agnew when he ran for and was elected to the Maryland governorship—the only time I have voted for a Republican. He was a moderate back then running against an overtly racist Democrat. It was an easy choice for me; how sad to have such a choice. How grand to have a choice.

Adam called last night. He is still tired from his trip but it went well enough; there were glitches that did not prevent the team from doing a lot of much needed surgery. It was the eighth time he has been to Colombia; he has been to four different regions there. If he keeps going back the Feds will suspect he's a mule. There are plenty of dangers in Virginia but I, nevertheless, feel relieved that he is safely back with his family.

I am watching bits and pieces of an eight-part PBS series, "The West." It uses snapshots and narration and attempts to present a balanced account of our nation's conquests and expansion to the west coast. It is a powerful story full of adventure, gore, suffering, deceit, hope, despair, victory and defeat. We forced and connived our way westward and squeezed out or defeated the indigenous population, English, French, Russians, Spanish and Mexicans. Our claim to moral and racial superiority excused a lot of grossly unfair behavior and killing on a grand scale. It is not always easy to differentiate killing from murder. There can be a fine line between glory and baseness.

How do you regard me? That question looms large and persists; we want an updated report at frequent intervals. I hope to get over that need for reassurance. My self-assessment ought to suffice without reinforcement. Authenticity ought to be all that matters. If the "authentic you" does not bring you respect and admiration, you might try some modifications that you yourself will admire and respect. That need for outside approval can stay powerful and lead to deception. Even toward the end we may misrepresent to gain the regard of others. I remember the dying macho man who asked his doctor to put the cause of his impending death as gonorrhea, not diarrhea.

Some people exude self-confidence and competence; it can take them a long way but it tells little about how they feel about themselves and less about their vulnerability to disruption if things go badly for them. My appearance of competence and self-assurance has been more than a facade, but I have always perceived myself as vulnerable and several times I have felt upset and disrupted when I failed to meet my own standard or it became clear to me that an important other found me unsatisfactory. Happily for me I have settled down and come to terms with my shortcomings or found a way to behave that felt acceptable to me. Not everyone finds a way to forgive himself.

Thinking awakened my nose, I think. When one thing follows another I tend to suspect they might be causally related. A lot of people are just getting to bed and here I am, up very early. My thoughts were about leadership and trustworthiness. We have a political system that encourages self-promotion and makes it very unlikely that one will be chosen on the basis of performance alone. Generals have been pressed into seeking high office; they have a record of very satisfactory service and have not been perceived as self-aggrandizing. The ideal candidate isn't a candidate at all but someone who has served well and impressed us as wise and dependable. A willingness to serve in high elective office is probably not enough; it must be followed by actually running for that office and getting contaminated by the process. It is a puzzlement.

My ruminations are for my amusement; I have no conviction that a philosopher or poet would do a better job than the professional politicians who are required to spend so much time selling themselves to the voters. If an outstanding non-political leader appears on the scene it is likely that she will be pressed into service and, if we are lucky, she will serve us well.

How did elite and elitist become pejorative labels? Who decided that liberal and conservative are polar opposites? Are we awaiting the appearance of the messiah, and if he declares his identity do we want to elect him? Would it be an improvement? Would he get contaminated by the political process? Religious Christians and religious Jews are separated by one appearance: the Jews await the appearance of the messiah and the Christians await the Second Coming.

The passenger pigeon is extinct; we hunted it out of existence. Congress passed legislation to protect the American bison but President Grant refused to sign it; the slaughter continued and led to further bloody conflict with hungry Americans who felt betrayed by the United States government. Actions that seem pragmatic and uncomplicated are seen in retrospect to have been despicable, morally insupportable and even criminal. This past week several admired administration workers resigned, unwilling to serve after President Clinton signed the Welfare reform legislation that many view as Welfare repeal. It seems tragic to us bleedingheartliberaldemocrats that President Clinton did the dastardly deed. No matter that he disclaims it, he did it. We must not do to the poor what we did to native Americans, their sacred buffalo or the passenger pigeon. I am aware that some people take a vow of poverty but I have never known anyone who wanted to be poor.

Yom Kippur, the holiest day of the year, and the first full day of fall coincide today. We celebrate the end of a successful year (we survived) and our hopes for the new cycle. Protective rituals abound as we try to wipe the slate clean and begin anew. Yom Kippur means Day of Atonement. In ancient times a scapegoat was sacrificed as people expressed sorrow about their wrongdoing and promised to be good in the new cycle. Before the scapegoat, no doubt, there was human sacrifice. We killed others in an effort to protect ourselves. That sounds familiar.

Yesterday Deb spent several hours helping me get some of my thoughts from computer to paper. When my thoughts are on paper they are there for you to see and that feels more self-revelatory. When I like what I have written I feel both embarrassment and pride. I think the embarrassment is about the pride. It's amazing, but I believe that even at this late stage and after all I have been through, I could blush.

We were only a little bit late for David's birthday party. There was a good sized crowd, all family, and lots of good food. Roy looked very well but he is still experiencing some postoperative discomfort. I enjoyed the afternoon. I did the driving and felt only moderate physical discomfort. When I dropped Deb off we could hear her newly acquired dog barking.

I only vaguely remember the asthma attacks I experienced until I reached puberty. Allergies run in the family: Deb had angioneurotic edema, Adam and I have a lot of allergic rhinitis and Allison has asthma. My asthma gave Mother an excuse for not allowing a dog in our house although I was permitted to play with neighborhood animals and on one occasion I was responsible for the care of the neighbors' dog while they were away for a week. My kids wanted a dog and we had a dog most of the time. When Ria left in early 1983, she took the dog with her. Since then I have had the world's best pets: outdoor goldfish. They are faithful, undemanding and, if I only ask them to swim or eat, obedient.

Deb's work has brought her in frequent contact with an old friend, Patti, who has been talking about giving her a puppy. Patti gave and Deb accepted a dog, not a puppy, that was presented as disturbed and in need of special care. I was told, warned, about it as I left for her house and I declared at once that I was not the grandfather. It is a wonderful, appealing, smart and handsome little bundle of joy, so maybe I am its grandfather. I can be tough as a marshmallow.

The holiday has ended and the new season has arrived. Deb and I broke fast with the Eisenbergs who have invited me to join them for that end of Yom Kippur tradition for several years. It was very pleasant to be with their family and friends, most of whom I see only when I am with Diane and Lloyd.

President Clinton was at the United Nations meeting in New York today to sign a nuclear test ban treaty while Bob Dole had to settle with warning us that Clinton is a liberal who must be stopped. A Republican columnist predicted today that Dole will win the election; he compared the expert unanimity about Dole's impending defeat with expert unanimity about the direction of the stock market: always wrong.

A Catholic bishop in England upset the mother of his fifteen-year-old son when he left the church and declared his intention to marry the woman he loves, not her. Nobody is perfect.

Ross Perot is getting a lot of air time and press coverage as he sues for inclusion in the presidential debates. The first debate, originally planned for this evening, was declined by President Clinton, who indicated that he had other important matters scheduled. Both Dole and Clinton are on the stump daily. What they say does not clarify much; they are trying so hard to persuade us that they fail to project verity. It is a sad spectacle.

Tonight the temperature will dip into the forties for the first time since last spring. The squash plants have died and the tomato plants are down but not out. The habanero pepper plants seem vigorous but there have been no peppers and I see no blossoms. All of last year's rhododendron cuttings have died and not one of the pink dogwood seeds germinated; maybe next year. Except for the wonderful tomatoes, my green thumb has not functioned well this year.

My number came up on the dermatology clinic Rolodex, I was examined, several small new lesions were treated with liquid nitrogen and I am scheduled for the biopsy of several nasal lesions on October 29. That will be the eleventh anniversary of my melanoma surgery and the day after my seventieth birthday. Time sure does fly when you are having fun. I tried to talk Dr. Davis into using cryotherapy on the nasal doohickeys, but I could see he was obdurate and I meekly acquiesced to the proposed biopsies. Some battles are not worth fighting.

We are nearly as helpless as leaves being buffeted about by the breeze—not quite, perhaps more like butterflies caught in a storm and ready to redirect themselves if not crushed or torn asunder. The luck factor looms large. We can influence the course of events and we often do, sometimes wisely. Still, it can be frightening to have so little influence over the trip one takes. Mumbo jumbo and talismans can have a calming effect when no clear-cut action is apparent. What if ... There are so many close calls where the balance could swing in either direction with vastly different results. Accurate information sometimes helps; if you have it you might use it wisely to get what seems desirable.

As I prepared to retire I helped some of my patients pick a new psychiatrist. I developed a short list of people whom I thought would be trustworthy and capable and who would probably remain in practice and outlive my patients. Perhaps I was being overprotective in my efforts to have them avoid a repeat of losing a therapist. Maybe it's worthwhile to repeatedly experience losses and learn to go on and form new important alliances; losses, after all, are an important part of life. Patients often outlive their physician—the same physician who predicted the patient's death. "Old Doc Soandso died ten years ago after he told me I'd be dead in a year if I didn't stop drinking, and I still drink." That statement was often accompanied by a hearty laugh and I would sometimes join in. Yes, knowledge is power and often useful and protective, but there is a very large luck factor. I am thinking about that physiology laboratory session with the turtle hearts: some hung on much longer than others.

War in and around Jerusalem gave President Clinton air time and he did not smirk. The Senate did not override his veto of the bill banning partial birth abortion. Candidate Dole was in Florida telling the old folks that Clinton is trying to frighten them. He makes a point and then repeats it, sometimes twice. Four congressional freshmen—two Democrats and two Republicans—were interviewed on "The News Hour"; each expressed great confidence about reelection. If there is truth in campaigning, I can not discern it.

Bela, the new family member, went to the beauty parlor today and is going on a shopping spree tomorrow. I'm told she's a bit of a nudge. Deb is surprised that she, Deborah, is being trained so quickly.

Fighting continues around Jerusalem where the orthodox Jewish influence has resulted in an offensive assertion of power that aroused the Palestinians to forceful face-saving action. The Israeli religious right shows itself to be as coercive and oppressive as all other such groups when they are in power. The horrors of persecution have not resulted in wise restraint and respectful toleration of difference. Some lessons are very hard to learn; once in power the Golden Rule is replaced by the rule of intolerance and revenge: Do unto others as they have done unto you. Binyamin Netanyahu and Yasser Arafat are doing what has been done repeatedly around Jerusalem for many centuries. Chalk up another one or two hundred battle casualties; it's a drop in the bucket. Martyrdom is very popular.

An Islamic militia coup overthrew the government in Afghanistan today and proclaimed that women would be banned from holding government office and men should grow beards.

In the United States the Christian right might overthrow the government by ballot and have autos-da-fé for those they find heretical.

The Republicans have coughed up a lot of money that they had withheld from legislation. It is time to go home to campaign, and haggling about money or principle must not delay their departure. President Clinton has them by their timetable and will not let go. The polls indicate that concerned citizens are not greatly pleased with the candidates: Dole is a good guy who is too old and out of touch with the people after decades in Washington; Clinton does not set a proper moral tone and, although he has done a good job, he is seen as slippery and sleazy; Perot is too weird. That's it; there are no others. What is a voter to do? This voter plans to vote the straight Democratic ticket and hope for the best.

Last evening PBS presented David Frost interviewing the three vice-presidential candidates. I turned it on and it turned me off. There is not much to feel enthusiastic about. The candidates are required to blare their messages and pose for votes; they do it and it takes on a beauty contest quality. They think there are still enough undecided voters to reverse the balance so the performance will continue until Election Day.

I have a clear memory, perhaps accurate, of leaving my office on Election Day 1980 with considerable confidence that Jimmy Carter would be reelected. My judgment about political outcome is comparable to my judgment about financial matters; with good reason, I lack confidence about these matters. The experts have confidence, but they always hedge because they have been burned. Political science is not a precise science. The weatherman, with all of his fancy equipment and satellites, makes mistakes. I'm trying to keep the race exciting. Wes was serving on an aircraft carrier in the Pacific when Truman was elected. Dewey was considered a shoo-in; the odds were twelve to one and Wes won six dollars. Anything can happen.

Slim pickings from the tomato plants this morning; summer is over and things do not look good out in the garden. I'm headed for the bridge game and following it I'll join Marilyn and Dick Schaengold for dinner at their home.

My body is asserting its influence; it acts up if I fail to put it into a reclining position every few hours. Yesterday I did not lie down for over nine hours. This morning the old crotchety bod is doing its thing. I take it with me almost everywhere and we did not dissociate for the bridge game or the very pleasant evening spent with the Schaengolds and their guests. The long drive home in a pouring rain was unpleasant but I felt OK and was in bed and asleep a little after 9 o'clock. Early in this new day I was alerted to the folly of sleeping on my right side with a full stomach. Call it dyspepsia or gastroesophageal reflux or heartburn; call it a wake-up call. I woke up with an uncomfortable bellyache. My neck hurt also and as soon as I turned over I began to sneeze. A series of sneezes cured me of all other sensations and soon I was busy blowing my nose and laughing. Now I have returned to my usual abnormal state and I am wide awake. Living alone has its advantages.

Dick and I met in medical school; I was one or two years ahead of him. Our friendship began here in Washington and we have several mutual friends but none of them were there last evening. Marilyn and Dick tried to continue friendships with both Ria and me and I have been pleased with Marilyn's persistence. Their guests last night were married couples, except for the grandson and me, and I had previously met all of the men and most of the women. I was the lone retired person. Several of the five psychiatrists are on the verge or are being urged to take the plunge by their spouses. Most of the talk was about travel, children and grandchildren. I was the first to arrive and the first to leave. I wonder if the talk turned to work and politics after I left. I'll ask about that when I call to thank them for the pleasant evening.

All important world events become fodder for our impending election. President Clinton has brokered a meeting in the United States between Netanyahu and Arafat with participation by Jordan's King Hussein and Egyptian President Mubarak. It becomes a test of Clinton's foreign policy success and has some politically disruptive potential. While our president tells us about these developments, candidate Dole is holed up in his condominium in Florida where he is boning up for the debate a week from today. Every hour or two Dole appears and shouts, "He's a liberal, liberal, liberal!"

This afternoon I was told about a recent occurrence and then asked to refrain from writing about it. I would have preferred that the request that I keep a confidence preceded the telling; I might have declined. People want to know how you regard them and often get indignant when you tell them and show them. They conclude that your level of respect and admiration is insufficient. I suppose that everything must be grist for the mill if one tells the tale truly.

My mother kept an immaculate home; she did most of the work herself. I remember drying the dishes occasionally and I was expected to pick up after myself, but nothing more in the way of housecleaning. I remember that a laundryman delivered and picked up each week, but Mother spent a lot of time washing and ironing and seemed burdened by it. All of us felt burdened by it when Mother would insist on washing clothing on a Sunday morning. We did not have a washing machine; just as I am my own breadmaking machine, Mother was her own washing machine. We could not leave for our Sunday outing until Mother was ready.

My brother and I started saving money for an anniversary gift for Mother and we saved for over a year. The money was kept in a jar in our bedroom closet and, in retrospect, it is unlikely that Mother was unaware of that jar and its contents. Our plan was to buy a washing machine for Mother. I had no realization that a washing machine would be for our convenience, not Mother's. When the plot was revealed, Mother seemed furious. She accused me, I think, of trying to get her to do all of the laundry and she was adamant that there would be no washing machine in her house. It was a big trauma for all of us. I have no idea what was done with that money, but I remember feeling that it made little sense to expect Mother to feel pleased. That was quite sad. She was obviously pleased with her grandchildren and viewed them as a grand gift. That felt good.

It can be very difficult to find the gift that will feel just right for both the giver and the recipient. No gift will correct or make up for interpersonal problems. Maybe an extremely expensive gift can make an unsatisfactory arrangement seem more or less fair. Remember the Kaplotsky diamond? The woman who owned it was quite pleased to have it but it came with a curse: Mr. Kaplotsky.

The cover article in *The Washington Post Magazine* today is about Wayne Curry, our Prince George's County Executive. He grew up here in what was a highly segregated county with a white police force that was known for its harsh treatment of blacks. Now he heads a county that has been called the most affluent majority black county in America. His mother taught him racial tolerance and the writer, Peter Perl, quotes her: "I came to see that there is one race, the human race. We tried to teach them (the children) to be colorblind. We drummed it into them." I believe what Mrs. Curry taught her kids; it does not, however, keep me from an awareness of the prevailing system of classifying people by race and the reality that most people use that system. This afternoon I walked across the street to greet my new neighbors, wish them happiness in their new home and give them a loaf of my bread. I was aware that Wayne Curry thinks he is black, my new neighbors think they are black and I too am stuck with such notions.

The President does not look boyish; there is a downturning of his mouth and a serious demeanor that leaves no doubt about his determination and authenticity as he announces that he has arranged a summit meeting to help establish peace in the Holy Land. He will get credit for giving it a good try whether it works or not. I am now so cynical that I see it as being important primarily as part of the campaign. In five weeks we will elect a man, Clinton or Dole, who will be a lame duck for four years. Everything they do between now and then will be at least partly political.

Congressional Democrats and Republicans have displayed the contentiousness and abuse of power that we find so appalling. Those in power exclude and disrespect the minority and justify their behavior with historical precedent. They do unto others what was done unto them. The Democrats misbehaved for many years; now they are getting it back and squawking about the lack of comity and fairness. The world has Serbs and Croats, Tutsis and Hutus, Palestinians and Israelis and Democrats and Republicans. No one is trusting enough or big enough to break the cycle of abuse and give up the us against them mentality.

Perhaps we are so hard-wired to be domineering and selfish that it will always be with us; family values in action.

Deb and Bela came for dinner last evening. It went well but I'll not invite Bela again—at least not for awhile. She is a nudge and a distraction. A dog is a lot like a child once you take it in and assume responsibility for its care. Deborah is thinking about that. The present arrangement is more like foster care than adoption. There is a lot to be said for outdoor goldfish.

The summit has begun but it is not certain that the participants will get beyond individual discussions with President Clinton. A large paid ad in the morning newspaper proclaims that American Jews strongly support the peace process. Almost everyone wants Netanyahu to subside and relent as a show of good faith in the peace process. Candidate Dole has not yet weighed in, but other Republican leaders are busy criticizing the President for what he has done and what he has not done. Polls show that a high percentage of Jews vote and tend to vote Democratic. Do you think the Republicans would welcome and encourage something that might erode that tendency? It's possible. There is a rumor (I'm starting it) that Grinch Frankly Newrich is Jewish and that he was videotaped wearing a yarmulke and davening. Oy, heaven help the Jewish people; and everyone else.

There is a great deal of aircraft noise this afternoon, including a lot of helicopter sounds, as traffic goes in and out of Andrews Air Force Base. I wonder if it is connected with the summit meeting. Less than an hour ago I was on the base and all was quiet except for long lines at the commissary. I went to the air terminal to inquire about space available travel to Florida and the terminal was very quiet. No doubt there is a separate, special facility for VIP travel and the President's activities. I'm eager to hear the 4 o'clock news for an update on international affairs and how they will impact on my preoccupations. It is a cool, refreshing day; just right for some yard work, but I'll bake a cake and read until the news starts.

Candidate Dole, formerly thought to be an honest man, put aside his debate study book to criticize President Clinton for creating a photo opportunity. He then arranged to meet with Netanyahu following the summit meeting. There has been no indication that he attempted to arrange a meeting with Arafat; there aren't very many Arab votes that he is concerned about. Of course, he will bar the media and all photographers from the meeting with Netanyahu because it will be about serious business, not a photo opportunity.

Arafat and Netanyahu met face to face yesterday for three hours, the killing has stopped around Jerusalem and no details have been released other than the obvious: they have resolved little. The summit is ended. President Mubarak of Egypt did not attend because he doubted it would be fruitful.

The lead story this morning was not about the summit meeting, the campaign or the crash of a Peruvian passenger plane; it was about the baseball playoffs. Washington is a baseball town without a baseball team, so it has adopted the Baltimore Orioles and spirits are high after the Birds won the first game of the playoffs. A small complication developed in a previous game when a great and much admired Baltimore player spit in the face of an umpire after he was called out on strikes. The spitter compounded his egregious behavior by bad-mouthing the spittee in a public statement. The umpires were distressed about this behavior and were not satisfied with routine procedures for handling such a matter; it will be dealt with further tomorrow. Public reaction is mixed about appropriate punishment for such an adolescent assault by a baseball hero. Almost no one openly condones the behavior; the question is about appropriate punishment. I suspect that there are some fans who feel the spitter did right by expressing his disdain about a bad call, but they are too discreet to say so.

Family values make it easy to resolve the punishment issue. If the spitter is part of your family, you secretly admire him for his intensity and his desire to advance the family fortunes, but you keep that reaction within the family and you reprimand him and take away his dessert for a whole week so the world will know you have disapproved his expression of pique and exuberance. If he is not a member of your family, you cut off his baseball. It gets a bit complicated when the families involved are in collusion about important self-serving matters and want to continue with those activities. Family values will help them to work it out. Pragmatic and cynical families will let him help win the battle and then sacrifice him. Why hasn't the public prosecutor charged the spitter with battery? I hope the spittee will file a civil suit against the offensive saliva dispenser.

Sports can be almost as much fun as politics. Outrageous behavior is not unusual in the arena; boys will be boys. Legislators have knocked each other unconscious as if they were gladiators or boxers. Trumped-up charges and countercharges are part of the game in the sport of politics. Always use the home team advantage and be deceptive and bluff when you think you can get away with it. Hit first and let the other guy get caught when he retaliates. Win. It is a pleasure to watch champions in action.

Candidate Dole interrupts his debate studies with periodic criticism of his opponent, but both men are boning up for Sunday. Dole has a slight advantage because expectations of him are low; he has never been known for debating skills while Clinton is an acknowledged master debater. Perot has been denied participation but will be permitted to watch with the rest of us. They can't take that away from him.

Tomorrow will be a critical day for me; there are frost warnings for tomorrow night and I risk losing all remaining tomatoes if I don't harvest them prior to the first frost. I will study the matter carefully and then decide. My tendency, you may be surprised, is to be conservative about such matters. I am a dyed-in-the-wool liberal who advocates self-reliance, efficiency and conservation. I am still working on being more generous but it is difficult for me; too critical.

Congress adjourned today just in time to miss the first frost, but you can bet many of our legislators are in for a deservedly frosty reception in their own bailiwick. Everything is up for grabs; both the House and the Senate could go either way. If the past two years have taught a lesson, both parties may be ready to accept that a mandate is a mandate for moderation rather than carte blanche for a sharp move to the left or right. It's probably too much to expect of them.

Islamic militiamen in Afghanistan have pistol-whipped women for being on public streets and beaten men for what they decide is improper attire. They have closed the schools temporarily and indicated that girls will not be permitted to attend classes. They declare that they are imposing strict Islamic rule. Quick justice has led to the killing of former communist officials; their bodies were hung from poles in public squares. I have seen no reports of high Islamic officials decrying such acts or declaring that they do not represent true Islamic rules and teaching. The zealots are behaving the way zealots behave when they are in power. Will something similar happen in America if the Democrats or the Republicans gain control of both the executive branch and the legislative branch in November?

The original zealots were Jews in Judea who fiercely fought Roman efforts to heathenize the Jews almost two thousand years ago. They did not proselytize or try to impose their rules on the Romans, but they were not in power. They were committed to imposing strict religious law on all Jews in a theocracy free of strangers. They expected a great religious battle that would lead to the coming of the messiah who would bring victory. They were fanatics, terrorists, assassins, freedom fighters, guerrillas, ... Zealots. Today we are subjected to echoes of that sect. Religious murderers wear smiles of beatitude when they are tried for their acts. There is no chance that such people will gain power in America, is there?

Yitzhak Rabin's assassin, a modern day Jewish zealot, and two who conspired with him were convicted of meticulously planning the assassination because they did not approve of Rabin's policies and goals. The religious fundamentalists have succeeded in derailing the peace process to the joy of both Islamic and Jewish fundamentalists. They want communities that command uniform compliance with religious law and exclude and condemn strangers and nonconformists. Clannishness avoids unwanted outside influences that might threaten traditional values and rules of behavior.

Poor rich Ross Perot has been excluded from the debate and can't get a major television network to show his latest infomercial. What good is all that money if it can't buy love or TV time? Well, maybe it can buy love. A late night TV comedy skit showed the candidates debating. Clinton was portrayed as silly and raunchy while Dole was mean and died when an alien, Perot, came out of his chest. The debates have the attention of the campaign watchers, but polls show little interest among likely voters and a lot of people do not plan to watch. I'm looking forward to it and it is my intention to stay awake to the very end.

There is heavy frost west of here. I pulled up the tomato plants and brought in about fifty scrawny little green tomatoes that won't be worth eating; the splendid season is over and I'll soon switch to grapefruit, but won't bother you with them. Excellent apples have been available; I'm enjoying them. I eat a very healthy diet and then add large quantities of cake and ice cream. Nobody is perfect.

I welcome the calls I have been receiving from former patients; they check in with me and check up on me. I have heard about vacation trips, illnesses, operations, retirement, business ventures, joys, important losses, legal difficulties and a pregnancy. I decline invitations for lunch. There are a couple of people I expected to hear from who have not contacted me and a couple who I think will avoid contacting me until they are ready to include a check when they check in.

The end of the season, the beginning of a new cycle, is a time that, for me, includes review with some nostalgia. I am surprised when I awaken thinking about Ria and, with the disorientation accompanying awakening, feeling that she is still with me. I depended so heavily on her for a very long time. That dependency was the best stuff in life for me and I missed it for at least a couple of years before we physically separated but I still recapture it on occasion in my sleep. Now I demand much less of myself and my needs from others are much reduced, but I have some nostalgia for the old arrangement. Would I like another go at it? No, thank you. Do I wish I had managed it better? You bet I do.

There is a traditional, paternalistic aspect of me that persists, although I feel it is not desirable or rational. Somehow I was supposed to guide and control the members of my family and protect them from outsiders and themselves. I tried to suppress that part of myself and was largely successful, but in the process I did not protect the family the way I might have. I did not keep very close tabs on what was happening in the home and when I was aware of potential difficulties I resisted authoritarian suppression of what I found. I did not keep Steven from going to Florida on his motorcycle. I did not throw out the marijuana plants on the back porch, although I did make it clear that if they were not gone I would be. I did not somehow get Ria to stop smoking and save her from a dreadful final illness and death. No matter what path we take, some things are gained and some things are lost. About twenty years ago Adam reprimanded me for failing to force him to learn to play a musical instrument. Perhaps I can forgive myself for such dereliction.

The Earth is pouring out its core in anticipation of the first Clinton Dole debate. A new island is being formed in the Hawaiian chain by the volcanic extrusion of huge amounts of magma. In Iceland another volcano has burst through and melted a tremendous hole in a massive glacier; floods could destroy most of that country. Our dear Earth is having a bowel movement. Perhaps it is just a coincidence that these humongous excretions occur at this time, but when things happen in close association, I tend to consider that they might be related. I'm not saying that I believe it, just that it is something to consider. People believe a lot of things that have not been proved. These events may be a sign and require the expertise of a sign reader. A third sign would be a sure sign. A committee could be formed to decipher and explain the significance of it all. I am thinking about whom I would include in such a group. If after their deliberations they decided to play golf, I would recommend that they get Scalia to be their caddie.

The town council met and decided to put a park bench on the south side of the library. When the vote was completed, Abraham declared that God told him that the bench belonged on the east side of the library. The council told him that the vote was completed, but he persisted and told them that as a sign of God's wishes the nearby mountain would move. The mountain moved but the council decided it was too late; the vote had already been completed.

I am ready to rumble. Past campaign debates were examined in the newspaper and on all the political talk shows this morning. The consensus is that it will not be a debate at all but an opportunity for Clinton and Dole to present themselves again in a way that voters will find appealing and not threatening. Also, it is a dangerous occasion where one might stumble. I think of it as round eleven in a twelve round heavyweight championship fight; the second debate will be round twelve. The incumbent is very far ahead on points and the challenger knows he must score a knockout; it's the only way he can win. It is the American way to root for the underdog and there would be no interest in the contest if it were not for the possibility of that knockout.

I will have dinner at the Behre house and then watch the big event there or come home and watch from my usual recumbent position. My Dukakis–Bentson button is ready. I'm getting sleepy just thinking about it.

Dinner and mostly non-political talk with Alice and Herb, Bob and Jean Markley and Jean's sister, Helen, was an excellent warm-up for debate watching. As soon as I stopped eating, my physical discomfort increased and I excused myself, drove home and got into bed to watch the debate. I remained wide awake for the full ninety minutes plus the half hour of commentary on PBS; it had my attention.

My partisan impressions did not quite match the expert opinions that were expressed. I was pleased when Mark Shields used prizefighting analogies and said that Dole had not buckled Clinton's knees or come close to scoring a knockout. The experts seemed unanimous that Dole had shown his sense of humor, his concern for the American people and restraint in his attacks on President Clinton. I found Dole less appealing than ever before. In seeking the office he has sullied much of what I found admirable about him. He did not show me that he is a direct, truthful and authentic person. He attacked by allusion while denying his willingness to engage in such behavior, he avoided the new question by going back to the previous one and, worst of all, he hedged and dodged when asked directly about the character issue, and yet he repeatedly told us that only he is believable. I thought he was disingenuous.

Those who characterize President Clinton as slick had their feelings confirmed last evening. He was well-prepared, firm, polished, vigorous and defended his record while promoting his vision and himself. I think that in round eleven Clinton did not throw a single punch; he defended himself and looked good. Dole threw all the punches and landed a few on his opponent and a few on himself. Any knockout will be self-inflicted. I must remind myself that Dole is a lot like some of those wonderful Mexican fighters: they never give up.

Ross Perot managed to get a lot of air time, including one of his infomercials that I thought he had been denied. He seems to be preparing us for the realities to come after the election. First, one must get elected.

Nothing happened to change the mind of the decided voter and the undecided must have been impressed by both men; that is probably slightly in Dole's favor. The President, with the consent of the Senate, will probably appoint three or four Supreme Court justices between 1997 and the year 2001; this is a very important election. Reporters were out in force this morning asking people who won the debate. The response was overwhelmingly, "My man." It is as if two different debates were conducted, one for the supporters of each candidate. During the debate Dole mentioned a young student in Ohio whose family wanted school choice and was denied it. The young man and his father were interviewed and asked about their reaction to the debate. They watched a movie last night, not the debate. The movie was described as boring.

The human volcano erupts again in Northern Ireland: Christian against Christian with few Christian acts included. The Protestant march through Catholic neighborhoods has been effective in keeping hatred alive and violently expressed. Terrorist and freedom fighter are synonymous; desperate men use desperate measures.

The IRA has claimed credit for yesterday's bombings that few find creditable. The perpetrators of our American bombings are more difficult to identify; those bombings are unsolved crimes. The primary suspect in the Olympics bombing had his property, including his guns, returned to him by the FBI and no one has been charged for that crime or for the train bombing that occurred one year ago.

The middle class ghetto in which I grew up was quite safe, but the message was clear that the world is a dangerous place for Jews: be admirable but cautious. I was entirely unprepared for and ignorant of the intense hatred and distrust Christians felt toward each other. If someone told me that those Christian Jew-haters were divided into competing sects, I missed it. The gentiles I knew were uniformly friendly and helpful, but they lived or worked in my parish and I understood that they were exceptional. Work outside of my safe place put me in a gentile environment for the first time while I was in high school. Any uneasiness I felt about my safety was ameliorated by my realization that those gentile people hated each other much more than they hated me. They seemed a bit wary of me but I detected no hatred toward me; they used it all up in their internecine struggles.

The University of Cincinnati was a municipal university when I was in medical school. It served the community and the tristate area of Ohio, Kentucky and Indiana. No Negro students were admitted to the medical school while I attended. There were no quotas, but each year twelve Jews were admitted and it was usual to have one student from New York and one from New Jersey. I remained at the Cincinnati General Hospital for four years after medical school and it was during that time that some changes began to take place. Exclusionary practices were slowly eroding and opportunities were opening up. It was not until the 1950s that the first Negro medical students and house staff were allowed, and at the same time departments that were closed to Jews made occasional exceptions. The mayor's son, a Jew, was admitted to the surgery residency program; that was a breakthrough.

I had a colleague who grew up in a small town in Wisconsin where there were no Negroes or Jews. He recalled that the community was divided into two camps that interacted minimally. His family was Catholic and his father was a dentist. All of his father's patients were Catholic. I do not know if there was a Protestant movie house and a Catholic movie house, but there was at least one of each for almost all activities, businesses and services; some melting pot. What do Christian people pray for? Let them pray for a more charitable heart.

The Pope is recovering from an appendectomy and is strong enough to watch the big debate tonight between Gore and Kemp. The candidates have indicated that they will try to avoid personal attacks and rancor. It sounds very dull, but I will watch it and try to stay awake.

Dole may decide to get more personal and nasty. When the final debate begins he is considering leaning over to President Clinton and telling him, in a stage whisper, that his fly is open, again. He cannot score a knockout by being subtle or gentle, but if he gets very mean he may knock himself out. The people believe in redemption.

My excitement about the debate sapped my energy; I fell asleep long before it began and then I was up and wide awake for all of it. Vice President Gore was solemnly repetitive while Kemp was exuberantly repetitive. They were messengers with a check list and each completed his mission over and over again. I was too well rested to succumb to the soporific quality of their mantras.

There is a fair chance that Gore and Kemp will be candidates for the presidency in four years. If that happens and if they stay dedicated to their convictions, it will be very difficult for me to tell one party from the other. I read that Jack Kemp once said he was not smart enough to be President; he jokingly hinted about that last night. I think he is not mean enough to be a modern day Republican. He is a sincere man who believes in helping all citizens achieve fulfilling lives with the help of well-planned federal government policies and action. That may be consistent with the Republican Party of Lincoln, but it is ground now held by the Democratic Party.

A woman has not lived in this house for going on fifteen years. Every once in awhile Deborah will let me know that something is amiss and she might recommend that I take action to correct it. I have developed an imaginary job jar that sits on the kitchen table. I know what is in it, but only rarely do I take on a project or hire someone to do it. Some things demand attention; those things I do. When the grass gets very long, I mow it. Every January or February, on a day that is very cold, I defrost the big freezer; it needs it badly after a year of use. A few years ago I swept out the garage for the first time since my father did it around 1980. I had the house painted several years ago and for the past two years I have hired someone to clear the drains and gutters. Most things are not very important. If the job is small enough and easy enough I might take it on just to empty the jar a bit. I like to do the things that I like to do, not things that need doing.

Ah, the smell of fresh baked bread; it covers the smell of mildew very well. Last week I replaced most of the old rug pads with a new mildew-resistant product that is guaranteed for ten years; I hope that is not long enough. Very soon I will re-caulk my bathtub and, with Deb's assistance, replace my toilet seat. I've been sitting on that same old seat for over thirty-three years and yet it holds no sentimental value for me; it is worn out and has lost its looks, just as I have, but I'm staying and it is going. The windows probably need cleaning; it has not been done for at least fifteen years. The rugs and curtains get vacuumed, I think.

Some things take care of themselves with time. Several years ago a small animal, probably one of the squirrels that own the attic, died in the wall between a back bedroom and bathroom. The smell was terrible, but after three or four months with those doors closed and those windows open, those back rooms smelled sweet again. In this house we have no skeletons in the closet; they are in the wall.

The Earth is entering its final phase; barring an accident that leads to its premature extinction, it has a little less than a billion years to go. The election, however, is more than three weeks off and the experts claim that the campaign is already in its final phase. Targeted messages are being sent by both candidates. A targeted message is one that is meant to be sneaked by most of us, because we are likely to find it offensive and it might turn us away from the vote seeker. This heavyweight championship bout has all the authenticity of professional wrestling.

A nice old lady worked at the admitting desk of the emergency room at Cincinnati General Hospital when I worked there. Her job was to register each new patient and to record the chief complaint. According to that nice old lady, about half of the people complained that they were "Out of whack below the belt." The Republicans want Bob Dole to hit Bill Clinton where they feel he is most vulnerable: below the belt. I do not understand why the Republicans think that my once-and-still married president is sleazy while their serially monogamous leaders are pure and faithful. Nevertheless, since the low punch is their only hope, they are using it while disingenuously pretending to argue about whether to use it. Sleazeballs abound.

Bob Dole tells us repeatedly that he alone is the presidential candidate who is trustworthy. He characteristically repeats himself three times in a mechanical way that reminds me of old cigarette commercials; say it three times and the dummies might remember it. What I remember is that he repeats himself a lot; maybe he forgot that he said it, but more likely he has been coached to smile more and repeat himself. We are being fed a lot of phony baloney.

My negativism about religious people continues to surprise me. I like religion when it helps people to have hope and to be more generous, tolerant and forgiving, but what I encounter is too often quite the opposite. Religion seems to breed fear, meanness, disparaging and punishing intolerance and vendettas. The religious people I encounter do not display the charitable heart that I want for myself and for others. I believe that charitable and nurturing alliances are the essence of goodness and ought to be considered the sine qua non of civilized people whether they are religious or not. Concerns about God and about life after death distract people and keep them from engaging in humane and refreshing activities. I'm sermonizing again.

The Sunday morning political entertainment is focused on the internal Republican debate about using the so-called character issue. They call it the character issue because it does not fit their purpose to call it fighting dirty. Dealing with issues has not worked for them and alluding to character deficiencies has not worked for them; nothing has worked for them and they are desperate, unwilling to quit and still looking for a knockout. I fear that they have time to pull it off.

President Clinton will not return low blows; it can not help his cause to attack Bob Dole based on Dole's character flaws and specific undesirable acts. The voters do not care that Dole left and divorced the wife who was so important to him as he adjusted to his terrible war wounds. It is only of passing interest that when his Senate seat was at risk he fought a very dirty fight. We already know about how he served Richard Nixon and continued that service beyond any semblance of respectability or patriotism. I do not admire Dole as much as I did a few months ago, but I am still impressed with his good intentions and tenacity. If he is guilty of anything, this bleeding-heart liberal finds a great deal of mitigation. When he cries I am reminded of the agony Abraham Lincoln experienced.

When Dole was in a close race against an obstetrician, he sent out flyers showing a baby in a garbage can and called his opponent an abortionist; he won a very slim victory and retained his Senate seat. I am pro life and pro choice and I do not believe in the soul. It is tragic when people who believe in the soul participate in the killing of someone they believe is a person with a soul. Abortion is often tragic even for those who do not believe in the soul. Once upon a time the world was flat and the developing fetus did not have a soul during the first trimester of its development. Things change but change is not always progress.

The Jains are religious people who believe in the sanctity of all animal life; they attempt to avoid even the accidental killing of a bug. I have never met a militant vegetarian—pushy but not militant, encouraging and persuasive but not insistent or coercive. Most people are content to follow their beliefs without imposing their ways on others, but some believe that they are obligated to impose their ways whenever they can manage it. Watch out for them; they are proselytizing zealots who will impose a totalitarian theocracy on us if we let them.

No chores were included in my dulcet, languorous weekend; it was strictly pleasure. Wes and I played only a little better than average at the bridge tournament Saturday morning. Following that I returned home and spent my time reading, writing and watching my favorite stuff on TV while making frequent trips to the refrigerator. Before cousin Raymond and Marlene arrive on Thursday, I hope to trim the bushes, mow the lawn, caulk the tub and replace the toilet seat. Dinner for them is ready to go.

Jimmy Carter was elected with a great boost from the Christian fundamentalists who were delighted when he declared that he is a born-again believer. Those same people deplored and abandoned him when they decided that he did not support their agenda. How could it be that President Carter was an authentic, practicing, born-again Christian and somehow not support their agenda? He taught and still teaches by example. He would not support efforts to coerce others to follow his religious principles and rules. Can one be an authentic religious fundamentalist and not try to eliminate all noncompliance? Some accused Carter of sanctimoniousness and self-righteousness but never of sleaziness or slickness. His style is mediation not coercion. The good example he set was nullified, from a fundamentalist point of view, by his eagerness to include and have a dialogue with all of us.

William Jefferson Clinton is our second announced born-again President. Clinton and Carter are soul mates. Both are strong, smart, ambitious men who try hard to do good and do right. They are Southern Baptists who have had one wife and one daughter. Each was a state governor. Only Carter has admitted that he has had lust in his heart. My special psychiatric acumen tells me that Clinton is, in his heart of hearts, a virgin.

The high ornamental hollies are bushes that would be trees. Those that grow around the perimeter of the pond area form an impressive privacy fence. The three that are close to the house are trimmed to keep them below roof level; each year we battle it out and they gain a bit despite my efforts to keep them contained. Last evening before dinner, Deb held the ladder while I trimmed and pruned, and when I quickly wore out we reversed roles. We made a good start, but we did not finish the job because I got shaky and weak from the effort and my wrist hurt.

Deb brought red snapper fillets that I poached in apple and tomato chutney. Perhaps I overcooked them, as we were not impressed with the red snapper; I'll go back to flounder or perch. We finished the last of the beef and barley soup that I made in February, just before I began this journal. Deb will be here again Thursday for dinner with Ray and Marlene. I started falling asleep as soon as she left and was zonked out before 8:30.

Candidate Dole is shouting that the Clinton administration is unethical and that he will address that during the big debate tomorrow. The Republican list of complaints is extensive and some of the actions they deplore strike me as obnoxious and ignominious. I hope Dole brings these matters up during the debate and I feel that doing so is entirely consistent with fighting a fair fight. I want the next four years to be administered far better than the last four. A couple of Republican columnists feel that Dole still has a good chance to win the election and tomorrow is round twelve: his last chance. I don't think the airing of the administration's ethical lapses will score a knockout, but the unspoken, subliminal message, the low blow that Dole dare not have seen by the voters, will permeate the proceedings and might do the job: Don't trust or vote for a perfidious womanizer.

It may be accidental that the Archer Daniels Midland Company yesterday agreed to pay a one hundred million dollar fine for price fixing. Top company executives face further legal action. That company has been an important source of funds in American politics and no one in her right mind believes that they gave the money for patriotic reasons. There are no innocents in this sad story of purchased influence that includes what most of us would call outrageous, unethical and illegal acts by politicians. Would I vote for a change of (I almost said Republican but could not get myself to do it) administration if I believed it would result in a clear improvement in the ethics of politics? Maybe; I hope so.

Anticipation of guests on Thursday threw me into premature labor. This afternoon I delivered a nicely mowed lawn three weeks ahead of schedule. While I was at it I also finished pruning the tall holly that seemed so resistant yesterday. I felt refreshed and strong after a long sleep and managed the work comfortably and safely. Now I am paying for it with increased movement and discomfort in my neck and right upper extremity. Life is a balancing act.

Bob Dole has played a dirty trick on himself. He left the job that he performed so effectively to engage in a wretched campaign that will take him to an unwanted retirement or an onerous position that would probably sully him in the view of his supporters and detractors alike.

Our culture presses us to be ambitious. Any lack of progress might be characterized as stagnation or failure. We are bombarded with the notion that we should fulfill our potential and be all that we can be. There is little support for the comfort of staying put in a life situation that is comfortable because it is well within one's capacities. Onward and upward, never give up; only wimps and weenies settle for less. Maybe one can get an exemption in very old age, but so many of the elderly will not grant themselves such relief.

Dole's timing is unfortunate. He prepared us for today's debate with a list of complaints about the ethics of the administration. He got specific and included a demand that President Clinton promise that he will not pardon anyone convicted in the Whitewater scandal. Bad timing: the former Iran-contra special prosecutor, Republican Lawrence

Walsh, was outraged by Dole's "hypocrisy" and announced that Dole was the foremost advocate of pardoning former Defense Secretary Weinberger before Weinberger was tried—a unique use of the presidential pardon. The bucket of worms is open, on to the debate.

Almost everyone used the prizefighting analogy. The audience formed a ring around the contestants and there was a referee and millions of judges. Dole began the final round with surprising strength, considering how far behind he was on everyone's scorecard. His jab was very strong, but President Clinton ignored many of those jabs and never seemed hurt. He responded with defensive moves and struck very few offensive blows. Dole needed to hurt Clinton severely, while it was important that Clinton not savage Dole or do anything that might annoy the judges. Fighting is a dirty game, judging is quite subjective and decisions are too often inexplicable. Don't humiliate a respected gladiator who is at the end of the road. There was no knockout, so a decision will be rendered. This cake will bake for three weeks and some will attempt to jar the oven.

A lot of important contests are being fought around the country. The results might change my world; yours, too.

The overnight visit led to an eating orgy; I gormandized from their arrival in the afternoon until they left this morning and was so full that I ate nothing at the bridge game. Perhaps Marlene and Ray will stop here again on Sunday to break up the long trip back to New Jersey from North Carolina and help finish the leftovers. I served several things that are strongly reminiscent of what Ray's mother and my mother served.

Phyllo cups with hummus and spicy tidbits
Salad with cheeses and sautéed asparagus
Potato blintzes with sour cream
Chicken soup
Roast lamb with seasoned rice
Brisket in onion gravy with potatoes and onions
Peach pie (Marlene's) with ice cream

For breakfast we had Dutch apple cake made from my mother's recipe and pecan coffeecake buns that are better than those from our childhood. I'll be hungry again soon.

Deborah and Bela joined us for dinner. Marlene and Ray have had large dogs for many years. They said that Bela would be less than a bite for their dogs. I think that Deb and Bela are now stuck with each other.

The week whizzed by. Are we there yet? We are practically there before we start; the whole megillah is over in a flash; life is just a flicker. The intrinsic importance of the trip is chimerical; it's there to be enjoyed and shared no matter how evanescent it is, and in the scheme of things it is very brief. Share it and make the most of it for it is the only game in town. Hear the holiday sounds, smell the spring rain, see the butterfly drink from the edge of the pond, taste the apples, touch life. Notice it before it is gone. That concludes my Sabbath sermon.

Grinch Frankly Newrich is trying to jar the oven and spoil the cake for the Democrats. He claims the Democrats are involved in a scandal much bigger than Watergate, because it involves foreigners and their sinister interest in influencing American policies. Grinch represents the xenophobic party that tells us to beware of outsiders and immigrants. The Democrats accepted a large contribution from an Indonesian family. The Republicans question why so much was given and suggest that there was an improper quid pro quo. Common Cause calls for an investigation of both parties and for campaign finance reform. It is a corrupt system that will not fix itself unless we insist on it.

Bob Dole says, "It's your money; it's your money; it's your money." He has been shouting a lot since he lost the debate and he continues to say things three times. Did he do that before he won the Republican nomination? This campaign has not been in his best interest. His dignity and probity are diminished. He tells us that he always tells us the truth and follows it with promises that are as meaningless as promising someone how you will feel in the future. He looks foolish. I think I am still dealing with and trying to justify my decision to retire. I will be retired one year on Thanksgiving Day; it's about time I stop ruminating about it.

The Republicans have declared victory: the American people realize that Clinton has failed them and they will elect Bob Dole and fifteen additional Republican senators and congressmen to insure that the Republican agenda for America is adopted. I heard it on TV this morning. That declaration was combined with further efforts to identify the Clinton administration with sinister foreign forces. Once again they play upon our xenophobic tendencies.

The Virginia senatorial campaign is appalling. Two reasonably decent men have spent lots of money to deceptively savage each other. It is difficult to think of them as intelligent, upright people when they behave so shamefully. Candidates would not use such tactics if they believed we could be persuaded by the truth told in a dignified manner. The term limits advocates believe we would have a more desirable system if incumbents had to be replaced. Then there would be no need to attack them or disgrace them to get rid of them.

Election Day is two weeks away. While recognizing that anything can happen, the experts seem to agree that President Clinton will be reelected and that both the House and Senate are up for grabs; it is too close to call. The cynics predict that both parties will go back to business as usual after the election, no matter who wins. I'm pleased to feel more optimism about the near future. The revelations and pressures during the past year have moved all parties toward bipartisan action to correct obvious defects and to fix the big ticket programs that are not sustainable unless modified. Powerful special interests will not go away and we will continue to resist having our own ox gored, but even thick-headed elected officials will recognize that the public is ready to accept reasonable bipartisan reform and correction.

The big picture is made with millions of teeny brush strokes. My minuscule part in that picture is very important to me and its importance is not diminished by my recognition of its inconsequence. My lucky life is not yet over. I agree with the notion that it is a mistake to judge a person's life until it is over. The remainder is still to be reckoned with; it can make a dramatic difference. My seventieth birthday and the eleventh anniversary of my surgery for malignant melanoma is near. I hope to celebrate my survival with some of my most important connections, my children and their families.

This morning I received a telephone call from a friend who calls me only when in need and who was aware of that and embarrassed about it. Still, he fits under the category of friend and I try to respond to him in a helpful and professional way. One of his kids has been troubled and in trouble repeatedly for many years. Our important partnerships greatly affect us and often seem the source of our joys and sorrows. If you don't have children what do you do for aggravation? The people who have no children seem to experience the full range of emotions anyhow. Very few of us seem suited to a life of isolation without important partnerships. Most of those who choose to isolate themselves are saints, disturbed or disturbed saints. How lucky it is for me and my kids that we more or less approve of each other and that we remain well connected. If all goes well I will predecease them. It feels tragic when the child dies before the parent.

Shortly after writing the above line I nearly killed myself. This weekend I cooked several things, including a new batch of beef and barley soup. I tried the soup on Sunday and served it last evening when Deb was here. We agreed that it was very tasty but not as spicy as expected, considering the many spices that I included. This afternoon I had a bowl of that soup and in the process I chewed and nearly swallowed a habanero pepper before I realized what was happening. It was a close call, but after chewing a lot of bread without swallowing any of it, I stopped feeling discomfort and it is likely that if I am careful I will live to see my seventieth birthday. Any little movement can have a large impact.

The old folks, those who receive Social Security and are covered by Medicare, vote; the candidates dare not defy them. The rest of the electorate feels less threatened and is less likely to show up on Election Day. Voter indifference adds power to the zealots and those who feel threatened. If the next two weeks are numbing enough there will be an even smaller than usual voter turnout. Both Dole and Clinton have become nigglers: Dole niggles about Clinton's character and Clinton presents us with niggling programmatic details; it's a turnoff. Low voter turnout makes it more likely that President Clinton will be reelected since he is so far ahead, but it makes the other races even less certain. I'm trying to stay interested and involved; there is less than two weeks to go.

The house was cozy this morning. My neck and arm discomfort increased as I read the newspaper and watched the TV news. So many people are having a difficult time. Terrible fires are destroying homes in California and there is severe flooding in parts of New England. Locally two children disappeared yesterday and hundreds of people are searching for them. Things are much worse on other continents. It is far from cozy for most of humanity. I'm a very lucky guy.

Why is this lucky and moderately secure fellow immodestly pandering to you with this prattle? There were a few things that I wanted to say, I said them and discovered a few more and said them. Recently I have been unwilling to have my output flag. It seems likely that this is connected with my concerns about how you feel about me, but such uninspired and perspiration-free activity is not going to garner admiration or approval. Some of this has been fun and a bit has felt important; not lately. Maybe I'm experiencing a letdown as my seventieth birthday and the election approach.

It's 3 A.M. Halloween morning; the goblins aroused my neck, right arm and right foot and drove me to get up and break my silence. My self-reprimand quieted me for over a week and I thought it might persist until after the election.

The scary creatures of the night make it difficult to rest comfortably. I wonder if they are visiting the candidates. The Republican drumbeat is loud and persistent. They attack the ethics of the administration and emphasize the need to keep the Democrats in check. Bob Dole has become a scold who criticizes all and sundry. Many Republican candidates have distanced themselves from him and Grinch. Dole is becoming a pathetic character; his dignity and credibility are gone.

The notion that Americans have become less honest, ethical and moral is nonsense. We have become more open about what is going on and we try to deal with it constructively. That's progress. Reports of cheating by trusted people appall us even when they do not surprise us. Breach of trust and deceptive self-promotion are not new.

Something important happened this week: Pope John Paul II, a very conservative pope, declared that the theory of evolution is probably correct. It takes a known conservative to effect important changes in entrenched policies and doctrine. The Church is an evolving institution no matter how much its members think of it as static. Thank you Pope John Paul for helping us to move forward with greater rationality.

All of my children were attentive and affectionate as we celebrated my seventieth birthday. I like them a lot.

Two days ago I was Patient Billet at the Andrews Hospital. First, Dr. Greenberg injected two hundred mouse units of botulism toxin into my neck, then Dr. Davis biopsied a couple of probable skin cancers on my extraordinary proboscis and finally I had a flu shot. It will take a while to see if the injections are helpful this time; so far my discomfort is increased. The biopsy reports will take a few weeks. Maybe I will not get the flu. I received the best that medical science has to offer from one of the finest health maintenance organizations in the world. It is far from perfect, but it is excellent.

My doctors put up with a lot from me. Every time I have a skin cancer removed, the doctor goes though a litany about all that might go wrong and when the surgeon is finished I ask if the surgery will prevent me from securing a proper bride. My question usually draws a straight response.

Yesterday I had lunch with Jenny and Elliott. Jenny prepared a delicious Chinese style beef with mixed vegetables. Elliott has been uncomfortable and is readying himself for his first transurethral resection of his prostate. The procedure is called a TURP. Since I have had three of them, I am a minor expert and was able to answer some of his questions and, I hope, reassure him that it's not so bad and can provide great relief from symptoms. I was reminded that prior to each of my three TURPs my butt would sweat severely if I did not respond quickly to the sensation of urinary urgency. Just try to impress a urologist with the distress that accompanies that symptom. Impossible.

I have donned my Superman T-shirt, my nose is painted with mercurochrome and my big blond wig is at the ready; let the candy beggars appear.

My struggle with The Classics Club 1942 series is nearly over; I have been unwilling to read each word and sometimes I have done little more than turn the pages, but now only two of nineteen volumes remain: *Robinson Crusoe* and *The Selected Poems of Robert Browning.* If I designed this project to educate myself, I have failed. Worse yet, I have not enjoyed the process and I envy those who have joyfully done what I attempted. One educated man suggested that group study might help me to relish these works. Maybe studying the classics is a partnership game, just like the rest of life.

Only a few trick or treat kids came to my door last night; my candy cornucopia runneth over. I sat by the door in my costume and read John Locke's "Letter Concerning Toleration." I skimmed through his "Some Thoughts Concerning Education" and for dessert I read Edward FitzGerald's first version of Omar Khayyam's "Rubaiyat." I was at my station with four bags of candy from 5 o'clock until 8:30 and only four kids and one mother showed up. What is happening to America and how can Bob Dole fail to blame it on the Democratic administration?

I wore my Halloween costume through the bridge game today; it got an amused response and reinforced the reality that I'm a ham and a character. The food game had an elaborate variety of delicacies; it was a special occasion to recognize Alice and Herb who are moving to a retirement community in southern Maryland. I ate just desserts, enjoyed myself and felt comfortable while playing fairly well. My walk to and from the game was quite pleasant. There was a fine drizzle and I wore my old winter jacket and knit cap. There were snow flurries nearby today. Deb and I ate the last homegrown tomato on my birthday, the leaves have turned color and many have fallen, Halloween is done, the election is four days away; the grand summer season is over and it will soon be spring. Natural disasters have caused terrible suffering around the world this year, but none of that touched me personally except that I slipped on the ice in February; spring and summer have been grand for me. I moan and groan a lot, but save most of it for when only I will hear it. My uncomfortable body sometimes frightens me and interferes with my sleep, but it has not kept me from enjoying most of my activities and observations.

Bob Dole started a ninety-six hour nonstop campaign finale that will end when he votes in Kansas. The assault on President Clinton by Dole and Perot is fierce and unrelenting, but so far his reelection seems secure. The candidates put themselves through an awful ordeal when they seek office. Why has Bob Dole done this to himself? It is such a dirty, unsavory business. Maybe all the close scrutiny this time around will help to clean it up. Campaign financing has made them too much like whores doing tricks. Politics ought to be an honorable profession.

The Sunday bunch that Bob Dole calls the elite liberal media was very critical of the political process today and was especially hard on President Clinton. If they are worth their salt, they will remain diligent after the election in their pressure for campaign finance reform. Each maven made predictions about the big game Tuesday.

One of my favorite political reporters, David Broder, suggested that Bob Dole would make an excellent ambassador or chairman of a bipartisan committee on Social Security or Medicare. I wonder if Dole will be up to such tasks after what he has imposed on himself in the campaign. Dole is in his ninety-six-hour marathon finish that ends when he votes. His practice of repeating himself three times persists, he has become mechanical and his sentences are more fragmented; he must be very tired. He claims that he is quite optimistic. I hope he retains the resilience he has shown in the past.

Openness might help us to make decisions about whom we want to represent us. Openness might dissuade some from accepting financial support that would put them in cahoots with sinister or unsavory forces. I like it when the Republicans complain about the big money the Democrats have received from the labor unions; that is where I want the Democrats to get their support. I like it when I hear that the Republicans got big money from the tobacco, sugar and wine companies; it reinforces my view of them as allied with corporate greed and neglectful of the ordinary citizen. I want my stance to be supported by facts, but I am eager to have the facts even if they prove unsettling.

The political parties admit that over $500,000,000 were contributed (or extorted) in connection with tomorrow's election. That is not so much when compared to the national debt or the number of stars in the heavens, but it still strikes me as a big number. When I first worked for pay, the starting wage was twenty cents an hour and I knew that my grandparents had worked for much less than that. It's easy to glaze over when the big numbers are thrown around just as it is easy to stay unaware that thousands of human beings are starving each and every day. It is too disruptive if we keep such matters in the forefront of our awareness. Both Clinton and Dole knew poverty and the need for parsimony in their youth, but they have become accustomed to big bucks. There is nothing to suggest that Bob Dole or Bill Clinton is embarrassed about his net worth or about how it was accumulated.

Several years after I started doing fee for service medical work, I saw a blind man. At the end of our meeting he asked me how much he owed for my work. I told him and he proceeded to pay the bill by counting off one dollar bills. It was always important to me that my fees be modest and reasonable. It took a long time for him to count out that money and afterwards I felt less pleased with myself. The blind man gave me perspective and helped me to see more clearly.

When Ronald Reagan defeated Jimmy Carter, I was very surprised and disappointed. I expected Dukakis to lose; America was not ready for a president named Dukakis. Today I am hopeful that Clinton will win and prove himself deserving of another four years in office. I am interested in what is in his heart, but I care a lot more about how he will perform as the important problems that affect America and the world are addressed. My best wishes to the winner.

My father's warning was explicit: "Sanford, never bet on the horses." He knew what a burden that activity could become; he had friends and associates who devoted themselves to the sport of kings and who suffered greatly from their preoccupation. I took his warning seriously and was able to generalize from it. I understood but did not yet feel that I might be vulnerable to some self-destructive, addictive behavior. In retrospect I was already addicted to cigarettes and on my way to the disruption that controlling that behavior would have on my life. It is so difficult to learn some things in a way that is usable. I have never been inclined to take things on faith; show me and then maybe I'll believe you. Some things are not understood until they are experienced. Oh, so that's what they were telling me about.

A local football hero was released from jail today; he served over a year after his conviction on drug charges. Prior to his conviction he had participated in many drug rehabilitation programs. Many of his fans were disappointed when he failed to stay clean and his drug use ended his career. It will be sad but not surprising if he resumes illegal drug use; some behavior is very compelling and hard to resist. You can imagine living your life without sex, but consider living without food or without air. Eating and breathing are rather compelling activities; it's hard to imagine life without them.

Djavotyet? It is an exciting day; democracy is at work. I waited until 9 A.M. to vote and I was pleased to see a crowd of retired old-timers at the polling place. There were about forty people ahead of me and before I left there were about forty more behind me. All but two of that crowd were old. I hope there will be a high voter turnout.

Soviet President Boris Yeltsin underwent coronary bypass surgery early today. Pakistani Prime Minister Benazir Bhutto was dismissed and placed under house arrest. The world is full of turmoil, provocations and uncertainty. It is very quiet around here; I'll take a nap before walking to the bridge game this evening and after the game the election results will be coming in. It has been a very long campaign, but over in a flash. It seems like only yesterday that I looked forward to this political year as the icing on the cake.

Children, stop fighting and do your chores now or we will disown you. That is the clear message sent by the voters to the Democrats and the Republicans. Voter turnout was about fifty percent and the balance of power is essentially unchanged, but there is wide recognition that the citizenry wants the legislative branch and the executive branch to work out the important matters that have been neglected because of partisanship, hubris and misconceived self-interest.

When I returned home last night it was already certain that President Clinton had been reelected and it was predicted that the Republicans would gain slightly in the Senate and the Democrats would gain only a little in the House. The voters did not throw the bums out; as usual, most incumbents were kept in office.

Bob Dole seemed refreshed and entirely intact when he delivered his gracious, reparative concession speech. He seemed very relieved and I wondered how much of it was relief that he had not been elected. I suppose I'm having an eccentric reaction; I scoured the paper for some agreement but found none. He is much more at ease when he is not being self-serving, or am I describing myself?

President Clinton gave his victory speech before the day ended. He felt grateful and honored and expressed his appreciation and a determination to achieve important bipartisan action during the next four years. Good luck, Mr. President.

The final bridge hand last evening was not complicated. I was the declarer in a doubled, vulnerable game contract that could have been beaten with perfect defense, but the defenders were not perfect and I was on my way to a top score when I pulled the wrong card and defeated myself. I was tired and sloppy and I let my partner down. It could have been about something important. How lucky that it was just a bridge hand.

The campaign and the election are over, my crutch is gone and it is time to move on. I wish you good luck. Wish me continuing good luck.

Postelection Rehash and Addenda

Preprandial Sex Is the Answer

What do I want in my old age? My requirements of myself are lax: it is sufficient that I enjoy myself without being mean. This quondam mensch is cautious about taking on serious responsibility. I admire but do not envy old-timers who effectively stay in the fray while I gambol; I cringe when one remains too long and messes up. I am still concerned about how I am regarded, but the focus has moved toward self-evaluation. I'm meaner than I would like; greater generosity would be preferable, but it doesn't come easily to me.

The big question in our relationships is, "How do you regard me?" So much of what I have done has been in the service of receiving approval from important others, yet I was unaware of it and suspect I would have denied it if confronted about it. Maybe, as I now deny it, it continues to motivate me.

I love you; tell me that you love me and prove it. Admire me greatly and don't fake it. I have a checklist that will help me to assess your love for me and I'm going to figure out what is on that list. When I know every item on my list I will be able to accurately grade your love and admiration for me. Then what? Love is a multipotent thing. I wonder how much I will value your devotion when I feel certain of it; it might repel me.

The love campaign is about gaining power and security. If you love me enough I can possess you until I'm ready to be rid of you, no matter what; your unconditional devotion makes you my love slave. Love is grand.

The old bumper sticker read MAKE LOVE NOT WAR. The new version reads MAKE LOVE NOT SEX. I'm trying to figure out what this love stuff is. For years I've been telling people that it is better to love than to be loved, but hardly anyone believes it and I know it is too vague to make sense. It is more clear when I claim that it is better to be left than to leave, but most people who think they are in love sneer at that assertion. They want to know how it can be better when it feels so awful.

I thought I had demonstrated how highly I value you. I have tried to be attentive, responsive, respectful, affectionate, helpful, entertaining, constant, authentic, protective and available. Perhaps I have been too ardent or not ardent enough. Maybe I've been too needy and suffocating or too independent and not around enough. You got bored with me; I was not innovative enough to keep you interested. You had heard all of my jokes at least once and you lost interest in me and my song and dance. Was I just another conquest or perhaps too predictable? Maybe you just tired of my repetitiveness and decrepitude. Our relationship was as a beautiful bouquet; has it faded irreparably?

I have been too explicit, not romantic enough; too prosaic, not poetical enough; obdurate or perhaps squishy. My dancing embarrassed you. That's it: I should have taken dancing lessons to renew your enthusiasm for me.

I was in love once. I was sixteen and severely smitten with an older woman, nineteen, whom I met at the seashore. We were in proximity for two weeks and I remained in love with her until the moment I saw her the following summer. It ended quite magically the moment I saw her. That was lucky; I might have become a stalker or a rapist. Even luckier, it never happened to me again.

Enough about being in love; it is unsustainable, undesirable and tragicomical. It is the generous, nurturing friendship that is worth cultivating and is worthy of the appellation, love. Better yet, drop the word love altogether since it so often is used to obfuscate rather than clarify what is felt or desired. Unconditional love, commitment, is, at best, meaningless and, at worst, bizarre.

I married to secure the availability of the person I lusted after. I probably knew that marriage is about creating a family and taking responsibility for that family, but it was lust that motivated me. My passions have weakened; I'm no longer pushed around by them. If I marry again, suspect senility. My capacity to meet my own standard of proper marital responsibility is now limited to writing checks and I can do that without marriage.

Clarity is so businesslike and unromantic; it leaves little to the imagination. What do you agree to? Is it fair, reasonable, enforceable, renegotiable and do you desire it? First grade ought to include a course in contract law to prepare us for life with others. The good faith contract is a wonderful thing.

If you want to hook up with a partner who would have great difficulty managing without you, get a dog and serve it well. It might help you to try a relationship with a less dependent partner: a cat or maybe a person who might leave you even if you are fair and reasonable. Life can be risky. I changed my mind once, how about you?

I live alone. When the freezer door is left open I know who did it. It's not a disadvantage to have that kind of certainty. Periodically I miss the physical and emotional comfort of a friendly woman, but I sometimes missed that when I did not live alone and I know how easy it is to arrange such a therapeutic treat. The married old folks I know, those who live together, don't seem better or worse off than I; so many of them are unpleasant with each other, waiting to be released from an until death do us part contract. Our culture insists that a marriage is a success if the couple stays together until at least one of them dies. If you murder your spouse and don't get caught you have had a successful marriage.

I have always been in charge ... of myself, but I didn't figure it out right away. The house rules felt oppressive; my parents made those rules, claimed that they were in charge and tried to enforce their rules. I chafed under that system, but I bought into it and looked forward to establishing my own place where I made the rules. It was not yet clear to me that wherever I was, I was making my own rules and that I was in charge ... of myself only. It's obvious, but it sure doesn't feel that way. My parents were often affectionate and always dutiful. Mother's main job was to teach and enforce her rules, rules designed to protect and direct her children. She was traditional and strict. I knew that she cared very much about us and that she called it love even when I felt unnecessarily restrained.

Whether or not it is called love, traditional parents assume responsibility for their children. The nurturing caring that they provide is very rewarding for many parents even though the parent often feels more oppressed than the child. When a Jewish child is confirmed, the father will sometimes shout out, "Thank you, Lord, for relieving me of this heavy burden." Up until that time it was the parents' obligation to ensure that the child properly follow the religious rules and regulations. The child has become an adult; a parent may try to be helpful until death, but the responsibility for the behavior of the young adult is no longer borne by the parents.

Here is a packet of special talismans. Think of each amulet as a prepaid chit that will provide you with friendly and enthusiastic nurturing on request, guaranteed with no hidden charges. It sounds marvelous, but who paid for this wonderful gift? Why you did, of course, by being such a phenomenal, admirable, generous, nurturing, magnificent person. Take it and use it in good health. Read the small print in the guarantee; it will reveal that these amulets are more reliable than people for they are devoted exclusively to you and are available for use on demand. They are never tired or preoccupied and they are unerringly enthusiastic to serve you. It sounds a lot like having a personal geisha. If what you request is that you be provided with an authentic person who will enter into a two-way relationship with you, throw away the packet and start a search.

The fable tells us that a love potion can be purchased for a few pennies and its antidote is extremely expensive. Be careful about whom you select to win over. A love slave can be a very heavy load to carry. Don't kid yourself, it is not pleasant to be pressured to care more and to want more and to give more than suits you. Service with a smile has a price. If you think you want someone who craves you more than you want them, think again and be careful. If Puck offers to throw some love dust for you, decline or suffer the consequences. You might want a raving beauty and wind up with a ravenous biddy.

Authenticity does not always win the day in our search for mutually fulfilling relationships, but disingenuousness is doomed to failure. Misrepresentation can work to your advantage in many transactions—it can be lifesaving—but it is destructive when you are trying to develop mutual respect in an ongoing friendship. If I am not scrupulous in my presentation of myself, a favorable reception does little to reinforce my positive view of myself, which is more important than what others think of me and it is bound to backfire in the quest for mutual respect. Take the risk; present yourself accurately. I would do it if I could figure out who is and what is the authentic me. I know it when I'm misrepresenting myself; it is much the same as lying, but the truth is not so clear. Part of what I must present is my uncertainty about myself, still uncertain after all these years.

My best friends are people whom I see one-on-one only rarely. I am ambivalent about having greater intimacy and question my capacity to give in ways that would be of value to my friends. It is a pleasure and a relief when I can be available and effective, but I do not welcome being tested. My endurance and resilience are reduced and fatigue makes me sloppy and unreliable. These excuses make it easier for me to succumb to, rather than resist, my tendency to be lazy and ungenerous.

Connections matter most. All of my important connections have been people, not pets or gods or imaginary playmates. I do not require much interaction with the people I value most. I like very much to hear about my grandchildren and I am concerned about their welfare, but just a few minutes together every now and then is satisfying and sufficient. Recently I had my first conversation with my four-year-old granddaughter; it lasted about a minute but I will take pleasure from it, I suspect, for a long time. Some of my most important relationships have diminished or ended; those that remain are more precious, especially when I confront myself with my reluctance to seek out new connections.

The admonition was that I be admirable but cautious, a difficult balancing act. I was sometimes naively incautious and lucky to avoid disaster. Now, no longer a cocky youth but an old ca-ca, I err on the side of caution and have doubts about my supply of judgment and luck.

The frightened old man you have been listening to was moderately adventurous when it seemed that there was a lot that might be lost; it is strange that he becomes risk-aversive now when the trip is nearly over and there is so little to lose. My words suggest that I remain quite concerned about appearances: if I'm an old fool, I don't want it to be apparent. I did not know and I still do not feel that I care so much about the opinion of the hoi polloi. Perhaps I'm trying to avoid embarrassing that small cadre of family and friends who matter so much to me. It probably wouldn't greatly upset anyone if I went out on a ridiculous note and it would give some a good laugh. I like helping people to laugh.

My retirement from medical practice was predicated in part on my professional creed: First, do no harm. I have not retired from life, I'm just a lot more cautious. This prattle is, I suspect, part of an effort to discover new directions or to decide to stay put. I realize, now that I have said it, that I want to hold to the same standard that I held concerning my professional life. Yes, that is the proper test; it will guide me to the better course when my ambivalence is pushing me around.

There is a lot of anxiety in the air; it is contagious. Friends and relatives report their distress and indicate that they are limiting themselves because they are too uncomfortable to enjoy themselves. What underlies their distress? It is too simplistic to blame it on one's neurotransmitters, but there is no doubt that we are a complex bundle of chemicals without which there would be no mind, no perception, no desire and no anxiety. Some have a clear sense of direction that is unwavering; they pursue their goals to the end and are undeterred by anxiety or ambivalence. Any questions they may have about their motives and objectives go unexpressed. Perhaps they conduct an inner dialogue. Introspection is liberating for some and paralyzing for others.

Not long ago most people died before their thirty-fifth birthday and few lived beyond fifty. Now thirty is the one-third mark, fifty is the halfway mark and the last portion begins at sixty-five or seventy. People continue to wish each other long life even after they have visited the senile elderly. Death remains a terrifying pit rather than a desired resting point. We reject it as irrational when someone decides that too much is enough and they want out.

If you suffer from gastroesophageal incontinence, limit yourself to preprandial sex and you will avoid making a mess of things.

Postcoital Abstinence Saves Lives

The miracle of birth is followed by the miracle of living into old age while inviting disaster. My neighborhood in Newark, New Jersey, was like a small town. The cast of characters changed only a little during my childhood; people knew each other, observed each other and influenced each other. There were many kids; most of us stayed alive through adolescence when World War II took its toll. Most of the kids my age and younger missed combat; some of us died at home. The Burrel kid was killed by a car while riding his bike and I didn't get a bike. Next door, Herby Buddish died of a brain tumor. I'm not sure what Mother did to keep me from such a fate. A very athletic fellow died of pneumonia while in basic training and Eddy Margolis was killed flying in combat.

We went about our business as if the world was a relatively safe place; I tended to view my mother's fears as excessive and her admonitions felt too limiting. I was greatly influenced by the older guys in the neighborhood and mother did not like that at all. I did not have to jump off the Empire State Building just because Eddy Kostern did. Eddy was a minor bully who pretended he was a big shot, smoked a lot and spit gobs of phlegm. I didn't like or admire him, yet I imitated him. Smoking and spitting were a part of my act before I reached puberty and soon thereafter I added a large pompadour and what was later called a ducktail. Sex was in the air, but I was as yet uninformed and hormone deficient.

Spitting is not very important to me, although I still do a lot of it when no one is looking; smoking and sex are another story.

Smoking was an automatic part of life for most of us even though it was prohibited and done surreptitiously. Long before the Surgeon

General's first report on smoking and health, my parents knew that smoking caused illness and death. Cigarettes were called coffin nails and it was widely held that Mr. Kostern's laryngeal cancer was caused by his smoking; that was way back around 1942 B.A., before air conditioning, when on a hot summer night all windows were left open and his stertorous breathing could be heard throughout the neighborhood. I was not impressed until 1948 when my professor of anatomy in medical school proclaimed that the scientific evidence was in, smoking caused cancer and heart disease and that he would very likely die because he smoked. He was a young man, but he promptly dropped dead after a heart attack. I struggled mightily for the next ten years to control my addiction and in 1958 began my first prolonged period of abstinence.

My friends and I were very busy after puberty; it's hard to believe that we did so much. I was devoted to my schoolwork, enjoyed much of it and got good grades. I played ball almost every day and aspired, unsuccessfully, to become a basketball star. In addition, my friends and I spent an enormous amount of time concerning ourselves with sex. My age mates and I, no longer hormone deficient, were awash in semen and prurience. Few of us dated or had physical contact with girls or women, but we were immensely occupied with sex. We were chronic Peeping Toms. At least a few of the women we watched were either deaf and dumb or were pleased to display themselves to an eager bunch of appreciative youngsters. Old Faithful went off at predictable intervals and we appreciated her display. We would conceal the light from our cigarettes as we awaited her performance.

Smoking was easy up until the time I recognized it as an undesirable and dangerous addiction; you buy them by the carton and smoke them. Sex was less easy and I was much more aware of its importance to me. If I wanted a smoking companion, I was unaware of it; solitary smoking was just fine. I wanted a sexual partner, but I was fussy, ambivalent and not at all ready for an entanglement from which I might have difficulty extricating myself. If I were to have sex that included penetration with an eligible woman, I would probably be stuck forever; caught by the genitals in a powerful grip that would keep us together through the journey of life. That left avoiding penetration with women whom I viewed as eligible and finding ineligibles for penile insertion. It does not sound admirable, but I was following the zeitgeist and trying to be fair while indulging my passion. It worked out fairly well in that I did not take terrible advantage of anyone and I did not break my own rules.

My efforts to stop smoking began around the time I met Ria and, although I probably contributed to her becoming an inveterate smoker, it was clear that I was struggling to stop smoking before we married. We were both ready to marry in that we wanted to be together and we wanted to establish our own place apart from our parents, but we did not have a clear notion about when we wanted children and it was not until after two pregnancies and three children that we made the connection between coitus and procreation. Those were difficult times. We both felt overextended and often depleted. I was working very hard and Ria had great responsibility, little relief and felt trapped and resentful. Her dissatisfaction shook me. When I finished my training we had a period of reduced pressure, but we did not recover completely from those stressful times. All of our disagreements were about sex or smoking. Maybe they were about sex and smoking for they were connected.

I thought that Ria and I had agreed to smoke no more beginning in August of 1958; I was wrong. She had said the words, but soon indicated that she was trying to avoid a verbal battle that she felt she was bound to lose. She had not stopped smoking and she did not want to discuss it. She was surprised that I had stopped and I was surprised that I was not more upset about her continuing to smoke. It didn't last; each time I was confronted with her ongoing smoking I felt disrupted. I was an addict who stopped using and lived in a den of addiction. I suspect that she would have left me if she had felt secure enough—the children seemed to think that—but she made no move to go. I suffered a couple of smoking relapses that were brief but very troubling to me. Maybe I would have left if I had no children and no penis, but I did not think about separating until 1982 when our relationship was so unfriendly that it was not worth keeping. The kids were grown, we had still another confrontation about her smoking, she told me to accept things as they were and I gave up. What a relief. My keeping after her had been partly paternalistic and partly defensive; I was ready to quit. I don't know how much relief Ria felt then, but after a while I'm pretty sure we both felt better off without the other. Within a few months I was ready to find a new woman.

People who get to know me comment about my informality and humor; it contrasts with their initial impression that I have a peculiar combination of aloofness and flippancy. Life is there for enjoyment and to do good, or maybe it's to do good and to enjoy. I have been very lucky to avoid the notion that life is hard and then you die. Life is easy when one is inclined to be the way one thinks he is supposed to be. That has been my good fortune. I am greatly influenced by my passions and yet it has been quite easy, usually, for me to avoid behavior that I find improper or deserving of punishment. People have given me great power and authority through the years; I have tried to use that trust constructively to help them and it has been very rewarding work. When I have been invited to take inappropriate advantage of my position, it has been easy for me to politely decline and, sometimes, to express my appreciation about their concern for me. It might have been disastrous if I were strongly inclined to break the rules, for I view myself as ruled by my inclinations. So many of the major decisions I have made were significantly influenced by my sexuality.

Plagues come and go; they are, by definition, devastating. A hundred years ago our mental hospitals housed paretics, people with severe central nervous system syphilis, most of whom contracted their disease through their sexual behavior. The era of antibiotics created a brief period during which coitus seemed free of serious disease consequences. Adequate contraception added to the notion that sex need not have any serious consequences. Some religious people are pleased with the turnaround that includes a multitude of serious, undesirable consequences from sexual union. We have new plagues and some, not all, are connected with sex.

Pick the plague that is most devastating this year; it is caused by cigarette smoking and includes lung cancer and other debilitating and fatal diseases. Acquired human immunodeficiency syndrome is probably a viral disease that is most frequently transmitted sexually. AIDS has killed many thousands of people and may result in the premature death of millions before that plague ends. Sexually transmitted diseases are once again plaguing mankind. Informed people have become more cautious and selective in choosing sexual partners.

Encouraging new statistics indicate that for the past few years there has been a decrease in premature death secondary to cancer. Almost all of the change is due to the lowered rate of cigarette smoking. The word is out and people are pressuring themselves and others to avoid smoking as one would avoid the plague.

Therefore, be careful about whom you choose as a sexual partner and after the sex act abstain from lighting up; it could save your life.

The Damned Thanksgiving Day Dinner

Paul hung up the phone and contemplated calling Dolores, his daughter's mother-in-law. He had accepted Tob's invitation for Thanksgiving dinner with feigned enthusiasm, listened to her complaints about Dolores and remained silent when his darling daughter rejected his request that she make baby peas and mashed potatoes with gravy to go with the turkey. Dolores had declined to join the family for dinner, claiming that she did not feel welcome.

No one acknowledged that Paul and Dolores got together periodically for sex ever since Dolores seduced him during his wife's final illness nearly twenty years ago. He was shocked but pleased by her persistence and felt only a bit uncomfortable around her husband, a vigorous and friendly man who seemed oblivious until he died a few years ago. Her son and Tob, married nearly twenty-five years, managed well in a plodding sort of way in spite of conflicts about Dolores who had been regularly rambunctious.

Both Tob and Harah wanted him to intercede. What the hell; he pressed her number.

"Dolores, this is Paul calling. It's holiday time again; I hope to see you Thursday for the big feast.

" Yes, Tob told me you were reluctant about going, that's part of why I'm calling. I'd like more peace and contentment in my old age, but it isn't easy to come by. If you join us we can share the bird and try to avoid giving each other the bird.

"Yes, yes, things are far from perfect and that would be the case even if my Tob and your Harah were a lot more accommodating.

"It's not that we're not welcome, it's that we're not as welcome as we would like. If my own daughter has such a difficult time with me, why should she find her mother-in-law easy to treasure? Nobody expects mothers-in-law and daughters-in-law to be crazy about each other, but one might expect a daughter to cherish her old dad.

"Dolores, you are welcome. Make it easier for yourself and for all of us. Join us and we'll give thanks together. I'm almost eighty and I'm tired of the holiday guilt trips we play on ourselves and each other. The holidays confront us with our discontent and we blame all the important players including ourselves.

"OK, I'm talking about myself, not you. I'm calling hoping to be a peacemaker and maybe I'm stirring up more trouble. I'm most aware of how alone I feel around the holidays. It's at its worst when I'm with family and still feel terribly alone. I tend to decide how they feel about me by how I'm feeling. If I feel loved, then they must love me; if I feel lonely, then they don't care enough about me. It's a screwy way to figure it, but it seems to be my method.

"Of course, they could be more friendly and caring.

"Right, we are not as important to them as we would like. Listen, I told Tob what I wanted for Thanksgiving dinner. Instead of being pleased that I was making it easy for her to do what I want, she told me that it was not what she planned. I didn't ask for anything exotic or difficult, but she was unwilling to be guided by my wishes. Well, it's still a few days off, maybe she will make peas and mashed potatoes to go with the turkey. After all these years I was still optimistic enough to think I was making it easier for her by telling her what I wanted. It's as if she prefers to feel guilty about being withholding rather than risk being responsive. What a world.

"I can tell that Harah loves you even though you feel it's insufficient. You did a good job raising him. You wouldn't have liked it if his father loved his own mother more than he loved you. Why shouldn't Harah care more for Tob than for his own mother? It's not unnatural.

"Why am I defending your kid? I'm not any more pleased with how he treats me than you are about how Tob is with you.

"I'm not criticizing him, I'm telling you about myself in the hope that it will help you to gain perspective. I'm running out of time and would like to be less of a curmudgeon before I leave the scene. You could spread a little more joy yourself, kiddo.

"Yes, I care about you and your feelings. What about you? You know it will put a shroud over things if you don't show up. That's not what you want. Be generous even if it's not exactly the way you are feeling.

"Wait a minute. I'm not accusing you of anything.

"Oh, come on, lighten up and give yourself a chance to enjoy the holiday with the people who care the most about you, even if it feels as though they don't care enough. Let's not punish each other.

"Hey, I did not say you want to punish anyone. I said we ought to avoid behavior that might be perceived as punishing.

"It was not and it is not my intention to give you a hard time. I was hoping to help you to join your son and his family and me for Thanksgiving dinner. That's not a bad thing for me to do. We might enjoy the day.

"Yes, I would like to see you. No one put me up to this call. It was my idea.

"And how long has it been since you called me?

"We're both old-fashioned.

"Would it make it any easier for you if I picked you up and we went there together?

"Wait a minute, Dolores, you know I don't like phone sex.

"All right, I'll stay on the phone while you go ahead without me.

"No, I'm not trying to turn you off, I'm refusing to pretend that it's what I want. Since I'm old-fashioned I know that sex is never free. I want to know the charges before I make a purchase.

"Yes, that is very unromantic of me and it's sexist for me to assume that I'm the one who will be charged, but it's what I believe.

"Convince me.

"I'm a pushover. I'll come to your place before noon on Thursday, we'll spend a couple of hours in the sack and then we'll drive to the kids in separate cars. But no matter how much we wash, they will be able to smell the sex and it will make them jealous."

•

"Happy Thanksgiving, madame. I've been anticipating this tête-à-tête and tumble since our telephone conversation. This is a wonderful way to start the holiday season. You look very nice and you smell delicious."

"Paul, I'm glad you came. That smell is fresh-baked danish that I made for Your Highness. No coat? Come in, come in and give me a kiss. Your visits are more rejuvenating than a face lift. Let's sit in the living room a bit. Would you like a cup of tea?"

"Yes, a cup of tea, please, but no danish until after I've been in your pudding. Tell me what you've been up to."

"Not much. You know my routine. This place keeps me busy, since I've been doing all the upkeep myself. I get together with my friends and enjoy their company. We spend a fair amount of time complaining about our children, bragging about our grandchildren and commiserating about the people our children chose to marry. All of my friends are women who are widows or waiting to become widows. You are the only person I have sex with. I don't know if that concerns you. It's very different than married life. The focus is on what I want and I no longer have old whatshisname around to blame for my discontent. He wasn't so bad, but it is better without him. Stability is so unexciting. All passion between us died long before he did. After three decades with him, sex with him seemed incestuous: forbidden in a way that was not at all exciting. What you and I have is more exciting because it is forbidden and covert and because it might be detected. Isn't that grand?"

"Yes, it is grand, but I don't think of it as forbidden, though I'm willing to keep it covert. I go by the notion that everyone knows everything. Surely our kids know we service each other even if no one says it out loud. No confrontation is required. It might embarrass the grandchildren."

"You are so matter of fact that you come across as uncaring."

"You know that I care."

"Perhaps you do. My poor rumpled body can't be much of an attraction and yet you have been willing to come by periodically and partake of what remains. I miss being sexually attractive. I wonder if I would be promiscuous if I could still attract men I find attractive."

"You are suggesting I might have to share you."

"I'm suggesting it's unlikely that you will have to share me, because I'm unlikely to cleave to anyone who would have me. It's the old Groucho Marx line. Our long relationship seems to exempt us from the constraints that usually inhibit us."

"Neither of us is willing to suffer the indignity bright lights would bring in the bedroom."

"When I was a young woman I could create turmoil by shaking my chest. Now these sagging ribbon breasts are a superfluous nuisance."

"We'll see."

"I'm still very ambivalent about the family gathering this afternoon. I told you I would attend and, unless you release me, I will keep my word. But it feels like an unnecessary charade. I'm not very fond of my son, your daughter doesn't like me and the grandchildren could care less. None of that need be confronted just because I decline to attend a family holiday dinner."

"I would agree with you if you had not already precipitated the confrontation when you originally declined the invitation. Thank you for the tea. You've had a bit of sherry."

"Oh, yes, I've had a little drink. It helps me to think about how to make a stink. It dissolves my resolve to remain prissy and starched. It strengthens my urge to merge with you. These liquors go straight to my knickers and put me on the verge of... Why, yes, I've had a little sherry.

I know you prefer tea. You are always at the ready without chemical reinforcement."

"I don't want to make a stink."

"You can be a stinker without trying. A little sherry enlivens me. I can feel the alcohol surge through my body and settle in my brain and my genitals. A fire begins to glow at both ends and my juices begin to bubble. My stodgy mind and inspissated pudendum are transformed and readied for you to ravish. Perhaps you object to this resurgence of creative energy."

"No."

"Stop hogging the dialogue; can't you see I'm on a role? You will soon play a tune with your sax, but for now be lax to the max with your cracks. When this lascivious, luscious lush lubricates, she will longingly lead you to ... let's linger in the living room. I'm ready. Let's do it."

"We'll soil the sofa."

"Stop alliterating and take your pants off now. If you don't hurry I'll go off without friction. When this soufflé is ready it waits for no man. Hurry. You're old but you are not that old. Too late, but don't worry I'll be set for seconds soon. What's the matter? You look very uncomfortable."

"My back has gone out. I can't move. Please don't touch me, any movement is very painful."

"Paul, there must be a way we can do it without your moving. I won't be deprived while my fire is lit. Damn it, I made danish for you. How can you let me down like this? Let me get your pants off and we'll proceed while you stay still. I'll do all the moving."

"When the sofa moves it hurts. Please, don't rock the boat."

"You decrepit, defective, dilatory, doddering dodo."

"Please stop shaking the sofa."

"I'll shake the sofa. I'll shake it hard, you stinker."

"Ah, it's over. The pain is gone."

"Thank God, my sweet. Get your pants off fast and let's do it right away just in case it comes back again. I've been off my lithium tablets for five days to get up for this tumble and we must not let the moment pass. Ram me."

"You ewe you."

"Cut that out and stick to your shtup shtick. I'm working up an appetite. Instead of going to my son's, lets go toward the sun. After we've taken each other to heaven, I'll take you to the Caribbean. We can leave within the hour. No one is flying right now but us."

"I'm too old for this."

"Oh no you aren't."

•

Harah Eyen, fifty years old, smart and even tempered, has shown none of his mother's moodiness. He was subjected to her episodes of angry seductiveness until she started seeing a shrink and taking medication when he was ready to leave home and start college. He has not been haunted by the past. Mother and son are a lot alike when mother stays on her medication. He is quite aware of subtle changes that occur soon after she skips her lithium and he understands that it is not accidental. She decides that she is ready to release herself and experience the wonderful intensity of feeling that eludes her when her mood is stabilized. He worries about her, but no longer tries to get her to forego the expression of her self-indulgent sexuality. So far she has avoided serious consequences. He knows that potential disaster accompanies these periods of angry sexual exuberance. He decided long ago that he was unwilling to save her from danger by being available for her predatory sexuality. He found it amusing and reassuring when he realized that dear old mom had latched on to Tob's father. Harah has never discussed this with Tob and, amazingly, Tob seems not to know about it even though his mother has come close to rubbing her nose in it. His father had been a lot like that, too. Some confrontations are worth avoiding.

The Eyen household was in holiday mode. Harah started off the day by making googly eyes at Tob, who indicated that she was available for what she called a snuggle and what he called a hurried. He declined in order to avoid having his participation in the holiday work seem like payment for services rendered. He intended to participate fully in the drudge work and to avoid even the suspicion of a pout. He had a lot to be thankful for and he understood that marriage is not about fun and games. The kids were around somewhere, but not in sight when he got downstairs and reported for duty.

"Awaiting orders, my Captain. Your wish is my command, but please do not assume that I am a mind reader or that I can see the obvious."

"There is a lot to be done."

"Yes, ma'am."

"If I have to tell you each and every thing, it's a bother."

"Give me a list of several things and I'll do those things."

"Let's start by extending the table since it's a two person job."

"One leaf or two?"

"That's the right question. It's not clear who will be here for dinner. You and I are likely to attend."

"Joy and Grace are around here someplace. I picked them up at the airport last evening. Each of them has invited a friend to join us. Your father said he would be here and he told you that my mother had agreed to attend. Your friend Bela and her husband will let us know this morning if they are in town."

"Yes, we will be two, three, four, five, six, seven, eight, nine or ten."

"Well, then, two leaves it is, just in case everyone shows up."

"You are an optimist."

"A pragmatist, my Captain."

"OK, two leaves it is. I don't understand why I'm feeling uncomfortable about the day. We are fully prepared and there is plenty of time to get everything ready. It is a lot of work to make dinner for ten, but it wouldn't seem like such a big deal if our guests were card friends or business acquaintances. What's the difference? Of course, they wouldn't demand baby peas and mashed potatoes and they wouldn't leave us on tender hooks about whether they'll show up."

"Bela told you their attendance is uncertain and you know that she is a vegetarian. It sounds the same to me."

"I guess I feel more certain about her feelings."

"Or the other way around. You are probably more sure of your own feelings with Bela and less concerned how she regards you."

"Smart ass."

"Sorry. I'll put the pads on the table and we can put on the tablecloth. Show me one place setting and I'll do the other nine."

"It will look silly if only three or four show up."

"There's nothing silly or shameful about inviting friends and family for Thanksgiving dinner. We can live with their idiosyncrasies and be thankful for what we have."

"Of course, you are right. No one matters more to me than the potential no-shows for today's dinner. We can only do our own part in this true life drama. All the other players are too unpredictable."

"My mother is not unpredictable. I predict that she will appear or she will not appear, she will be high or she will be low, she will be terse or she will be exuberant and provocative. I'm pretty sure, nearly positive, that she's off her medication and that if she shows up she will be a whirlwind, so please be careful."

"Does my father know about this?"

"Tob, your father knows my mother."

"That sounds lascivious."

"I'll do the place settings later. What next, ma'am?"

Tob suggested that Harah watch television and read the newspaper while she got organized. He agreed after indicating his ready availability whenever she wanted assistance. The girls were not about. They were up and out quite early and had made no inquiry about how they might be helpful. Their eagerness to be home for the holiday had nothing to do with a desire to be with their parents. They wanted to see their friends and to compare notes about the college experience.

Joy and Grace were a lot alike but not identical twins. They chose different schools and it was their first separation. Tob expected their seeming indifference, but felt disappointed and put upon nevertheless. She reminded herself of the discomfort she continues to feel with her own father and the irrational notion she holds that father, not mother, was supposed to die twenty years ago. She continued to hold that against him. If mother were alive she would be right there in the kitchen with her, sharing and enjoying the holiday preparations... maybe.

Father did not help, he demanded. She reacted to his most tentative requests as imperious orders. She knew that she was too severe with him. She also had a vague notion that father kept Dolores from being even harder to deal with. She was grateful for it, but never was aware of the overt eroticism that took place between Dolores and Paul. It took a lot of psychic energy to keep that reality from her awareness. The girls, more than Tob or Harah, were exposed to the way Dolores would light up sexually and successfully attract Paul to their mutual satisfaction. At first the girls were startled that a couple of old fogies were still so horny, but that evolved into amusement and excitement. Not everyone is lucky enough to get turned on by the sexual play of their unrelated old grandparents.

Tob had dinner preparations under control, just as everyone expected. She decided to put the stuffing in the bird and exercise her suturing skills rather than bake the filling in a casserole. She'd ask Harah to clean the place up a bit and make the salad. That would please him and satisfy her. Maybe he could also make a corn pudding. She did not know that he would insist on making mashed potatoes and baby peas. Cook, before she left for the holiday, had prepared candied sweet potatoes, cassoulet with ham and both pumpkin and apple pies. Rolls were ready to be popped into the oven right before dinner. The turkey would go into the oven at noon and there was nothing much to do until shortly before it was time to eat. There was plenty of time to take a shower, nap, read the paper ... think about why no one had the courtesy to call and let her know who would be there for dinner.

Harah saw that things were progressing and that there was plenty of time for sex, but he refrained from repeating the googly eyes routine and Tob appreciated his restraint. She did not feel up to an emotional erotic exchange and she never used Harah for quick sexual relief, even though she thought he might like that. She asked him to put the bird in the oven at noon and she laughed when she reminded him to turn on the oven. She went upstairs, had a quick shower, got into bed and was soon asleep.

Tob was in an emergency medicine residency when she married. She and Harah anticipated that following her residency she would have regular hours and a high salary, both of which would be very compatible with having kids and being an available wife and mother. That's more or less the way things worked out, although she did often feel preoccupied with her patients and depleted by the intensity of her duties. Harah, a government lawyer then and now a circuit court judge, was consistently helpful and supportive. She felt lucky to have him and she, too, tried to be a helpmate. Before he proposed to her, he told her that his mother suffered from a recurring difficulty, probably a manic-depressive disorder. Tob told no secrets. She realized that the high degree to which she was sexually self-contained might create doubt about her suitability for marriage, but she was unaware that Harah knew about and put high value on how little need she felt. He wanted a wife who was not likely to stray, not likely to be sexually demanding, not likely to be like his mother.

She awakened feeling refreshed and relieved. Her naps were almost always accompanied by the same brief, orgastic dream. She was playing in the yard and the gardener appeared and startled her. She would awaken clutching her groin, feeling a special relief that occurred only rarely outside of sleep. Now she felt ready and available for an erotic exchange with Harah. She went downstairs and turned on the oven; it was almost noon. She put the turkey into the oven, went into the living room, made googly eyes at Harah and said, "The oven is hot. Let's go upstairs and put the turkey in." Upstairs they went.

•

Dolores used him and bruised him until Paul was limp and unresponsive. She went into her bedroom and returned wearing only high platform shoes and, under a see-through blouse, a brassiere that contained and thrust forward her pendulous bosom. Paul watched as she did a lewd dance, but only his eyes moved. She gave up in disgust, poured some sherry and plunked down on the sofa, spilling some liquid on both of them. She licked a few drops from his chest and then again gave up on arousing the old stinker.

Paul's trousers were crumpled down around his ankles. He was unable to reach down to pick them up. Dolores said that she preferred him with his pants down and refused to help him. It was urgent that he get to the toilet. After several tries he was able to struggle to his feet and waddle unsteadily toward the bathroom as Dolores pranced around him. When he arrived she tickled and pinched him as she directed his stream into the sink. She returned to the living room and he was able to sit on the toilet and carefully bend down to reach his trousers. His back was stiff but not painful as he carefully stood up, zipped and buckled and slowly returned to the living room. Dolores looked sullen and pensive when he did not join her on the sofa, but chose instead a wooden chair that would not test his back.

"Your back is out of whack, but you haven't lost your knack in the sack, you old hack."

"Too much is enough, Dolores. Please put away the sherry and take a couple of your lithium tablets."

"Don't be a pall, Paul. The ablation of masturbation and constipation in our constellation requires frequent fornication."

"You will still be high for the weekend if you start back on your medication now."

"Meany. Always thinking about yourself. As soon as you've had enough, I'm supposed to stop. Do you want me to start spreading it around? I will if you aren't obliging."

"Don't do that, Dolores. I love you. Take your medication and put on some clothes."

"I'm dressed now except for a skirt, a wig and my makeup. No pants on the holiday. No washing. Let's go. Your back is too uncertain; I'll do the driving."

•

Although Harah seemed spared, there was ongoing concern that the girls might inherit whatever it was that Dolores exhibited. Tob had a couple of tentative conversations with them in which she cautioned them to let her know if they experienced strong feelings that disturbed or frightened them. The kids did not feel vulnerable and they thought their parents were square and too conservative about drug use. Tob would occasionally tell the family about tragedies she encountered in the emergency room that were clearly related to drug use. They thought their mother was naive and overprotective.

Soon after she arrived at college, Joy began daily smoking and drinking and moved into the room of a Byronic young man who claimed that he was in great pain if he did not have sex with her twice a day. He majored in uppers and downers. Sex was more prophylactic: similar to brushing one's teeth to avoid cavities and periodontal disease. She had never before felt so wonderful. Her skin cleared up and her grades were excellent. It was Byron whom she had invited for Thanksgiving dinner and it was Byron she went to join early that Thursday morning. It was important that he not be deprived of her ministrations.

Grace was less happy at school. She did not have to move out of her dorm room to find love. Her roommate, Jo, was a beautiful, brilliant young woman who claimed that she was in great pain if she did not have sex with Grace twice a day. She called it making love. It did not feel like love when Jo proved jealous, possessive and restricting. Grace was strongly attracted to a Byronic young man who seemed interested in her but who already had a live-in.

Jo insisted that she be included in the Thanksgiving weekend. Jo and Byron were sequestered nearby at the home of Glory, a friend whose parents were away. When Joy and Grace arrived it was clear that all necessary sexual ministrations were completed for that morning. Grace was relieved and Joy felt devastated. All agreed that sharing a couple of joints would calm things down and give them time to think. It seemed like a good idea. Dinner was still a long way off. Glory was peeved that they had failed to invite her to dinner, but she felt a lot better about things after her early morning double dose of sex with people she did not know. Before they lit up, Glory had accepted the dinner invitation and was hoping for heavy appetizers before then.

•

Harah was feeling very lucky. He felt a shiver and hoped he was not jinxing things with his easy contentment. Tob and he had very different satisfactions from their communion. That was just fine.

"I'm thinking about how lucky I am."

"I'm wondering about who will show up for dinner. I predict we will be six."

"What would we do without six? One, two, three, four, five, seven, eight... What would we do without sax? We would have to rely on the clarinet. What would we do without socks? I would let you warm your feet on my wherever. It would be ever so inconvenient to manage without sucks. What would we do without Sikhs? Did I leave anything out?"

"Yes, you left it out. Do you want to put it in again? I have a convenient opening for it."

"Thank you, I think that I will."
"What dinner?"

•

Paul was sprightly and polished when he arrived. Now he was tatterdemalion and sagged as he was swept along by his exuberant playmate. They were nearly the same age and together totaled one hundred and fifty years, but he looked twice her age as they approached her car. She was wearing a "Don't you dare call me a whore" outfit, suitable for a country and western star. He was filled with trepidation about being a passenger as she drove, but he did not have the wherewithal to resist. His fears were confirmed when she smacked into the car in front and the car behind as she maneuvered out of her parking space. He was in the death seat. He calmed down when he reminded himself that it wasn't a big deal since he was very old and near death anyway. He would have preferred to die on the sofa while diddling Dolores, but dying in the car would be almost as satisfactory as dying in the saddle.

Holiday traffic was light and fast. He buckled his seat belt. Dolores declined his recommendation that she also buckle up. When they reached the interstate she got into the fast lane and sped up. Soon she was tailgating and honking. The guy in front of her gave her the finger and the duel began. Paul closed his eyes and tried to relax, but he could hear and feel the swerves and sprints and scrapes. He kept his eyes closed as the car screeched and skidded and came to a stop.

•

The five of them, Byron and his harem, sat in a circle on the living room floor, facing each other with their toes touching. All were almost eighteen; Joy and Grace, twins; each of the other three, an only child. The modern affluent family has one and one-quarter children. They were calm and smoked only a little. Joy was recurrently tearful: first when she thought about Byron's casual unfaithfulness and she realized that she was in love with him and later when she realized that she was no longer in love with him. Now she viewed herself as inconstant and perfidious. How could she stand being so fickle and so shallow?

Five young, slightly stoned adults sitting toes to toes with the world at their feet, thinking about their world and how they will participate in life. That is the big homework assignment: How will I participate in the world and how can I best prepare myself for that participation? Assignment must be completed prior to Armageddon. Joy sobbed and all looked to her.

"I found my love and lost my love all in a day. It happened today. I served my dear Byron gladly, without great desire. His claim that he needed me brought security, not fire. He said that I had a special touch that would keep him mine and that I was divine. Lulled by his need for unique me, I did not see that no matter what he might say, he might stray from me. This morning I learned that he was not my possession. Only then did I experience the obsession that I must have him, that I was in love with him. My yearning required his turning away from me.

"It did not last; so soon it has passed. My feelings seemed pure, but they did not endure. I hope that what I learned about myself today will inure me and that I will never be in love again. Go to college and gain some knowledge about yourself. These dear tears you see are for me. I cry for the self I lost today. That accounts for this display. My constancy is no more. I flit from adore to abhor to ignore the bore. I am no longer a child beguiled by self-deception. How strange that I am sad, not glad, about my more accurate perception. Joy should be joyous, on reflection. It is time for me to give up the diversion of this used, up and down, randy man and to move ahead with discovering my own grand plan. I lost myself and found myself all in a day. Today."

"They named me Glory; I fulfilled their need for an adornment. That's all my being born meant. Who would think it? I'm merely a trinket. Mother and father don't bother about me. They have gone west to ski and left me here, bereft and lonely. Your visit has eased the pain, but there is little that I will gain from touching toes and telling tales with wails and woes. Our early morning union that filled my emptiness and brought me happiness was too ephemeral and could not raise me from my private hell. I require a deep and permanent connection to lift me out of my dejection and preoccupation with parental rejection. I hate. I don't feel whole and won't until I find my soul and a soul mate."

"My name is Jo, without an e, born without a dingus to hold when I pee; another instance of failure to achieve parental fulfillment through progeny. This extreme microphallic state does not abate my desire to compete; I aspire to conquer and win, not tolerate defeat. I can be sweet when I choose, but if you challenge me, be prepared to lose. I am smart, powerful and beautiful. Hook up with me and learn the art of being dutiful. Don't label me dyke; I'm a three-way girl who goes both ways as I like. It is not a sin to fight hard to win. I am hardhearted, but in my dreams I sometimes seek someone who will open my heart so that I can let them in."

"Sing along with me.

I'm Byron the chemical man, beep, beep.
I do what I do when I can, beep, beep.
I do uppers and downers with all kinds of bounders.
I'm Byron the chemical man.
My life is a merry-go-round. Why not?
You may think that my mind is not sound. Why not?
I know life's a brief sojourn
And then we will all burn,
So I'm Byron the chemical man. Why not?
I don't try to give meaning to life.
Through the miracle of chemistry I avoid strife.
While you look for purpose,
I know death will soon usurp us.
I treasure the brief pleasure of life.

"Seriously, when I first realized that our species arose out of the feces of some lizard, I despised the notion. Magically, my certainty that I am special ended as did my devotion to some grand wizard in the sky. Suddenly I lost deity, piety, dignity and everlasting life. I felt bespattered, bereft of all that mattered. Soon I learned that I could get high and perhaps stay high until I die. Some strive hard for nirvana; not me, I get it for a small fee. Whee! Call them pain killers, that's what they are. They provide a Weltanschauung that is better by far than the sandstone rock of the church or Olympian pillars. Blasphemous, I hope, I rely on dope, not some religious pap, no better than crap, fed to us by well-meaning, frightened mothers. False hope or dope, take your druthers.

"Please forgive my bravado. What I seek is a soul city El Dorado where I will feel whole again, with a soul again. I envy those lucky people who were taught truth from the start and require none of the God and soul part to go on with their lives with the belief that they can create for themselves a brief life worth living. Amen."

"The phallus went fourth, but I nevertheless feel like the cleanup hitter. I hope I don't sound graceless or bitter. I was taught to be graceful and sweet and to be cautious and gentle when I compete. Grace, not Ace, is my moniker and it does not give me license to spit, whistle or play the harmonica. I can do all three, but not for an audience. I'm under surveillance: I'm a budding genius who is kept under close supervision and observation as she evolves into a stupendous sensation. Don't get your nose out of joint yet, there's a fly in the ointment: If my loony grandmother's genes prevail, they will smother my talents and all the careful watching and guiding will be to no avail. Grandma's genius genes are expressed only through her speciality: sexuality. Such narrowness is a bore; I want much more. I'm hauteur; it's not enough to be an expert fellate and frotteur. My genius seeks sanctification through diversification.

"They watch me almost every place I go, but not in the john or my dorm room, so they miss much of the show. I've looked for the surveillance camera and found none. It's time for fun; I can glow with Jo. She thinks she's very strong and that she has all the power. I've no reason to prove her wrong; I watch her glower, pretend to cower, and watch her perform her song and dance as I take romance. Well, it's too frantic to call it romantic; it's juicy and hot and I like it a lot and wonder how much of my grandma I've got. That is the question raised by dear mater and pater; we'll all find out sooner or later. In the meantime, I'm a budding genius; watch me flower.

"A little bit of self-revelation was the price of admission to this feeble verbal competition. I declare myself the winner. Let's all go to dinner."

Tob and Harah were in the kitchen finishing dinner preparations. She was stewing about not hearing from anyone and he was sautéing onions to add to the instant mashed potatoes. They heard a car door slam and soon the front door bell rang. When Tob opened the door she was startled to see a strikingly handsome young man in uniform. Her heart went to her throat when she noted five slouching people, including Joy, Grace and Glory, behind him. Before she caught her breath he spoke.

"Dr. Eyen, ma'am, I'm Police Officer Occhio. There's a bit of a problem".

"Oh my, have you kids gotten into some trouble?"

The patrolman turned about and was surprised to see the crowd behind him.

"Ma'am, there's no problem with these young people. May I speak to you in private?"

Tob asked the kids to please go into the house and without introductions they filed by with red eyes and a strong, sweet pot smell that was very obvious to Tob.

"Doctor, I think I'm doing the right thing coming here like this. I've seen you many times at the hospital emergency room and I've testified before Judge Eyen. I admire both of you very much."

"Please, tell me what's going on."

"Yes ma'am. I was finishing up for the day when I spotted an accident in the making, so I was on the scene at once. No one was seriously hurt. One car sped away after forcing the other into a spin and skid before it left the road and miraculously stopped on the shoulder. The driver of the car seemed high as a kite. She claimed to be Judge Eyen's mother, but she had no driver's license, no identification at all. The passenger confirmed her claim and showed his identification. He says he is your father. They were only bumped about a bit, even though Mrs. Eyen was not wearing her seat belt. I thought I would just charge her with failure to use her seat belt, but she was so high and he seemed so worn out that I decided it was best that I drive them here in the patrol car."

They walked to the car and there in the back seat were the expected culprits. Paul looked bedraggled. Dolores smiled brightly, but said nothing. Her wig was just a bit askew. She looked garish with her see-through blouse, and her short skirt was hiked so high that a wisp of pubic hair was visible between her thighs. Tob blushed for the first time in many years. Paul broke the ice by telling them that it was important that he get to the bathroom quickly.

Despite the flurry of activity, Tob ascertained that Sesso Occhio was on his way to an empty apartment and a turkey pot pie. She invited him to join them and, although he was initially reluctant, he gladly accepted. Dinner could wait a bit. Harah had put out snacks and was pouring beverages. Tob quickly briefed Harah and introductions were made before Tob took Dolores upstairs for a more sedate costume.

When Dolores and Paul reappeared, they looked like proper old folks, but no one forgot the picture they made on arrival. There were more introductions, but little clarification about Jo or Byron. The officer was getting a lot of attention. He reminded the older generations of Rudolph Valentino while the college crowd found him intriguing and potentially threatening. All relaxed a bit after he asked Harah to put his weapon and gun belt in a secure place. He had saved the day for all of them by what he did and by what he did not do. He was pleased with himself and they were grateful.

Dolores exercised considerable restraint as she warmed up to Sesso. She was looking up at him as they stood by the fireplace. Although she was over seventy, now primly dressed and did almost nothing, she still managed to exude a sexual interest in the handsome young man. He was used to such attention and quite comfortable with it, but he didn't let that show. He seemed rather shy as he played a young Gary Cooper, not Rudolph. Everyone was aware of their exchange and most were embarrassed by a sense of complicity and an accepting understanding of what they saw. Tob found it unnerving and decided to intrude by asking everyone to gather around to let the guests introduce themselves. Dolores chimed in suggesting that each of them take a turn and so they did. How modest, brief and unrevealing they were.

Harah went first. He identified himself as the father of Joy and Grace, Tob's husband, Dolores's son and a circuit court judge. He said that he was proud of his family, pleased with his professional accomplishments, thankful for all that he had and grateful that they were gathered together safely to celebrate the holiday. No one wanted him to reveal more.

I'm at the halfway mark on life's quick journey,
A time for reflection
And introspection.
I'm still full of life and yet so close to the gurney.

Surrounded by the ones I love most,
I try not to boast.
All the accoutrements of success
Don't protect me from making a mess.

Sometimes I feel a terrible dread
That I'll fumble
Or stumble
And cause big trouble ahead.

I'm not a believer, not religious,
But a judge must be judicious.
So no matter what I say,
I have started to pray.

I chose my path inventively
To protect
And deflect,
But can one prevent what is meant to be?

What is fated
Can be debated.
My internal soothsayer
Has directed me to prayer.

It's not clear if it's nature or nurture,
Most confusing
And not amusing,
That determines our future.

My genetic links
Have produced some scary kinks.
My mother's a minx
And I fear that I am a jinx.

There is some evidence of it.
I must stay alert
And never blurt
Out that I love it.

Perspicacity
And alacrity
May deny
The evil eye.

What horrors might be brought
To my fair innocents
And those with other bents
By the power of my thoughts?

If there is power in prayer,
Thoughts that fly through the air,
You'd best be very careful
For the consequences could be baleful.

On the surface I'm calm and logical.
One can't see my need for control.
If it were seen, I'd seem droll,
Less sensible and more comical.

When your mother periodically tells you she's hard up,
You learn to keep your guard up
With all your might
To avoid the fright.

Oh, Father, now in heaven, why did you fail me on Earth
When I needed your protection
And affection?
I suffered from your weakness right from my birth.

This story must never be told;
It would be too bold.
This tangled history
Shall remain an unspoken mystery.

Tob started with thanksgiving that they were gathered together and that their lives were so bountiful and promising. She delineated many of her roles: mother, wife, daughter, friend, physician and cook.

Don't doubt that I'm an achiever.
I have a ball
While I get it all.
Watch me and become a believer.

I keep much of my toughness hidden;
Too much of it is forbidden.
It's required that I balance the mental
With being both strong and gentle.

The rules are not fair,
So I bend with the wind
For they will not rescind
Them; I do not despair.

To succeed under these unfair rules,
Perpetuated by old male fools,
A woman must have both class
And a shapely ass or a lot of sass.

It's not easy to remain decorous
When, by and large,
The people in charge
Are so lecherous.

So I learned to play
And they let me stay.
Now I loom large
For I am in charge.

I work with death and dying each day:
With violence
And pestilence,
That's how I earn my pay.

I'm a heroic life saver.
There are none braver.
Too often I'm drenched
By the bleeding I've quenched.

This work takes its toll.
It's sometimes depleting,
Defeating,
But I manage to stay in control.

Too often my skills are deficient
And our resources insufficient
To secure the survival
Of the latest arrival.

I'll try to save her;
That young woman with the disfigured face
Might be my precious Grace.
Her life depends on my behavior.

Each time a new tragedy has appeared,
Often even worse than I had feared,
I think that we are victims, all,
Since the original fall.

The world is one big horror show.
Put aside the dissembling
And you'll see the fear and trembling,
But there is no other place to go.

It's true that we are complicitous
In some of the trials that visit us.
We did ourselves in
With original sin.

Plagues abound;
They are a blight
That we fight;
They are always around.

I don't think we've deserved
What God has served.
There is too much with which we must grapple
Just because Adam plucked that damned apple.

Glory was next in the circle. She said she was a neighbor and high school classmate of Joy and Grace; no more.

They used my house as a motel
And I wasn't invited to this dinner.
I know I'm no winner
But they can all go to hell.

I could have told them a lot of baloney;
It's easy enough to be phony.
If they don't like it, too bad.
The truth would surely make them mad.

I'm just a poor little rich girl,
Home alone,
Waiting by the phone,
Hoping someone will bring me into the whirl.

Jo and Byron were great in the sack,
But there is so much that they lack.
They were divine,
But they'll never be mine.

All of these people will be gone from my life tomorrow.
It's easy to see
That they don't care about me.
And I don't care about them, to my sorrow.

I need a strong connection,
More than some stud with a perpetual erection.
I enjoy impurity
But I crave security.

The house I live in feels empty.
Whether my folks stay
Or go away,
Their agenda preempts me.

Sure, I resent their deficiency;
Still, I fear it was meant to be.
They don't seem to have the wherewithal
To care at all.

I'll probably be as stunted as they are.
From the lack of their backing
I'm emotionally lacking.
Without help I don't stand a prayer.

Is it already too late?
Am I stuck with my fate?
Like a crippled bird that can fly no more,
Will I never soar?

So far I've avoided the quick fix of dope.
If I can lovingly connect,
I may gain self-respect.
That is my hope.

There is so much that I need,
Since I've an ego to feed.
Would I feel respectable
If someone found me delectable?

When my neediness is on display
It's destructive,
Not productive;
It frightens people away.

I dwell
In my private hell.
I need help to embark
Out of this terrible dark.

Surely my loneliness is not meant to be.
Someone strong and insistent,
Someone persistent,
Will save me from this bleak destiny.

Save me, love me,
Save me, love me,
Save me, love me.
Please, save me by loving me.

Byron identified himself as Joy's friend and classmate.

Doing drugs and sex are my main activities.
I have no doubt
That they've figured me out;
They understand my proclivities.

Though they are doing some preening
And suggesting that their lives have meaning,
It's my hunch
That they're not a bad bunch.

They don't trust me.
I'm poking their daughter
And they don't think I ought'a,
But they're not going to bust me.

They have found life somewhat mysterious
And quite serious.
I have found
Life's a playground.

Put aside all care;
Don't worry,
Let's hurry
To the fair.

I've decided college is my career.
When graduation is near
I'll decline it
And redefine it.

I've no important projects that cause strife.
Since life's just a flicker
I will not dicker,
I will enjoy my life.

Don't tell me I have no humanity;
It's you strivers who suffer insanity.
You propose some grand plan
For trivial man.

I'm protesting too much.
If you could hear me, I suspect
You would detect
My uncertainty that life is such.

I'm well sponsored. Is it a curse
To have no concerns about the purse?
Do I envy those who must scrounge
While I lounge?

It's the affliction of plenty.
Having it all
Led to my fall.
That has rent me.

The death of the grand master, Tim Leary,
Has put a bit of fear in me.
Perhaps I want more
Than to live and die a druggie bore.

I'm Byron, so aesthetic.
With naught but diversion
On my playful excursion,
I'll soon be pathetic.

It's how I regard myself that counts;
That's from whence the pressure mounts
To change my course
Or feel remorse.

In just a few moments
I've swung from arrogance
To questioning my competence.
A strange turn of events.

I had furled all ambition
Without contrition.
This unintended soliloquy
May turn things around for me.

Jo's eyes twinkled with delight as she considered identifying herself as Grace's lover; she settled for roommate.

They'll think I'm sweet, but wait;
Before this is done
And I've had my fun,
They'll suspect I'm the devil incarnate.

Old Bill said the world is a stage.
I agree with the poet sage.
When the action starts
I play my many parts.

Each character I present is ephemeral.
The reprise
Is my desire to surprise
And to damn you all.

Partnership Games

I'll enrapture you
To capture you;
I flirt
To hurt.

Before you realize that I'm not sincere,
That I'm playing a game
That's designed to defame,
You will know fear.

Just when you think I'm not serious
You'll awaken, feeling delirious,
Knowing I'm a succubus and more,
Someone to abhor.

Once I decide whom I'll nail,
I'm relentless.
They're defenseless;
I never fail.

I'm not exaggerating about my power.
Within the hour
This live wire
Could set the house on fire.

I make the high and mighty stumble.
I play rough
And after I've done my stuff
They're meek and humble.

I'm an expert at creating the double bind
Where you will find
There is no right path
That avoids my wrath.

If I target you when I dissemble,
Playing vixen or lambkin
Or Chimera, I will win
In the end and you will tremble,

For you will know your future's at stake
And you'll be seen as a lecherous rake.
Our encounter is one you will never forget
And forever regret.

Once I was the victim; no more.
I'll go to great length
To demonstrate my strength:
It is I who will score.

When our exchange is completed
And you've been defeated,
You might despise me,
But you will never trivialize me.

Hear me.
Think about me every day.
Know that I will have my way.
Fear me.

I will use you
And abuse you.
I have no fear
For I am not the puppet but the puppeteer.

The young policeman looked at each one of them. He expressed gratitude that he was invited to join them, to be their companion on the holiday. It would make the day more holy for him.

These people express gratitude for what they've got,
But they are just mouthing it,
Not espousing it.
They seem unaware that they're a privileged lot.

Oh, they know they have lots of stuff
But would take it as a rebuff
If I questioned their sincerity
Or noted their failure to see reality.

Partnership Games

The doc and the judge try to be fair.
They see the conniving,
The clawing and striving,
So they think they are aware

Of the real world. They do meet
Many who regularly suffer defeat.
They don't feel that they are a part
Of the corruption that defeats us right from the start.

I'm part of the hoi polloi,
One of the penurious
That our injurious
System can destroy.

The doctor and judge
Don't have to fudge
To remain unaware
That my handling of Dolores was unfair.

They view it as generous and thoughtful
That I protected her
When another might have neglected her.
They don't know I was being artful.

They are so accustomed to special consideration,
They tend not to question its motivation.
They feel righteous and deserving,
Entitled to the best serving.

I saved them from embarrassment and disruption.
They can ignore
And fail to deplore
That mine was a convenient act of corruption.

Convenient for them, that's easy to see,
But it remains to be seen what's in it for me.
I've ingratiated myself in their favor;
It's more than dinner that I'd like to savor.

I'm well-mannered and good-looking.
Although I'm not profound,
They might tolerate having me around.
I'll see what I can get cooking.

Joy and Grace are cutie pies.
They were quick to note my sexy eyes.
One might be my ticket in;
I could become kin.

I don't want them to get suspicious
That the helpful cop
Wants their help to get to the top
And is duplicitous.

I'd have a very different life
With Joy or Grace as my wife
And influential in-laws
Who can open doors.

I could do big things
With the confluence
And confidence
Such a union brings.

I feel no contrition
About such highfalutin' ambition.
I must avoid getting queasy;
This could be very easy.

Joy told her name and said, somewhat provocatively, that she is the sweet older twin.

Yes, I am the sweet one:
Almost always compliant,
Only rarely defiant.
My twin is the smart one.

The folks will deny they perceive an asymmetry
Or that they, in any way, want to limit me.
Of course, I chose the path I have taken,
But when they claim no influence, they're mistaken.

I am very intelligent.
In a family where all are so superior,
I seem almost inferior
And inelegant.

The race is not all intellectual,
There are areas where I'm the most effectual.
I use with utility
My considerable sensibility.

I know what's going on around me.
Compared to Grace's, my IQ is just so-so,
But I'm no bozo.
There's not much that will astound me.

My insight cuts two ways
And obviates delays.
Often I will know secrets
And of secret regrets.

Grandpa claims that he does assume
That everyone knows everything.
Oh, what chaos that would bring,
Without a sound, more disruptive than a sonic boom.

Wait, maybe not;
Confronting one's self is quite a lot,
But without interpersonal confrontation
We can usually avoid a conflagration.

My life's course is not yet clear.
Seeing things is my special ability.
If I use my talent with facility
I could become a seer.

Such ambitiousness sounds conceited.
I might be defeated,
But I hope to use my ability
With nobility.

Most of what I see, as today,
Is interesting, humorous stuff,
Mostly just a lot of fluff
As we put ourselves on display.

We prance
And romance;
We strut
And we rut.

This group reeks of hot coitus.
So many lubricious receptacles
Are enough to steam up your spectacles.
It's with semen that they will anoint us.

I want to do more than just mate;
I'd like to be great.
I will not abjure the whore,
But I want and expect much more.

So, I've entered adulthood.
Having loved and lost so quickly,
I know that life is not risk free.
I would not go back if I could.

I savor, right from the start,
Dancing my brief part.
It's so auspicious,
I expect it to be delicious.

Grace looked coy as she identified herself as the baby of the family.

I am the future of the world.
I may be its savior;
Watch my behavior
Once my great talents are unfurled.

Did they mean to encourage in me
Such grandiosity?
They did inspire it
And I did acquire it.

From the very beginning
They've told me I'm precious,
Precocious and marvelous
And that I would be winning

Whatever I desired,
Whenever I aspired.
I could have anything I wanted
And never feel daunted.

Such praise without cessation
From all and sundry,
Telling me what I could be,
Created quite an obligation

For me to push in the direction
Of perfection
And to keep it light and breezy,
To make it look easy.

Even for this God-like creature
Who was born to succeed
And has the spirit of a steed,
That's quite a squeaker.

I must never relent,
Work until I'm spent
And look fresh as a daisy
While I feel suicidal and crazy.

Where do I go from here?
I have decisions to make.
What road will I take?
Nothing seems clear.

Grandma's genes may be at work
And by some strange quirk
I'll become the first woman president
And a permanent mental hospital resident.

The burden is oppressive
But it would be a cop-out
To take the hospital route.
Grandma says it's better to be manic than depressive.

Enough of the dramatic;
I will be emphatic
And continue in the direction
Of perfection.

Where it takes me, we will see.
I hope to serve humanity
And avoid insanity,
But things could get filthy.

My parents encouraged me to put on this yoke,
But I was answering my own voice
When I made the choice
That I will not revoke.

So, upward and onward and never say die;
I will live,
I will give,
I will fly.

Live.	*Live.*
Give.	*Give.*
Die.	*Fly.*
Fly.	*Die.*

Dolores looked all nine of them in the eye.

Old women are permitted to speak out loud.
I won't be discreet,
I'll get right to the meat.
I want the attention of the entire crowd.

Life's one big contortion,
A late-term abortion.
First comes de feet, then mangle the head.
Soon after you're dead.

I've painted a pretty picture.
It's only fools
Who don't flout the rules;
I have tolerated no stricture.

I'm a grand old hag,
A high flying hag.
Listen carefully, sonny,
Not everything I say is meant to be funny.

When I come up from my bleak, dark cave
Into the fulgent sunlight,
With all my might,
I want a love slave.

Once out of that pit,
I must have it.
When you see how I behave,
You will know that I am the slave.

Sex with me isn't beautiful:
It's kinky and wet,
It's the best you can get,
It is never dull.

Sanford L. Billet

I've had a long relationship, love-hate,
With lithium carbonate.
It brings me up from the mire,
But it also dampens my fire.

I am the now generation:
For me it is now or never.
Before they pull the lever
I want veneration

As the world's oldest love goddess.
Come, rip my bodice.
Stick it to me hard,
Pard.

Don't get sanctimonious.
My life has been more than sexual.
Don't conclude I've been ineffectual,
That's erroneous.

With all my up and down excursions
And my erotic immersions,
I've had an almost ordinary life
That's included the roles of mother and wife.

Although my life is nearly completed,
I'll continue to pun
And try to have fun
Until I'm unseated.

What about you, young snotnose,
What do you propose?
Will you use your time better than I?
Think about it, don't reply.

Unless you believe in reincarnation,
This is your one time flight.
Get it right.
Waste it and you deserve eternal damnation.

Whether you are constrained or let it rip,
Life is a very brief trip.
Take your choice
And rejoice.

Tob was ready to get the dinner started, but her father, the tenth person, had yet to speak.

Too hungry to listen?
I could speak a lot
Or not.
I have no special mission.

Paul is my name.
Pall is pronounced the same.
After I cover the gathering with gloom
Let the festivities resume.

I'm almost eighty.
You may expect to hear something portentous
Or contentious,
Something weighty.

Don't hold your breath,
For I confess
That I have much more to say about pee
Than about philosophy.

I have a very slow stream,
Urgency,
Hesitancy
And a prostate that will soon feel the ream.

My bladder capacity is ever so small,
It holds almost nothing at all,
So I'm on a very short tether,
For it doesn't matter whether

Sanford L. Billet

I restrict my fluid intake,
Or distract my mind.
I still find
That suddenly I must make.

I'm out of whack below the belt.
Oh, the symptoms I have felt.
My ass itches a lot,
One of the most aggravating symptoms I've got.

I have been dutiful
With exercise and diet.
You name it, I've tried it,
In an effort to keep the body beautiful.

It's hard to be fit and well rested
When your body is infested
With gremlins that compact your stool
And pluck at your tool.

Who said life is too brief?
That's not born out
When your body is worn out.
I'm ready to go; it will be a relief.

Well, no need to hurry
Or go out in a flurry.
My unresolved fears
May keep me hanging in there a few more years.

I almost forgot to mention my fright:
I'm embarrassed.
I'm harassed
By the Furies of the night.

Why this anxiety about death?
Why do I treasure each breath?
It's because I'm an old sinner
That I stay on for my next dinner.

If I didn't have this fear,
I would get into the saddle
And try to die in the heat of battle
When I knew that death was near.

I'll end on a high note;
Don't let it stick in your throat:
It would be neat
To die locked in an embrace with Dolores in heat.

Tob asked for assistance in getting dinner on the table. Paul went to the bathroom and everyone else offered to help. Harah noted that the table was set for ten and that they were ten. What good luck. He shuddered and feared that he had put a jinx on it.

As she worked Tob was thinking about Bela, Sister Mary. They met in medical school when they were assigned to share a cadaver for dissection in the first year gross anatomy course. They became good friends and provided each other with support for the next seven years. Most of their classmates did not know that Bela was a nun who was preparing herself for a career as a medical missionary. There were one hundred and thirty classmates and Bela was most admired by those who knew her.

Bela had written recently that she was returning to America and expected to arrive on Thanksgiving Day. In a matter-of-fact way, she wrote that she was accompanying her husband and, on arrival, would call to confirm that they would join the family for the holiday dinner. There had been no call.

Harah and Tob took the end seats. On one side Dolores sat next to the cop whom she called her sexy boy in blue, then Joy and Byron. Paul, Grace, Jo and Glory had the side facing the kitchen. As soon as they were all seated, of course, there was a knock on the door: Sister Mary, Dr. Bela, had arrived with her husband. Everyone got up to greet them.

Her smile was beatific and yet twinkled as she introduced herself and her husband. She laughed when she said that although his name is Jesus, he is not Puerto Rican. Jesus was in a wheelchair. He was a tall, frail wisp of a man and he did not speak.

She explained that they had been detained by the immigration people who felt that Jesus was too near death for them to allow him admission. They relented when told that the trip was part of an effort to revive him and that he was covered by excellent health insurance. The insurance was the clincher.

Another chair was brought to the table. Sesso Occhio made his getaway to the other side of the table and sat between Grace and Glory. Jesus was wheeled in and placed between Dolores and his bride. When Bela hovered around him, Grace thought of the Pietà. Bela spoke.

My dear Jesus speaks rarely.
He is watchful and hears
My hopes and my fears.
He deals with all matters fairly.

The missionary life
Is a life filled with strife,
A tiny band
In a foreign land.

We try to avoid being self-serving.
We serve others;
All are brothers
And all are deserving.

The world's in a crisis of disbelief
From which it has found little relief.
All of humanity
Seems on the verge of insanity.

While our Earth is careening,
Full of corruption
And approaching a fiery eruption,
There is scant search for meaning.

It is not just the cannibals
But all human animals
Who must learn to believe
So that they can receive

The beneficence
That our dear Lord
Will afford
In His munificence.

We missionaries renounce material wealth;
We attend to the physical health
Of the sick and the needy.
We are greedy

For the souls of the spiritually deprived.
If they never bend a knee,
They will not see
Heaven; it will be proscribed.

Though I have striven to,
I know belief can not be given to
Those in need,
But we can plant the seed.

That's what I have tried to do.
I have plowed the field
And prayed for some yield.
Perhaps I have helped a few.

Here in the United States
Affluence creates
A different picture,
A different mixture,

But the same lack of fulfillment.
There is a feeling of dread
That God is dead.
It is felt even by the well-meant.

That is why Jesus and I have come here;
Our mission is to allay that fear.
We will revive His spirit
And have everyone hear it.

The Messiah is here on Earth.
He walks with us,
He talks with us;
It is a time of spiritual rebirth.

Remember, He does not slumber.
Remember, He's got your number.
If within you His spirit does not dwell,
You will roast forever in hell.

The natives were beginning to lose their appetite and get restless. Harah suggested it was time to say grace. Jesus leaned slightly toward Mary and whispered very clearly, "The Twenty-Third Psalm." None of them, not even Bela, could recite the psalm. Jesus called softly for the Bible; there was none in the house. He began to slowly deliver grace. After the amen there was silence and awe.

The sentry,
Who stopped us at your border,
Feared we were here to create disorder.
We were reluctantly granted entry.

Will we have the art
To steal into your heart
Or will you steel your heart
And keep us apart?

He who hears my voice,
My message of redemption
And ascension,
Will rejoice.

My big surprise,
The grand prize,
Is everlasting life
Without strife.

Our goal is to draw you in,
Get you to stop preening,
To find life's meaning
And to live without sin.

The Jew
Gave his life for you.
He has forgiven those who smit Him;
Now is the time for you to admit Him

Into your very essence.
Learn to rely,
Not defy;
Learn obeisance.

You have so much to gain
If you will refrain
From your lustful excursions,
Your licentious diversions.

Okay, you've heard my whole recruitment spiel,
My refrain
About what you can gain,
Now here's the deal.

There has been too much corruption.
I've suffered too much disruption.
I hate it
And won't tolerate it.

You pip-squeaks have no taste for redemption.
You indulge every whim
And don't give a damn about sin.
Don't think I'll grant you an exemption.

It's my game and my ball.
I created it all.
I could play with my clapper
And flush all of you down the crapper.

You're a restless, motley crew.
You deserve this rebuke,
You make me puke.
Sit still, I'm almost through.

Now I'm getting sore.
Let's see what I have in store
For you dumb suckers,
You dirty chicken pluckers.

You are defiled.
I see the way.
It will be by auto-da-fé ;
You deserve to be reviled.

Now I'm going to play rough,
Now I'll show you I'm tough.
Right after dinner I'll show you my ire.
I will start the final fire.

All right, everyone has said their piece. Let's eat.